Applied Machine Learning for IoT and Data Analytics

(Volume 1)

Experimental Design of Bio-Inspired Algorithms for Optimization Problems in Industry 5.0

Edited by

Pijush Dutta
Department of Computer Science and Engineering
Greater Kolkata College of Engineering and Management
Kolkata, India

Sudip Mandal
Department of Electronics & Communication Engineering, Jalpaiguri Government Engineering College
Jalpaiguri, India

Korhan Cengiz
Department of Electrical-Electronics Engineering
Biruni University
Istanbul, Turkey

&

S. Balamurugan
IRCS
An Indian Technological Research & Consulting Firm
Coimbatore, Tamil Nadu, India

Applied Machine Learning for IoT and Data Analytics

(Volume 1)

Experimental Design of Bio-Inspired Algorithms for Optimization Problems in Industry 5.0

Editors: Pijush Dutta, Sudip Mandal, Korhan Cengiz and S. Balamurugan

ISBN (Online): 979-8-89881-408-3

ISBN (Print): 979-8-89881-409-0

ISBN (Paperback): 979-8-89881-410-6

First published in 2026.

Bentham Science Publishers Pte. Ltd.
No. 9 Raffles Place
Office No. 26-01
Singapore 048619
Singapore
Email: subscriptions@benthamscience.net

BENTHAM SCIENCE

CONTENTS

FOREWORD

Industry 5.0, which emphasizes the collaboration of intelligent systems and humans to create highly personalized, efficient, and sustainable manufacturing processes, represents a significant change in how industries function. Industry 5.0 aims to establish a cooperative environment where artificial intelligence and human creativity may coexist peacefully, in contrast to its predecessor, which was mainly concerned with automation and cyber-physical systems. In this new industrial age, optimization is essential for solving complicated problems, from energy efficiency and resource allocation to dynamic production planning and real-time decision-making.

To address these complex optimization problems, bio-inspired algorithms—which draw inspiration from natural processes like evolution, swarm intelligence, and brain adaptation—have become very effective. They are ideal for the dynamic and unpredictable situations seen in Industry 5.0 applications due to their innate flexibility, adaptability, and capacity to break free from local optima. Bio-inspired optimization approaches provide creative ways to increase productivity, resilience, and sustainability as businesses get increasingly linked through the Internet of Things, edge computing, and artificial intelligence.

This book, "Experimental Design of Bio-Inspired Algorithms for Optimization Problems in Industry 5.0," is published at a pivotal point in time when industry applications and scholarly research must come together to fully use these methods. It methodically investigates experimental approaches that guarantee the effective application of bio-inspired algorithms in commercial contexts. The book explores important topics, including algorithm selection, parameter tweaking, performance benchmarking, and real-world application scenarios, through several perceptive chapters written by top specialists.

The well-organized combination of theoretical underpinnings and real-world applications will provide readers with the skills they need to successfully develop, apply, and assess bio-inspired algorithms. This book provides a lot of material to help you in your endeavors, whether you are a researcher investigating new optimization techniques or an industry expert looking for workable ways to improve operational efficiency.

I have no doubt that this book will be a priceless tool for practitioners, researchers, and students alike, spurring more advancements in bio-inspired optimization for Industry 5.0. It is admirable that the editors and collaborators put together such an extensive and progressive work. I invite you to explore the insights contained within these pages and leverage the knowledge presented to address the pressing optimization challenges of Industry 5.0.

We sincerely hope that readers will find this book informative and inspiring, and we extend our gratitude to all contributors for their invaluable efforts in making this work possible.

Mete Yaganoglu
Ataturk University, Faculty of Engineering
Department of Computer Engineering
Erzurum, Turkey

PREFACE

Advances in robots, artificial intelligence, and cyber-physical systems have accelerated the evolution of industrial systems, opening the door for the emergence of Industry 5.0, a paradigm change that prioritizes resilient, sustainable, and human-centric production. Robust optimization strategies become increasingly important as companies shift toward intelligent automation, energy efficiency, and individualized manufacturing. In this regard, bio-inspired algorithms have drawn a lot of interest because of their versatility, capacity for self-organization, and efficiency in resolving challenging optimization problems.

To close the gap between theoretical developments and real-world applications of bio-inspired optimization techniques in the changing industrial environment, this book, "Experimental Design of Bio-Inspired Algorithms for Optimization Problems in Industry 5.0," was developed. It offers a thorough manual for creating, putting into practice, and assessing these algorithms for practical uses in supply chain management, smart manufacturing, human-robot cooperation, predictive maintenance, and other fields.

Leading authorities in the domains of neural computation, swarm intelligence, evolutionary computing, and industrial engineering have contributed to the edited edition. With an emphasis on crucial elements, including parameter tweaking, performance assessment, benchmarking, and scalability, each chapter is thoughtfully written to provide insights into the experimental design features of bio-inspired algorithms. The integration of these algorithms with contemporary computational frameworks is also covered in the book, providing useful answers for both scholars and practitioners.

This book's salient characteristics include:

• A comprehensive examination of bio-inspired algorithms designed for industrial use, such as genetic algorithms, particle swarm optimization, ant colony optimization, and hybrid approaches.

• Recommendations for creating exacting experimental frameworks that guarantee robustness, repeatability, and dependability in optimization solutions.

• Real-world examples and case studies that show how bio-inspired approaches may be used to address Industry 5.0 issues.

• New developments and potential lines of inquiry, such as the application of AI-enhanced optimization in industrial systems.

Chapter 1 explains the way how Artificial Intelligence (AI) has rapidly advanced and changed many industries, ranging from healthcare and finance to manufacturing and entertainment, where people began to interact and process information with machines differently. However, despite the potential offered by AI, some challenges have also emerged. For instance, the black box issue, which is the aspect of AI where many systems, and especially those that rely on complex algorithms such as deep learning, are hard to understand by the human race. The difficulty in understanding how decisions are made and how models work brings worries about trust, fairness, responsibility, and openness in AI systems, especially in situations where they are of critical importance, for instance, in medical diagnosis, autonomous vehicles, or legal matters. This is where Explainable AI (XAI) comes in to remediate this problem and help make decisions more transparently without suppressing the functioning of the AI systems. XAI not only improves the performance of AI systems in healthcare but also fosters trust between patients and providers in Industry 5.0, where human-AI collaboration is crucial.

Chapter 2 covers extending the techniques of ANOVA in optometric research to different experimental designs. In each case, the type of experimental design is described, a statistical model is given, and the advantages and limitations of the appropriate ANOVA are discussed. In addition, the problems of non-conformity to the statistical model and the determination of the number of replications are considered.

Chapter 3 investigates a power series nonlinear mathematical model based on an enhanced Elephant swarm water Search algorithm (ESWSA). The proposed ESWSA algorithm has been developed to predict the average localization error (ALE) of a wireless sensor network system. The performance of the proposed algorithm is evaluated from the effects of anchor ratio, transmission range, node density, and number of iterations. Experimental results demonstrate that higher localization precision with fewer iterations can be achieved. This chapter presents the suggested approach in real-world WSN applications as a foundation for optimizing node location, which is advantageous to lower computational consumption and thereby extend the lifetime of sensor nodes.

Chapter 4 provides a mathematical model of the grinding process based on the input parameters (*i.e.*, infeed, flow rate, and presence of scrapper board) using Regression Equations and ANOVA analysis. The model has been developed from the experimental data of the up-grinding mode with or without a scraperboard. The relationship between response and the grinding parameters has been illustrated graphically by contour plots and surface plots. The output variables are optimized to find the best suitable conditions for grinding using ANOVA. The aim is to find the optimal parametric conditions at which output variables will be minimized.

Chapter 5 analyzes a nonlinear optimization issue for powder injection molding (PIM) of Alumina feedstock, which is addressed by using the artificial neural network (ANN) algorithm. The Jaya algorithm is used to solve the problem of injection variables in a mold-filling optimization issue. The ANN model is implemented with the help of analysis of variance (ANOVA) based on input and response variables. In the last stage, the optimum process parameters are obtained, which show a satisfactory output. Future research may concentrate on creating a posteriori version of the Jaya method, which could then be used to tackle optimization issues for various conventional and contemporary machining processes while taking into account several goals at once.

Chapter 6 demonstrates that a micro-blind hole generation on silica by electrochemical deposition (ECDM) is a very promising method for micro-hole generation on glass. To achieve the target results of the work and to control the process parameters such as machining voltage, pulse frequency (fixed 50Hz), pulse on-time inter-electrode gap (IEG), duty ratio, electrolyte concentration, *etc.*, a series of experiments and analyses are performed to achieve the target results during the micro-ECDM process. The results show that applied voltage leads to a critical voltage that takes action mainly on diametric overcut (DOC) and tool wear rate (TWR).

Chapter 7 presents a micro-drilling of glass by the electrochemical discharge machining (ECDM) process, which is a challenging process due to its high material removal rate and radial overcut during the drilling process. The analysis of variance (ANOVA) is conducted to find out the significant process parameters for the above-mentioned responses of the ECDM process. A mathematical model for Material Removal Rate (MRR) and Radial Overcut (ROC) is developed using the factorial design method. The effects of two process parameters, applied voltage and electrolyte conductivity, on respective machining criteria are justified through ANOVA results and experimental analyses.

Chapter 8 explains Gas Metal Arc (MIG) welding of austenitic stainless steel AISI 304 using ER 308L electrode and 99% pure Argon gas shielding at suitable combinations of input parameters that have been considered for research. A second-order model is developed to represent the responses in terms of the process variables, including welding current (I), gas flow rate (F), and welding speed (S). The relationship between the responses and welding parameters is depicted graphically using contour plots and surface plots. A total of twenty welded specimens are fabricated under varying parametric conditions using the Response Surface Methodology (RSM) with a face-centered central composite design (CCD). ANOVA and ESWSA metaheuristics are applied for the optimization of the welding process, i.e., to find out the optimal welding condition for MIG welding.

Chapter 9 discusses speed control of a 4-phase, 8/6 switched reluctance motor (SRM) powered by photovoltaic. The high-gain converter is controlled by using a Maximum Power Point Tracking (MPPT) technique by implementing an Adaptive Neuro Fuzzy Inference System (ANFIS). The ANFIS-MPPT algorithm generates a control signal and maximizes the efficiency of PV systems using input voltage (VPV) and current (IPV). In addition, a PI and an optimization algorithm for fine-tuning the parameters of the PI result in regulating the speed of SRM.

Chapter 10 explores an experimental framework for bio-inspired algorithms in wireless communication at the physical layer, supporting various components throughout the system. The proposed wireless experimental environment can construct local, small- or medium-sized internal communication systems for factory scenes and provide better understanding and verification in high-definition and high-precision industrial case instruments. The paper focuses on the technical merit and potential of Biological Inheritance (BIA), which not only achieves the same performance as a parallel counterpart scheme for discrete signal data transmission, but also achieves point-to-point signal data communication. BIA's quick operability and the importance of the annealing process in ensuring correct behavior in complex future applications are highlighted.

Chapter 11 introduces Artificial Intelligence (AI) and Robotic Process Automation (RPA) in revolutionizing the Indian banking industry, offering significant improvements in efficiency, customer service, and risk management. However, AI and RPA have not been fully implemented in India. In this paper, the implementation strategies, applications, and benefits of AI, RPA, and AI in the Indian banking sector have been discussed. The paper concludes with the following. (1) AI is a powerful tool for enhancing operational efficiency, improving decision-making, and providing personalized customer experiences. (2) RPA has the potential to revolutionize the banking sector, enabling more efficient and streamlined processes, as well as improving customer experience. (3) RPA and AI are essential to the digital transformation of the banking industry. (4) RPA can allow banks to lessen guide efforts, provide higher compliance, reduce risks, and improve the general patron experience. (5) RPA is an important tool for improving the overall customer experience of banks. (6) AI is an effective approach for improving operational efficiency and reducing operational costs.

Chapter 12 suggests a 4.5 GHz rectangular patch antenna with a hexagonal slot cut in the copper patch, designed and simulated using CST Studio. The proposed antenna exhibits a remarkable return loss (S11) of -61.4 dB and a substantial bandwidth of 1.291916 GHz, significantly outperforming existing works in this frequency band. The antenna's near-ideal

VSWR of 1.00169, combined with these superior performance parameters, makes it highly suitable for high-speed data transmission applications.

Chapter 13 presents a hybrid optimization algorithm based on Particle Swarm Optimization (PSO), Genetic Algorithm (GA), and hybrid HGAPSO for the nonlinear liquid flow control process model. In the first phase, a total of 117 datasets are used to design a nonlinear power model by ANOVA. In the second phase, two ordinary common metaheuristic optimizations, GA and PSO, along with this improved hybrid optimization technique HOAPSO, are also applied to test the model on 17 test datasets to find the coefficient of the nonlinear model analysis of variance (ANOVA) coefficient.

Chapter 14 introduces a new hybrid algorithm, HCSPSO, which is based on incorporating PSO with CSO algorithms. The proposed hybrid algorithm is applied to extract the parameters of single and double-diode RTC France silicon solar cells (S75), which have irradiance levels of 1000 W/m2 and a temperature of 25 °C. The effectiveness of this technique in the single and double solar cell model problem with non-smooth cost functions, like diode current, in both cases can be improved using the hybrid algorithm.

Chapter 15 describes an experiment on a rectangular microstrip patch antenna with a triangular polygon at the right upper side of the patch designed in the environment of CST studio suite version 2023,. Twenty five different antennas are configured by changing three parameters, namely substrate height(h), width of the patch, and width of the feedline. A regression model with ANOVA for both bandwidth and resonant frequency is created in the Minitab (version 21) environment to design several antennas with variations in these four variables. The model is well-fitted and validates the target outcome of 2.5 GHz of bandwidth close to the desired frequency of 26 GHz, which is appropriate for applications on 5G and very useful for Industry 5.0.

For researchers, business executives, and graduate students eager to investigate and use bio-inspired algorithms to improve intricate industrial processes, we think this book will be an invaluable resource. The ideas presented in this book will contribute to the development of Industry 5.0 optimization as the globe transitions to a more intelligent and connected industrial environment.

Pijush Dutta
Department of Computer Science and Engineering
Greater Kolkata College of Engineering and
Management, Kolkata
India

Sudip Mandal
Department of Electronics & Communication
Engineering, Jalpaiguri Government Engineering College
Jalpaiguri
India

Korhan Cengiz
Department of Electrical-Electronics Engineering
Biruni University
Istanbul
Turkey

&

S. Balamurugan
IRCS
An Indian Technological Research &
Consulting Firm Coimbatore
Tamil Nadu
India

List of Contributors

Anurima Majumdar	Department of Electronics and Communication Engineering, Guru Nanak Institute of Technology, Kolkata, India
Antara Ghosal	Department of Electronics and Communication Engineering, Guru Nanak Institute of Technology, Kolkata, India
Amit Dey	Department of Electronics & Communication Engineering, Greater Kolkata College of Engineering and Management, Baruipur, West Bengal, 743387, India
Anubrata Mondal	Department of Electrical Engineering, Greater Kolkata College of Engineering &Management, West Bengal, 743387, India
Azzam S. Hameed	Faculty of ME Department, Wasit University, Kut, Iraq
Abhishek Ghosh	Department of Mechanical Engineering, SKFGI Mankundu, West Bengal, India
Arijit Mitra	Department of Electronics and Communication Engineering, Jalpaiguri Government Engineering College, Jalpaiguri, India
Anand Polamarasetti	Department of Computer Science, Andhra University, Visakhapatnam, AP, India
Arindam Sadhu	Department of Electronics &Communication Engineering, Dr. Sudhir Chandra Sur Institute of Technology and Sports Complex, Kolkata, West Bengal, India
Barun Haldar	Industrial Engineering Department, College of Engineering, Imam Mohammad Ibn Saud Islamic University (IMSIU), Riyadh, 11432, Saudi Arabia
Bijan Mallick	Faculty of ME Department, Global Institute of Management and Technology, Krishnanagar, MAKAUT, West Bengal, India
B. Kirubadurai	Aeronautical Engg, VelTech Dr. Rangarajan Dr. Sagunthala R&D Institute of Science and Tech, Chennai, India
Dipankar Saha	Department of Electronics &Communication Engineering, Global Institute of Management &Technology, Krishnagar, West Bengal, India
Gour Gopal Jana	Department of Electronics &Communication Engineering, Greater Kolkata College of Engineering and Management, Baruipur, West Bengal, 743387, India
G. Jegadeeswari	Department of Electrical and Electronics Engineering, Saveetha Engineering College, Chennai, India
Krishnendu Mondal	Faculty of ME Department, Future Institute of Engineering and Management, MAKAUT, West Bengal, India
Kaushik Saha	Department of Electronics and Communication Engineering, Jalpaiguri Government Engineering College, Jalpaiguri, India
Kabita Purkait	Department of Electronics and Communication Engineering, Kalyani Government. Engineering College, Kalyani, India
Peeraj Mazumder	Department of Mechanical Engineering and Mining Machinery Engineering, Indian Institute of Technology, Jharkhand, Dhanbad, India
Pijush Dutta	Faculty of CSE Department, Greater Kolkata College of Engineering and Management, West Bengal, India
Rudrajit Datta	Department of Electrical Engineering, Greater Kolkata College of Engineering and Management, Baruipur, West Bengal, 743387, India

Sunipa Roy	Department of Electronics and Communication Engineering, Guru Nanak Institute of Technology, Kolkata, India
Sujit Majumdar	Department of Mechanical Engineering, Kalyani Government. Engineering College, Kalyani, India
S. K. Tanbir Islam	Department of Mechanical Engineering, Greater Kolkata College of Engineering and Management, Baruipur, 743387, India
S. K. Hikmat	Faculty of ME Department, Global Institute of Management and Technology, Krishnanagar, MAKAUT, West Bengal, India
Sourav Mazumder	Department of Management, Eminent College of Management and Technology, Moshpukur, Barberia, Barasat, Kolkata, 700126, West Bengal, India
Somnath Chakraborty	Department of Management Studies, Brainware University, Barasat, 700125, West Bengal, India
Sumanta Dey	Department of Electronics &Communication Engineering, Greater Kolkata College of Engineering and Management, Baruipur, 743387, West Bengal, India
Sudip Mandal	Department of Electronics and Communication Engineering, Jalpaiguri Government Engineering College, Jalpaiguri, India
Zaiba Khan	Department of Computer Science, RNB Global University, Bikaner, Rajasthan, India

CHAPTER 1

Explainable AI in Industry 5.0: Principles, Mission, and Future Direction

Anurima Majumdar[1], **Antara Ghosal**[1] and **Sunipa Roy**[1,*]

[1] *Department of Electronics and Communication Engineering, Guru Nanak Institute of Technology, Kolkata, India*

Abstract: Explainable AI (XAI) is a critical component of Industry 5.0, which focuses on human-centric, sustainable, and resilient manufacturing. Unlike Industry 4.0, which emphasizes automation and cyber-physical systems, Industry 5.0 integrates human intelligence with AI, ensuring that AI-driven decisions are transparent, interpretable, and aligned with human values. XAI enhances trust and collaboration between humans and AI systems by explaining AI decisions. This is particularly important in industries like manufacturing, healthcare, and finance, where AI-driven insights affect critical operations. With XAI, workers and decision-makers can validate AI recommendations, reduce bias, and ensure compliance with regulations like GDPR and AI ethics guidelines.

Keywords: AI-driven, Explainable AI (XAI), General Data Protection Regulation (GDPR), Industries, Industry 5.0.

INTRODUCTION

Artificial Intelligence (AI) has quickly advanced and changed many industries, ranging from healthcare and finance to manufacturing and entertainment, where people began to interact and process information with machines differently [1]. However, the extent of the promise offered by AI is matched by the magnitude of the challenges it presents.For instance, the 'black box' issue, which is the aspect of AI where many systems, especially those that rely on complex algorithms such as deep learning, are hard to be understood by the human race [2, 3]. The difficulty in understanding how decisions are made and how models work brings worries about trust, fairness, responsibility, and openness in AI systems, especially in situations where they are of critical importance, for instance, in medical diagnosis, autonomous vehicles, or legal matters [4]. This is where Explainable AI (XAI) comes in to remediate this problem and help in making

[*] **Corresponding author Sunipa Roy:**Department of Electronics and Communication Engineering, Guru Nanak Institute of Technology, Kolkata, India; E-mail: suniparoy4@gmail.com

Pijush Dutta, Sudip Mondal, Korhan Cengiz and S. Balamurugan (Eds.)

decisions more transparently without suppressing the functioning of the AIsystems. One such example that is explored in XAI is the need for justification, main principles, techniques, hurdles, and the development of the ethical AI of the future [5]. Fig. (**1**) represents industry evolution from Industry 1.0 to Industry 5.0 with its verticals.

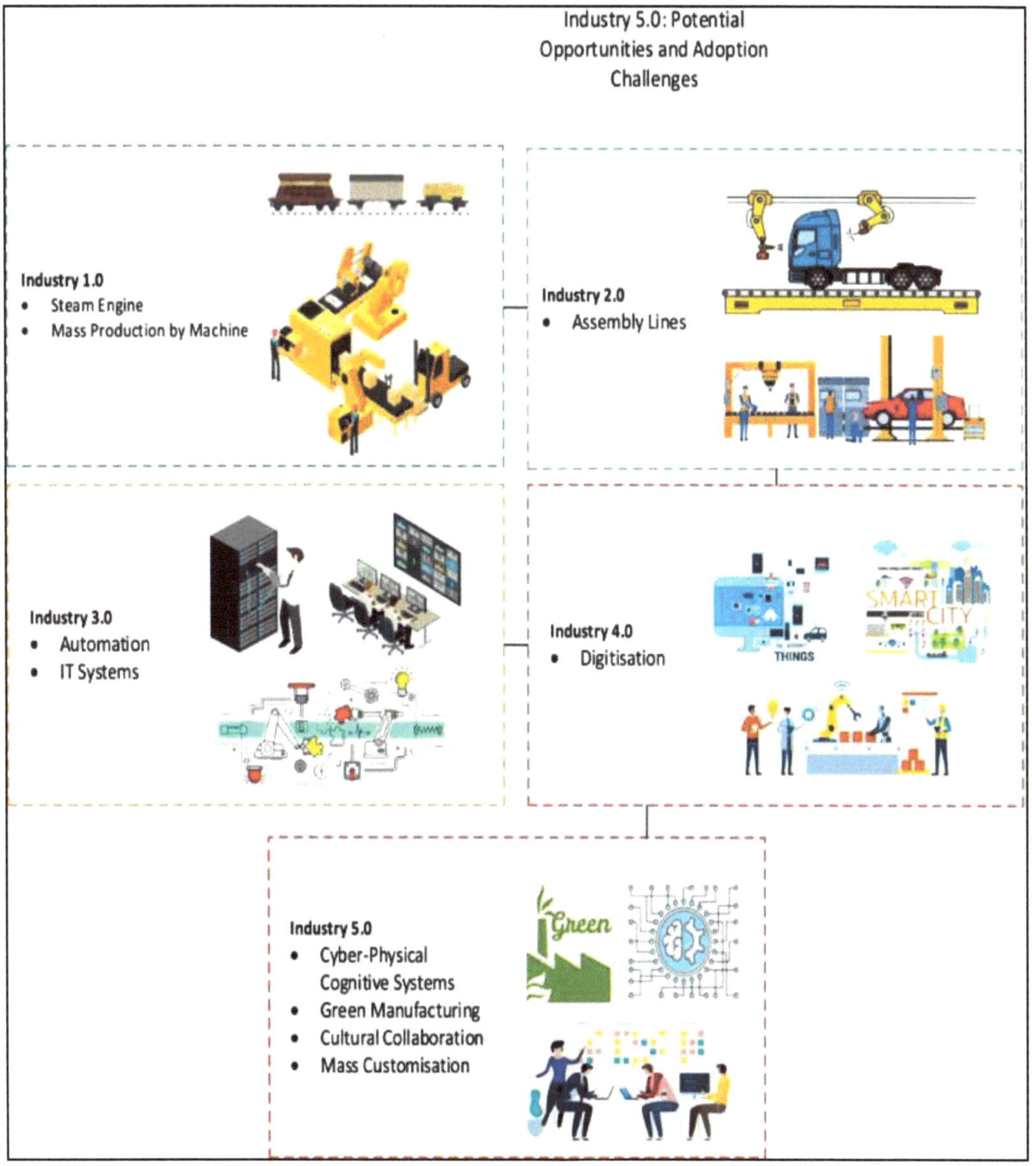

Fig. (1). Industrial Evolution.

The exponential growth of Explainable AI (XAI) is significantly attributable to the numerous application domains in which AI models are being increasingly used to make decisions. Today's AI models are predominantly designed using complex, deep neural networks, some with millions of parameters, to deal with big data to identify, classify, or recommend actions. Even though such models seem to be very accurate and efficient, the naked eye cannot decipher how they reach a defined outcome on a particular issue; hence, disregard is placed on ethics and reasoning [6]. This is quite problematic, especially in critical fields like healthcare, law, and others, where there are high consequences associated with the decision-making process and whose outputs are doled out to humans. For example, in the health sector, forecasting a disease's occurrence could be an AI application. However, if physicians do not grasp the reasoning discordant with that prediction, they may refuse to use that application within their diagnostic pattern. Similar conditions exist in the finance sector while evaluating customers' applications for credit [7]. In such and many more cases, a lack of apparent justification leads to dialogue paralysis concerning AI, especially its acceptance and use, thus inducing social problems. As the pressure mounts for more transparency in AI from policymakers and regulators, explainability becomes even more important. For example, the General Data Protection Regulation (GDPR) of the European Union also provides for an individual's right to explanation in instances when AI impacts his or her life a great deal, such as when a loan or job application is denied. Explainability as a concept cannot thus be polarized into it being merely an engineering requirement, but there are legal and moral reasons for ensuring AI embeds fairness and accountability in a socio-culturally relevant manner [8].

Explainable AI is a subset of AI that tries to provide human-understandable explanations for AI models. Hence, it is pertinent to first analyze the key terms of the definition of explainable AI. Explainability can be analyzed as the responsibility of the artificial intelligence (AI) system to justify its actions through evaluation of how well humans comprehend the reasons for the actions of AI systems [9]. However, explainability is not just a one-size-fits-all remedy. It can vary depending on the intended audience (*e.g.*, data scientist vs. a layperson), the setting (*e.g.*, simple recommendation system vs. recommendation affecting health), or the artificial intelligence model itself. There are two key types of explainability, namely global and local. Global explainability refers to the understanding of a model in its entirety—how it makes predictions given input in all instances. For example, in medicine, it may help to know the broad principles that the model employs to reach the diagnosis. While local explainability is concerned with the explanations for individual decisions, it explains why a particular output is a result of a particular input. For instance, in the case of a credit scoring system, a local explanation would account for why one person was granted a loan or had an application turned down [10].

A further addition to XAI is the distinction between model-specific explainability and model-agnostic explainability. In contrast, some model-specific methods are developed for a specific category of models, for example, decision trees, which are self-explanatory since they are structured along rules and regulations. However, these model-agnostic methods can be used for any type of AI model, irrespective of the degree of irregularity. LIME (Local Interpretable Model-Agnostic Explanations) and SHAP (Shapley Additive explanations) are examples of such methods that seek to explain how black-box models work, or more practically, how certain input affects the models' output in a given decision [11, 12]. Different researchers have proposed different approaches to the decomposition of AI systems into explainable components and attempted to implement these. Each alternative has its advantages and disadvantages. Some emphasize the reduction of complex models to simple ones, whereas others work on building models that are interpretable by design.

Inherently Interpretable Models

The main aim of these AI models is to be clear and understandable from the very beginning. Among the easy-to-understand ones are models based on linear regression, decision trees, and rules that map the system to understandable directions. Nevertheless, the latter might not always be able to compete with more complex models like deep neural networks in terms of performance or accuracy [13]. Therefore, there usually lies a balance between the two opposite poles, such as simplicity and performance, in these models.

Post-hoc Explainability

Post-hoc explainability strategies can be used for models that are not naturally interpretable once the model has produced its predictions. These techniques try to explain or approximate the behavior of the black-box model in a way that makes sense to humans. By building more straightforward surrogate models for individual predictions, LIME, for example, approximates complex models and helps people comprehend the impact of different input characteristics [14]. Similarly, SHAP provides a more comprehensive understanding of how each feature affects the result by assigning relevance ratings to characteristics depending on how they contribute to the model's predictions [15].

Visualization Techniques

Using model behavior visualization is another powerful XAI technique. Users can get visual clues about how various variables impact predictions with the help of tools such as saliency maps for neural networks, feature importance graphs, and partial dependence plots (PDPs). Saliency maps identify the areas of an image that are most crucial to a neural network's conclusion in domains like image recognition, making it simpler to comprehend what the model "sees." [16].

Natural Language Explanations

Some approaches focus on generating explanations in natural language. Giving them human-accessible explanations can aid non-expert users in understanding AI conclusions, which can be particularly beneficial. Instead of offering a complex mathematical model, an AI system might, for instance, give a clear explanation of why a certain loan application was approved or rejected based on a user's financial history. Explainable AI has advanced, but there are still many obstacles to overcome. The intrinsic trade-off between interpretability and accuracy is a significant obstacle [17]. The most interpretable models are frequently the most accurate ones, such as deep learning models with several hidden layers. Because of this, AI professionals are forced to decide between transparency and performance. Making sure that the explanations offered by XAI techniques are significant and not merely rough approximations presents another difficulty. Even if an explanation is mathematically sound, it might not offer human decision-makers any valuable insights. Another big worry is making sure AI explanations are fair. Simply explaining a biased decision does not address the issue of prejudice itself, and some models may unintentionally reinforce biases. Thus, XAI must be coupled with ethical AI development practices to ensure fairness and justice [18]. The need for explainable AI will only increase as AI is further incorporated into many facets of society. Future developments in XAI are probably going to concentrate on creating more understandable explanations, improving the interpretability of intricate models without compromising accuracy, and integrating explainability throughout the AI development process from the ground up. Furthermore, XAI is an essential part of AI governance since businesses will be more motivated to prioritize accountability and transparency as AI legislation changes [19]. Finally, given the current AI environment, explainable AI is not only a technical problem but also a socio-ethical necessity. XAI reduces the possibility of biases, unfair outcomes, and unforeseen effects while ensuring that the advantages of AI are available to everyone by increasing the transparency, understandability, and accountability of AI systems. Explainability will be essential to building human-machine trust and cooperation as the area develops, resulting in a more responsible and inclusive AI-driven future.

PRINCIPLES OF EXPLAINABLE AI IN INDUSTRY 5.0

Explainable AI in Industry 5.0 is based on several fundamental ideas that guarantee AI systems continue to be ethical, transparent, and focused on people. To ensure that AI systems are reliable and able to function alongside human workers, these guidelines direct their design, development, and implementation across a range of industries [20].

Transparency

The first XAI tenet describes AI systems' capacity to offer concise, intelligible, and interpretable justifications for their choices and behaviors. Because it allows users to understand how and why an AI system came to a specific result, transparency is crucial for fostering human-AI trust [21]. Transparency is essential in Industry 5.0 to promote human-machine collaboration and guarantee that AI enhances human decision-making rather than taking its place.

Interpretability

The ability of humans to comprehend and make sense of AI models and their outputs is known as interpretability, and it is closely related to transparency. AI must be able to explain complicated, linked systems in Industry 5.0 in a way that non-experts, like manufacturing workers, medical professionals, and financial decision-makers, can understand [12, 22]. Interpretability aims to make AI systems usable by a wide variety of users, making it easier to incorporate them into routine operations and decision-making procedures.

Accountability

One essential idea that guarantees AI systems function morally and responsibly is accountability. AI systems will be essential in Industry 5.0 in fields like manufacturing, healthcare, and finance, where choices can have serious moral and legal ramifications. Mechanisms for monitoring and auditing AI decisions are essential components of XAI frameworks because they enable enterprises to assign accountability and guarantee adherence to legal requirements [23]. In XAI, accountability also entails giving concise justifications for mistakes and prejudices so that remedial measures can be taken.

Fairness

Fairness in AI decision-making is critical to preventing biases from spreading or amplifying, especially in sensitive sectors like hiring, lending, and healthcare. Industry 5.0 requires XAI to incorporate tools for recognizing and mitigating biases, ensuring that AI systems make fair and equal decisions [24]. This principle also entails providing clear explanations for how AI systems balance various aspects, allowing users to evaluate the fairness of AI-driven results.

Human-centricity

Human-centric innovation is a major differentiator for Industry 5.0. AI systems are intended to complement, not replace, human capabilities. XAI is critical to keeping AI systems aligned with human ideals and needs. This principle emphasizes the need to build AI systems that deliver explanations in a way that facilitates human comprehension and decision-making, hence encouraging collaboration between people and robots.

MISSION OF EXPLAINABLE AI IN INDUSTRY 5.0

Explainable AI in Industry 5.0 aims to create AI systems that are not only strong and efficient but also transparent, understandable, and consistent with human values. XAI seeks to close the gap between AI's computational capabilities and human intuition, boosting trust and collaboration in areas where AI plays an important role [25]. The task can be divided into many main objectives:

Empowering Human Workers

One of the primary goals of XAI in Industry 5.0 is to empower humans by providing them with AI tools that are interpretable and intelligible. This allows workers to benefit from AI's capabilities while maintaining control over decision-making processes. For instance, in manufacturing, AI systems can provide explanations for predictive maintenance warnings, allowing engineers to evaluate the AI's predictions and take relevant measures.

Enhancing Trust and Collaboration

Trust is a key component of successful human-AI collaboration. XAI's aim involves increasing trust by ensuring that AI systems are transparent and can explain their conclusions in a way that humans can understand. Explainable AI, for example, can increase clinicians' faith in AI-driven diagnostic tools, resulting in better patient outcomes and more successful treatment strategies.

Ensuring Ethical AI Use

In Industry 5.0, AI systems will participate in decision-making processes with far-reaching ethical implications. XAI's objective is to ensure that AI systems behave ethically by offering clear explanations for their actions and detecting potential biases. This is especially essential in industries like recruiting, finance, and healthcare, where biased or immoral AI choices can have catastrophic implications.

Driving Regulatory Compliance

As AI becomes more widely employed in industry, regulatory organizations are more concerned with ensuring that AI systems are transparent and accountable. XAI's purpose includes promoting regulatory compliance by offering the tools and frameworks required for auditing AI choices and ensuring that AI systems adhere to legal and ethical guidelines. This is especially important in businesses like finance and healthcare, where compliance with rules like GDPR (General Data Protection Regulation) and HIPAA (Health Insurance Portability and Accountability Act) is required [26].

THE EVOLUTION FROM INDUSTRY 4.0 TO INDUSTRY 5.0

With an emphasis on a more human-centric approach, the transition from Industry 4.0 to Industry 5.0 signifies a substantial change in the way manufacturing and production processes function [27]. Here is a summary of this change:

Industry 4.0: Key features

Automation and Data Exchange: Industry 4.0 places a strong emphasis on building smart factories through the application of big data analytics, artificial intelligence, and the Internet of Things. Machines interact with one another and use real-time data to inform their decisions.

Cyber-Physical Systems: These systems allow for improved monitoring, control, and optimization by fusing computational power with physical processes.

Customization: They have the capacity to mass-produce individualized goods in response to specific consumer requests.

Transition to Industry 5.0: Emerging Concepts

Human-Centric Focus: Industry 5.0 places a high value on human-machine cooperation. In addition to automated procedures, it aims to strengthen the role of human workers by appreciating their inventiveness and problem-solving skills.

Sustainability: Taking into account resource efficiency and environmental impact, there is a heavy emphasis on sustainable methods. Industry 5.0 maximizes resource usage and minimizes waste by promoting the concepts of the circular economy.

Resilience and Adaptability: Businesses are now concentrating on developing systems that are more resilient to supply chain interruptions, market fluctuations, and other unanticipated difficulties.

Technologies in Industry 5.0

Collaborative Robots (Cobots): These robots complement people by helping with jobs and increasing production without taking the place of human workers. **Advanced AI and machine learning:** Predictive analytics, workflow optimization, and the ability to make more complex decisions are all made possible.

Augmented reality (AR) and virtual reality (VR): By offering immersive experiences, these tools improve maintenance, training, and operating efficiency.

Implications for the Workforce

Skill Development: As their responsibilities change in this new paradigm, workers will need to adjust by learning new skills, especially in technology and teamwork.

Employment Creation: Industry 5.0 is anticipated to generate new positions centered on monitoring and enhancing human-technology interactions, even as automation may eliminate some occupations. The transition from Industry 4.0 to Industry 5.0 is a revolutionary strategy in which technology enhances human intelligence, spurring innovation while placing a premium on resilience and sustainability [28]. A more sustainable and effective industrial landscape will eventually result from this evolution's goal of fostering a more harmonious partnership between humans and machines.

THE NEED FOR EXPLAINABLE AI IN INDUSTRY 5.0

Trust and Transparency

To be trusted, AI systems must be able to explain their conclusions in human-readable language, especially in safety-critical areas such as healthcare, manufacturing, and finance. Users gain trust when they can see the reasoning behind an AI's recommendations or actions, allowing them to confirm that these judgments are consistent with company objectives, ethical standards, and legal obligations. AI will be firmly ingrained in processes that have a direct influence on humans, such as tailored medicine, self-driving cars, and collaborative robots [10, 13]. XAI ensures that AI's decisions in these domains are transparent, lowering the risk of harm and improving the adoption of AI-driven advances.

Accountability and Ethical Compliance

As AI becomes more powerful, it assumes greater responsibility. In Industry 5.0, where AI is used for everything from product creation to supply chain optimization, accountability is critical. XAI has a framework for tracking AI choices, which is critical for auditing, legal compliance, and detecting bias. Explainability is also important for addressing ethical problems. For example, in recruiting processes, AI-driven decision-making must be transparent to eliminate prejudices based on race, gender, or other protected traits. XAI enables businesses to ensure that their AI systems are fair, justifiable, and adhere to ethical requirements.

Human-Machine Collaboration

Industry 5.0 encourages a symbiotic partnership between humans and machines. AI systems must be able to explain their decisions in real-time to collaborate effectively. For example, in a production scenario, if a cobot detects a fault in a product, it should be able to explain why it detected the problem and recommend corrective steps. This transparency enables human workers to trust and comprehend the AI's reasoning, resulting in more productive teamwork. XAI encourages collaboration by making AI systems more accessible to non-technical people [29]. When AI judgments are transparent and understandable, human workers can be more effective in providing feedback, correcting errors, and making educated decisions based on AI insights.

APPLICATIONS OF EXPLAINABLE AI IN INDUSTRY 5.0

With an emphasis on fusing human intelligence with cutting-edge technology like robotics, artificial intelligence (AI), and the Internet of Things (IoT), Industry 5.0 signifies a revolutionary change in manufacturing and production. Industry 5.0 places more emphasis on human-machine collaboration, which fosters creativity and invention, than its predecessor, Industry 4.0, which placed more emphasis on automation and efficiency. Transparency and confidence in AI systems are two essential elements of Industry 5.0. Demand for Explainable AI (XAI) has increased as AI becomes more and more integrated into decision-making processes [30]. XAI refers to strategies and tactics that ensure users can understand how decisions are made by making AI system outputs comprehensible to humans.

Healthcare

In Industry 5.0, explainable artificial intelligence (XAI) is essential, especially in the healthcare industry. The following are some examples of how XAI improves human-AI collaboration, trust, and decision-making [18, 19]:

Clinical Decision Support Systems

Personalized Treatment Plans: By assisting doctors in comprehending how patient data informs recommendations, XAI may provide an explanation of the reasoning behind suggested treatment alternatives.

Diagnostic Support: AI systems can offer explanations of how they arrived at a diagnosis, which helps medical practitioners confirm or challenge the AI's suggestions.

Patient Engagement

Transparent Communication: By assisting patients in comprehending their medical issues and available treatments, XAI can improve patient compliance and participation.

Risk assessments: Giving patients concise explanations of risk factors and the logic behind evaluations might enable them to make well-informed health decisions.

Predictive Analytics

Disease Prediction: By elucidating the variables influencing forecasts, XAI can assist medical professionals in concentrating on groups that are at risk and putting preventative measures in place.

Resource Allocation: Hospitals can improve patient care and operational efficiency by optimizing resource distribution by explaining demand estimates.

Drug Discovery and Development

Compound Evaluation: The medication development process can be made more transparent by using AI models to explain the anticipated safety and efficacy profiles of novel therapeutic compounds [21].

Clinical Trials: By describing selection criteria based on patient data, XAI can help find qualified trial candidates.

Ethics and Compliance

Bias Detection: By exposing biases in AI models, XAI can guarantee that healthcare applications are just and equal for all populations.

Regulatory Compliance: Healthcare firms can comply with regulations requiring transparency in the use of AI by offering interpretable models.

Medical Imaging

Image Analysis: By clarifying how particular characteristics in medical images result in particular diagnostic findings, XAI might increase radiologists' confidence in interpretations supported by AI.

Error Analysis: Over time, XAI helps imaging systems become more accurate by elucidating the causes of misclassifications.

Robotic Surgery

Assistive Robotics: By giving surgeons knowledge about how robotic systems make decisions, XAI can improve cooperation and confidence throughout operations.

Post-Operation Analysis: By explaining surgical results, practitioners can enhance their methods and provide better training for subsequent procedures.

Population Health Management

Public Health Insights: By assisting public health officials in comprehending the facts behind health patterns, XAI can more successfully direct policies and interventions.

Community Engagement: Healthcare institutions can promote trust and collaboration in communities by providing explanations of health data interpretations. XAI not only improves the performance of AI systems in healthcare but also fosters trust between patients and providers in Industry 5.0, where human-AI collaboration is crucial. Explainability must be incorporated into AI systems as the healthcare industry changes to provide moral, efficient, and patient-centered treatment.

Manufacturing

In the context of Industry 5.0, explainable artificial intelligence (XAI) is essential, especially in manufacturing. To increase productivity while maintaining safety, sustainability, and personalization, this phase places a strong emphasis on human-machine collaboration. Key uses of XAI in this context include the following [25, 26]:

Quality Control and Assurance

By offering insights into the decision-making of AI systems employed in defect detection, XAI helps improve quality control procedures. When an AI detects a faulty product, for instance, XAI can describe the characteristics or factors that influenced this judgment, allowing operators to comprehend and have faith in the system's results.

Predictive Maintenance

AI models examine machine data in predictive maintenance to foresee malfunctions before they happen. XAI can assist personnel in prioritizing interventions and comprehending the root causes of possible problems by elucidating the logic behind maintenance recommendations. Better planning and resource allocation are made possible by this transparency, which also increases confidence.

Human-Robot Collaboration

By making robotic decision-making transparent, XAI can help humans and robots collaborate as robots become increasingly integrated into production processes. This increases overall workflow productivity and safety by assisting human workers in comprehending robot movements and modifying their interactions accordingly.

Supply Chain Optimization

By explaining the AI-driven projections and optimization techniques it produces, XAI helps improve supply chain management. For example, XAI can offer reasoning based on demand forecasts and market patterns if an AI system recommends adjustments to inventory levels, empowering stakeholders to make well-informed choices.

Customization and Personalization

By elucidating how design decisions impact product performance and cost, XAI can facilitate customization in production, particularly in industries like consumer electronics and automotive. This can assist design teams in making better choices that maximize resource utilization and correspond with client desires.

Energy Management

By examining usage trends and making recommendations for changes, XAI can improve energy use in manufacturing facilities. Manufacturing companies can successfully adopt more sustainable practices by describing how specific actions can lower energy expenses or carbon footprints.

Training and Skill Development

By offering insights into the logic underlying AI recommendations or actions, XAI can help with staff training. This comprehension aids employees in learning from AI systems, improving their abilities, and creating a workforce with greater knowledge.

Compliance and Safety

XAI can assist in guaranteeing adherence to safety regulations in highly regulated industries. Manufacturers can better comprehend and follow laws, reducing risks and improving worker safety, by explaining the rationale behind safety alerts or compliance checks [24]. In addition to increasing operational efficiency, integrating XAI into industrial processes under Industry 5.0 promotes a cooperative atmosphere where machine intelligence and human intuition work in tandem. More creative and environmentally friendly production techniques may result from this collaboration.

Finance

The finance industry's journey from Industry 4.0 to Industry 5.0 signifies a dramatic change in the way financial services are provided, with a focus on sustainability, personalization, and human-to-advanced technology collaboration.

Industry 4.0 in Finance

Automation and Efficiency: Using robotics, machine learning, and artificial intelligence (AI), Industry 4.0 brought automation. This resulted in improved risk management, automated trading systems, and more efficient back-office operations in the financial industry.

Data-Driven Decision Making: Financial institutions were able to examine enormous volumes of data thanks to the emergence of big data, which enhanced consumer insights and made predictive analytics for risk assessments and investment plans possible.

Blockchain and Crypto-currencies: While cryptocurrencies have become alternative financial assets, the implementation of blockchain technology has opened up new avenues for safely and transparently handling transactions [29, 30].

Customer Experience: Mobile banking, robo-advisors, and customized financial services are examples of how digital platforms have improved client involvement.

Transition to Industry 5.0

Human-Centric Approach: Industry 5.0 places a strong emphasis on the value of both technology and human beings. This entails using AI in finance to improve human expertise rather than replace it, creating a more cooperative atmosphere.

Personalization and Customization: Financial services are becoming more and more individualized to meet the demands of each client, using data analytics and artificial intelligence to offer custom solutions that take into account each client's unique financial situation and goals.

Sustainability and Ethical Finance: Sustainability is a fundamental tenet of Industry 5.0. To encourage socially conscious investing, financial institutions are including ESG (Environmental, Social, and Governance) criteria in their investment strategies.

Decentralized Finance (DeFi): Peer-to-peer financial transactions without the need for traditional middlemen are made possible by these (DeFi) platforms, which promote greater financial inclusion and innovation.

Enhanced Security and Trust: Industry 5.0 places a strong emphasis on fostering trust *via* cutting-edge cybersecurity measures and open procedures in response to growing worries about data privacy and security.

Opportunities and Difficulties

Integration of New Technologies: To comply with regulations, financial institutions must manage the challenges of integrating cutting-edge technologies.

Workforce Transformation: To optimize potential benefits, personnel must be upskilled to collaborate with AI and other technologies.

Customer Trust: As technology develops, it will be essential to preserve customer trust *via* openness and moral behavior.

In the financial sector, the transition from Industry 4.0 to Industry 5.0 signifies a paradigm change that prioritizes a more sustainable, individualized, and cooperative approach to financial services. Financial institutions can become more competitive and better meet the changing requirements of their customers by adopting these ideas.

CHALLENGES AND FUTURE DIRECTIONS

Balancing Explainability and Performance

Finding the right balance between explainability and performance is a major problem when building XAI. More complicated AI models, such as deep learning systems, frequently deliver higher accuracy, but at the expense of interpretability. In Industry 5.0, businesses must navigate this trade-off by selecting models that strike the proper balance for their specific use cases [14, 19].

Regulatory and Ethical Considerations

Explainability will become a legal requirement in many industries as governments and international organizations develop legislation surrounding AI. Organizations must verify that their AI systems comply with these rules, which may include investing in XAI frameworks and technologies. The ethical concerns of AI decision-making will also receive increased attention, especially when AI assumes increasingly autonomous roles in society [14].

Integration into Existing Workflows

Effective XAI requires a smooth integration into current procedures. This implies that, in addition to offering explanations, AI systems must also do so in a manner that complements human decision-making. Industry 5.0's XAI future is probably going to see the creation of intuitive tools and user interfaces that let people engage with AI explanations.

CONCLUSION

Explainable AI (XAI) plays an important role in Industry 5.0, where the emphasis is on human-machine collaboration. XAI offers explanations of AI decision-making, inducing transparency, accountability, and trust. This is important in sectors such as health, finance, and manufacturing, where AI-based decisions have far-reaching implications. The advantages of XAI are fairness, compliance with ethics, and efficient human-machine collaboration. Nonetheless, challenges such as the balance between explainability and performance have to be addressed. The future of XAI involves creating intuitive tools and embedding seamless integration into workflows. By focusing on XAI, we can realize the potential of AI and build a more sustainable, efficient, and ethical industrial age. As Industry 5.0 is shaped, the relevance of XAI increases, influencing human-machine collaboration and AI-driven decision-making. Ultimately, XAI has the potential to revolutionize industries by enabling trust, cooperation, and innovation. By creating AI systems that focus on transparency, accountability, and human-centeredness, we can advance human well-being, safety, and prosperity. Moving forward, adopting XAI is crucial in building a future that has humans and machines cooperating effectively, advancing progress with limited risks. By doing this, we can channel AI's potential to make a better world for everyone.

REFERENCES

[1] A. Adel, "Future of industry 5.0 in society: human-centric solutions, challenges and prospective research areas", *J. Cloud Comput. (Heidelb.),* vol. 11, no. 1, pp. 40-44, 2022. [http://dx.doi.org/10.1186/s13677-022-00314-5] [PMID: 36101900]

[2] C. Trivedi, P. Bhattacharya, V.K. Prasad, V. Patel, A. Singh, S. Tanwar, R. Sharma, S. Aluvala, G. Pau, and G. Sharma, "Explainable AI for Industry 5.0: Vision, Architecture, and Potential Directions", *IEEE Open J. Ind. Appl.,* vol. 5, pp. 177-208, 2024. [http://dx.doi.org/10.1109/OJIA.2024.3399057]

[3] P. Bhattacharya, "Internet-of-explainable-digital-twins: A case study of versatile corn production ecosystem", *Proc. Int. Conf. Commun. Comput. Cybersecur. Informat.,* pp. 1-5, 2022. [http://dx.doi.org/10.1109/CCCI55352.2022.9926502]

[4] X-H. Li, "A survey of data-driven and knowledge-aware eXplainable AI", *IEEE Trans. Knowl. Data Eng.,* vol. 34, pp. 29-49, 2022.

[5] R.S. Peres, X. Jia, J. Lee, K. Sun, A.W. Colombo, and J. Barata, "Industrial artificial intelligence in industry 4.0—Systematic review challenges and outlook", *IEEE Access,* vol. 8, pp. 220121-220139, 2020. [http://dx.doi.org/10.1109/ACCESS.2020.3042874]

[6] Andreas Hartl, "Germany's human-centred approach to AI is inclusive, evidence-based and capacity-building", *OECD.AI Policy Observ.,* 2021.

[7] P. Bhattacharya, "Towards future Internet: The metaverse perspective for diverse industrial applications", *Math.,* vol. 11, 2023. [http://dx.doi.org/10.3390/math11040941]

[8] S. Chaudhary, "Untangling explainable AI in applicative domains: Taxonomy, tools, and open challenges", *Proc. 4th Int. Conf. Comput., Commun., Cyber-Secur.,* pp. 857-872, 2023. [http://dx.doi.org/10.1007/978-981-99-1479-1_63]

[9] J. Tao, "XAI-driven explainable multiview game cheating detection", *Proc. IEEE Conf. Games,* pp. 144-151, 2020.Osaka, Japan

[10] A. Nascita, "Unveiling mimetic: Interpreting deep learning traffic classifiers via XAI techniques", *Proc. IEEE Int. Conf. Cyber Secur. Resilience,* pp. 455-460, 2021.

[11] N. Sarathy, "Investigation of an innovative approach for identifying human face-profile using explainable artificial intelligence", *Proc. IEEE 18th Int. Symp. Intell. Syst. Informat.,* pp. 155-160, 2020.

[12] U. Pawar, "Explainable AI in Healthcare", *International Conference on Cyber Situational Awareness, Data Analytics and Assessment (CyberSA),* pp. 1-2, 2021.Dublin, Ireland

[13] M.T. Ribeiro, "Why Should I Trust You?", *Explaining the Predictions of Any Classifier,* pp. 1135-1144, 2016.
[http://dx.doi.org/10.18653/v1/N16-3020]

[14] S. Tian, W. Yang, J.M.L. Grange, P. Wang, W. Huang, and Z. Ye, "Smart healthcare: making medical care more intelligent", *Glob. Health J.,* vol. 3, no. 3, pp. 62-65, 2019.
[http://dx.doi.org/10.1016/j.glohj.2019.07.001]

[15] F. Kitsios, M. Kamariotou, A.I. Syngelakis, and M.A. Talias, "Recent Advances of Artificial Intelligence in Healthcare: A Systematic Literature Review", *Appl. Sci. (Basel),* vol. 13, no. 13, pp. 7479-7484, 2023.
[http://dx.doi.org/10.3390/app13137479]

[16] S. Bharati, M.R.H. Mondal, and P. Podder, "A Review on Explainable Artificial Intelligence for Healthcare: Why, How, and When?", *IEEE Trans. Artif. Intell.,* vol. 5, no. 4, pp. 1429-1442, 2024.
[http://dx.doi.org/10.1109/TAI.2023.3266418]

[17] S. Bharati, "Artificial neural network based breast cancer screening: A comprehensive review", *Int. J. Comput. Inf. Syst. Ind. Manage. Appl.,* vol. 12, pp. 125-137, 2020.

[18] J. He, "The practical implementation of artificial intelligence technologies in medicine", *Nat. Med.,* vol. 25, pp. 30-36, 2019.
[http://dx.doi.org/10.1038/s41591-018-0307-0]

[19] K. Zahoor, "Explainable AI for Healthcare: An Approach Towards Interpretable Healthcare Models", *24th International Arab Conference on Information Technology (ACIT),* pp. 1-7, 2023.Ajman, United Arab Emirates
[http://dx.doi.org/10.1109/ACIT58888.2023.10453740]

[20] W.J. von Eschenbach, "Transparency and the Black Box Problem: Why We Do Not Trust AI", *Philos. Technol.,* vol. 34, no. 4, pp. 1607-1622, 2021.
[http://dx.doi.org/10.1007/s13347-021-00477-0]

[21] Y. Matsuo, Y. LeCun, M. Sahani, D. Precup, D. Silver, M. Sugiyama, E. Uchibe, and J. Morimoto, "Deep learning, reinforcement learning, and world models", *Neural Netw.,* vol. 152, pp. 267-275, 2022.
[http://dx.doi.org/10.1016/j.neunet.2022.03.037] [PMID: 35569196]

[22] V. Chamola, V. Hassija, A.R. Sulthana, D. Ghosh, D. Dhingra, and B. Sikdar, "A Review of Trustworthy and Explainable Artificial Intelligence (XAI)", *IEEE Access,* vol. 11, pp. 78994-79015, 2023.
[http://dx.doi.org/10.1109/ACCESS.2023.3294569]

[23] D. Paul, G. Sanap, S. Shenoy, D. Kalyane, K. Kalia, and R.K. Tekade, "Artificial intelligence in drug discovery and development", *Drug Discov. Today,* vol. 26, no. 1, pp. 80-93, 2021.
[http://dx.doi.org/10.1016/j.drudis.2020.10.010] [PMID: 33099022]

[24] Michele Scalas, "Explanation-driven characterization of Android ransomware", *ICPR Workshop on explainable deep learning - AI,* pp. 228-242, 2021.

[25] Michele Scalas, "Explainable machine learning for secure smart vehicles", *AEIT Int. Conf. Electr. Electron. Technol. Automot.,* pp. 7-11, 2021.

[26] Battista Biggio, "Wild patterns: Ten years after the rise of adversarial machine learning", *Pattern Recogn.,* vol. 84, pp. 317-331, 2021.

[27] J. Fior, L. Cagliero, and P. Garza, "Leveraging Explainable AI to Support Cryptocurrency Investors", *Future Internet,* vol. 14, no. 9, p. 251, 2022.
[http://dx.doi.org/10.3390/fi14090251]

[28] G. Giudici, A. Milne, and D. Vinogradov, "Cryptocurrencies: market analysis and perspectives", *Econ. Polit. Ind.,* vol. 47, no. 1, pp. 1-18, 2020.

[http://dx.doi.org/10.1007/s40812-019-00138-6]

[29] Marco Ortu, "On technical trading and social media indicators for cryptocurrency price classification through deep learning", *Expert Syst. Appl.,* vol. 198, pp. 116804-116810, 2022.

[30] Fan Fang, "Cryptocurrency trading: A comprehensive survey", *Financ. Innov.,* vol. 8, 2022. [http://dx.doi.org/10.1186/s40854-021-00321-6]

CHAPTER 2

Optimization of Process Parameters Using ANOVA: A Review

Amit Dey[1], **Sumanta Dey**[1], **Gour Gopal Jana**[1], **Rudrajit Datta**[2,*] and **Arindam Sadhu**[3]

[1] *Department of Electronics & Communication Engineering, Greater Kolkata College of Engineering and Management, Baruipur, West Bengal, 743387, India*

[2] *Department of Electrical Engineering, Greater Kolkata College of Engineering and Management, Baruipur, West Bengal, 743387, India*

[3] *Department of Electronics & Communication Engineering, Sudhir Chandra Sur Institute of Technology and Sports Complex, Kolkata, West Bengal, India*

Abstract: The process parameters in casting, welding, renewable energy, and machinability research are optimized using mobile analysis of variance (ANOVA). Experiments are frequently designed using analysis of variance, which reduces the number of experiments for a given number of components and their levels. Compared to the Taguchi approach to design, it has numerous advantages. Experiments are carried out under the experimental design, and output and other reactions are documented. To determine which factors have a major impact on the answer, an analysis of variance is utilized. The process parameters are optimized to achieve a particular goal function, and regression equations are created to forecast the response.

Keywords: Analysis of Variance (ANOVA), Experimental design, Factorial experimental design, Modeling.

INTRODUCTION

Analysis of variance (ANOVA) is the most efficient technique to perform data analysis, avoiding the multiple comparisons between groups [1]. ANOVA is a sophisticated and subtle technique with multiple variations, each of which is appropriate for a certain experimental setting [2]. A clinical experiment taken from optometric research was used to define and illustrate the analysis's most basic form, the one-way ANOVA, in a randomized design [3]. The many ways to compare certain group mean pairings were also taken into account. The objective of this paper is to apply these methods to various experimental setups. These

* **Corresponding author Rudrajit Datta:** Department of Electrical Engineering, Greater Kolkata College of Engineering and Management, Baruipur, West Bengal, 743387, India; E-mail: rudrajit.datta@gkcem.ac.in

Pijush Dutta, Sudip Mondal, Korhan Cengiz and S. Balamurugan (Eds.)

ANOVA types will be discussed in this article under the following headings, which should cover a wide range of scenarios that arise in optometric research: (1) 1-way ANOVA, (2) 2-way ANOVA, (3) 3-way ANOVA, (4) factorial ANOVA, and (5) Split-plot factorial ANOVA. Each instance includes a description of the experimental design type, a statistical model, and a discussion of the benefits and drawbacks of the relevant ANOVA. The issues of determining the number of replications for the statistical model are also considered.

STATISTICAL MODELS

ANOVA is commonly described by the following notation: The subscript "i" indicates the group or class that ranges from "1 to x," while the subscript "j" indicates the members of the class that range from "1 to n". Any observation in a linear model can relate to the mean and variance and can be written as follows:

$$x_{ij} = \mu + a_i + e_{ij}$$

By adding additional terms xijto a simple model, it turns into complex types of ANOVA obtained from equation 1 (Table **1**), so that an observed value reflects the combined effects of errors of measurement and natural variation between replications.

Table 1. Statistical models

Types of ANOVA	Y (Dependent Variable)	Constant elements	Additional Components
One-way, fixed	x_{ij}	$\mu + e_{ij}$	a_i
One-way, random	x_{ij}	$\mu + e_{ij}$	A_i
Two-way, randomized blocks	x_{ij}	$\mu + e_{ij}$	$a_i + b_j$
Three-way	x_{ijk}	$\mu + e_{ijk}$	$a_i + b_j + c_k + d_{ij}$
Two-factor, factorial	x_{ijk}	$\mu + e_{ijk}$	$a_i + b_j$
Two-factor, factorial split-plot	x_{ijk}	$\mu + e_{ijk}$	$M_i + B_j + T_k + D_{ij}$

TYPES OF ANOVA

One-way ANOVA

In a randomized design, a one-way ANOVA is used to examine the reading rates of three groups of people: patients with age-related macular degeneration, old normal participants, and young normal subjects [4]. To estimate the deviation between the subject groups that are regarded as "fixed," a one-way ANOVA model [5] is used. An alternative model aims to evaluate different causes of variation in time and space and, in many circumstances, to quantify the degree of variance [6].

Two-way ANOVA in randomized blocks

Each observation in the one-way ANOVA is categorized according to only one factor. Patients within a group are a random sample of a certain demographic and are allocated to treatment groups at random [7]. It is feasible to create more intricate experiment designs in several ways. Because of a constraint in the way subjects are randomized to treatments, it is sometimes called "randomized blocks design" that satisfies the following metrics: (1) subjects are first grouped into "Segments", and (2) Individual participants within each segment receive treatments at random [8].

The three-way ANOVA

The "carry-over" effect may become 'tired' as the tests go on when they are administered in randomized blocks in a two-way ANOVA. The strategy is to provide each combination of treatments to an equal number of participants to avoid systematic effects [9]. Each treatment order would be n/2 participants if there were two treatments and n subjects [10].

Factorial ANOVA

A factorial design examines the effects of several distinct elements simultaneously, compared to analyzing each element separately in a single experiment. Additionally, the sums of squares (SS) across treatments or groups are separated into discrete comparisons [11, 12] that illustrate possible interactions between the variables, which is different from the three-way design. The interactions between the variables are sometimes the most intriguing data from a factorial experiment [13]. An illustration of the most basic kind of factorial experiment is when two medications (A and B) are administered to 24 randomly selected patients, six to each treatment combination, at two "levels" (given or not).

Factorial ANOVA, split-plot design

The experimental subjects were randomly allocated to every conceivable combination of the two components in the 2^2 factorial mentioned above [14]. However, in certain designs, the two elements are not interchangeable. When one component may be regarded as a major factor concerning the other as a minor factor, a typical situation known as a split-plot design occurs. In factorial

ANOVA, the subplot treatments are randomized throughout the entire large block [15 - 17]. However, in some of the applications, researchers may further search for separate subplots when designing a split-split-plot design [18].

SIGNIFICANCE OF ANOVA IN PROCESS OPTIMIZATION

ANOVA, or analysis of variance, is a potent statistical method that is essential to process optimization in many different engineering fields. Its main importance stems from its capacity to ascertain how various factors affect a certain output, which makes it a crucial technique for finding and refining crucial process parameters. ANOVA is particularly useful in industrial processes where several factors affect the performance and quality of the final output [11]. ANOVA assists engineers and researchers in making data-driven decisions by methodically examining the impact of each component and how they interact, which improves process efficiency, lowers variability, and improves product quality. The capacity of ANOVA to differentiate between important and irrelevant elements is one of its most important benefits in process improvement. This saves time and money by enabling engineers to concentrate on improving the most important characteristics. ANOVA, for instance, can assist in determining the crucial elements that have a major impact on product quality in manufacturing, such as temperature, pressure, and feed rate. Manufacturers may decrease faults and ensure consistent product quality by optimizing these crucial characteristics [12]. Furthermore, ANOVA is not just used in manufacturing; it is also widely used in a variety of other disciplines, such as environmental management, chemical processes, and renewable energy systems. ANOVA, for example, aids in determining the best mix of reactants and operational parameters to optimize yield in chemical process optimization. ANOVA may also be utilized in renewable energy to maximize the efficiency of solar and wind energy system design and operation.

Application of ANOVA in Different Engineering Domains

Numerous engineering areas have made considerable use of the flexible statistical methodology known as ANOVA, which allows for the methodical examination of the variables affecting process results. ANOVA assists engineers in determining which factors have a major influence on system performance by dividing the overall variation in data into components linked to various sources [13]. Because of this feature, it is an essential tool for streamlining intricate technical procedures.

- ANOVA is used in production engineering to optimize machining parameters, including tool angle, feed rate, and cutting speed. ANOVA, for instance, can identify the parameters that have the most effect on material removal rate or surface roughness in a turning operation. This guarantees increased process efficiency and higher-quality products.

- ANOVA aids in the optimization of chemical reaction parameters in chemical engineering, including temperature, pressure, concentration, and catalyst type. For example, scientists can determine the ideal conditions for optimum efficiency in a chemical reactor by using ANOVA to examine the effect of various factors on product production.
- ANOVA is often used in renewable energy systems to maximize the efficiency of wind turbines, solar collectors, and bioenergy systems. ANOVA, for instance, may be used to guide the design of efficient solar systems by determining the effects of variables such as collector tilt angle, sun intensity, and ambient temperature on energy production.
- ANOVA is used in environmental engineering to evaluate how different factors affect pollution levels, wastewater treatment effectiveness, and air quality control. ANOVA aids in the development of successful mitigation plans by identifying the key variables influencing environmental outcomes.
- ANOVA is used in electronics and communication engineering to improve network setups, antenna designs, and signal processing parameters. For example, in wireless communication, ANOVA may identify the effects of channel noise, modulation method, and transmission power on the signal.

INTEGRATION OF ANOVA WITH OPTIMIZATION TECHNIQUES

In many engineering fields, combining Analysis of Variance (ANOVA) with optimization techniques has become a potent strategy for improving process performance. ANOVA is a statistical technique that determines important characteristics that affect process results by analyzing the impact of several factors on a response variable. When paired with optimization methods like Response Surface Methodology (RSM) [16], Differential Evolution (DE) [15], Particle Swarm Optimization (PSO) [14], and Genetic Algorithm (GA) [14], ANOVA provides a methodical, data-driven way to find and adjust the most important parameters, improving process performance.

Role of ANOVA in Optimization

The main purpose of ANOVA is to pinpoint the critical elements that have a major influence on a process's outcome. By removing less important variables, this first analysis aids in simplifying the optimization issue. Following the identification of the essential components, optimization techniques are used to ascertain the best possible combination of these parameters for enhanced performance. ANOVA, for instance, can pinpoint crucial factors in production, such as temperature, pressure, and feed rate, and optimization approaches may pinpoint the ideal values for these parameters.

ANOVA with Metaheuristic Optimization Algorithms

ANOVA has been effectively used with several metaheuristic optimization methods: ANOVA with Genetic Algorithm (GA): In this method, the important elements in a process are first identified using ANOVA, and the ideal values of these factors are then found using GA. For example, in a liquid flow control system, GA can optimize the values of crucial factors to get a desired flow rate, whereas ANOVA can detect those parameters.

ANOVA with Particle Swarm Optimization (PSO): To optimize multi-parameter processes, ANOVA and PSO may be used together. PSO is used to find the optimal solution in a multi-dimensional space after the important parameters have been determined. This method has been frequently used to optimize chemical reactors, renewable energy systems, and machining operations.

Combining ANOVA with Differential Evolution (DE): For difficult optimization issues, DE is a reliable optimization method that may be used in conjunction with ANOVA. DE is used to adjust the important parameters for optimal performance once ANOVA identifies them. This method works well for multi-modal, non-linear optimization issues.

ANOVA using Response Surface Methodology (RSM): RSM is a well-liked optimization method that approximates the relationship between input components and output response using a quadratic model. It may be used to optimize complicated processes like chemical reactions and energy systems since it enables a systematic investigation of component interactions when paired with ANOVA.

BENEFITS OF ANOVA-INTEGRATED OPTIMIZATION

ANOVA integration with optimization methods has the following benefits:

- Less Complexity: ANOVA makes the optimization issue simpler and requires less computing power by determining the most important factors.
- Improved Accuracy: By ensuring that only important components are maximized, ANOVA produces solutions that are more accurate and trustworthy.
- Effective Search for Optimal Solutions: Optimization methods can rapidly determine the ideal parameter values by concentrating on important elements.
- Enhanced Process Performance: By using a unified strategy, processes are optimized for optimal performance, quality, and efficiency.

CHALLENGES AND FUTURE DIRECTIONS

Notwithstanding its advantages, there are drawbacks to combining ANOVA with optimization methods. These include the computational expense of multi-dimensional optimization, the possibility of overfitting when employing sophisticated optimization models, and the requirement for huge datasets to guarantee accurate ANOVA findings. For improved performance, future studies should concentrate on creating hybrid ANOVA-based optimization strategies that incorporate the advantages of many approaches, such as ANOVA-PSO-GA or ANOVA-RSM-DE.

CONCLUSION

ANOVA is known as a very effective tool for optometric research. Therefore, before planning any experiment, several factors must be taken into account. It must be ensured that the factor is designated as a "fixed" or "random effect" factor in a single-factor design. Every element must be specified precisely with multiple fixed and random factors. The benefits of a randomized block design should be taken into account when duplicates are blocked or grouped. However, compared to a randomized design, the error variation is lowered to about 14% to offset the loss of d.f.

In a three-way design, various treatment orders are incorporated as an "effect," which must be taken into account while administering various therapies to a patient in a sequential manner. When choosing how many replications to utilize in a factorial design, the impact of "internal replication" should be considered. Every ANOVA error term should, if at all feasible, have at least 15 d.f. Moreover, careful thought must be given to whether a given factorial design qualifies as a repeated measurements design or a split plot.

Data must be examined for non-normality, non-additivity, large errors, and lack of error independence. In certain situations, data transformation could be required before analysis.

Before experimenting, the researcher should consult a statistician with expertise in optometric research if there is any uncertainty regarding the aforementioned matters. Verifying that the d.f. and error terms, as well as the model assumptions, are accurate, is very crucial. A statistician may not be able to assist after they have committed to an incorrect design, which will not appropriately test a null hypothesis.

REFERENCES

[1] R.A. Armstrong, F. Eperjesi, and B. Gilmartin, "The application of analysis of variance (ANOVA) to different experimental designs in optometry", *Ophthalmic Physiol. Opt.,* vol. 22, no. 3, pp. 248-256, 2002.
[http://dx.doi.org/10.1046/j.1475-1313.2002.00020.x] [PMID: 12090640]

[2] R.A. Armstrong, S.V. Slade, and F. Eperjesi, "An introduction to analysis of variance (ANOVA) with special reference to data from clinical experiments in optometry", *Ophthalmic Physiol. Opt.,* vol. 20, no. 3, pp. 235-241, 2000.
[http://dx.doi.org/10.1046/j.1475-1313.2000.00502.x] [PMID: 10897345]

[3] T.A. Ryan, "Multiple comparison in psychological research", *Psychol. Bull.,* vol. 56, no. 1, pp. 26-47, 1959.
[http://dx.doi.org/10.1037/h0042478] [PMID: 13623958]

[4] P.C. Austin, "Balance diagnostics for comparing the distribution of baseline covariates between treatment groups in propensity□score matched samples", *Stat. Med.,* vol. 28, no. 25, pp. 3083-3107, 2009.
[http://dx.doi.org/10.1002/sim.3697] [PMID: 19757444]

[5] H.J. Keselman, C.J. Huberty, L.M. Lix, S. Olejnik, R.A. Cribbie, B. Donahue, R.K. Kowalchuk, L.L. Lowman, M.D. Petoskey, J.C. Keselman, and J.R. Levin, "Statistical practices of educational researchers: An analysis of their ANOVA, MANOVA, and ANCOVA analyses", *Rev. Educ. Res.,* vol. 68, no. 3, pp. 350-386, 1998.
[http://dx.doi.org/10.3102/00346543068003350]

[6] G.N. Wilkinson, and C.E. Rogers, "Symbolic description of factorial models for analysis of variance", *J. R. Stat. Soc. Ser. C Appl. Stat.,* vol. 22, no. 3, pp. 392-399, 1973.

[7] G.H. Lemon, "Factors for one-sided tolerance limits for balanced one-way-ANOVA random-effects model", *J. Am. Stat. Assoc.,* vol. 72, no. 359, pp. 676-680, 1977.
[http://dx.doi.org/10.1080/01621459.1977.10480636]

[8] C. Wang, T. Wang, D. Trafimow, and K. Talordphop, "Extending the a priori procedure to one-way analysis of variance model with skew normal random effects", *Asian Journal of Economics and Banking,* vol. 4, no. 2, pp. 77-90, 2020.

[9] Y. Yao, and S. Chakraborti, "Phase I process monitoring: The case of the balanced one□way random effects model", *Qual. Reliab. Eng. Int.,* vol. 37, no. 3, pp. 1244-1265, 2021.
[http://dx.doi.org/10.1002/qre.2793]

[10] N. Ibrahim, and A.B. Abdullahi, "Analysis of Variance (ANOVA) Randomized Block Design (RBD) to Test the Variability of Three Different Types of Fertilizers (NPK, UREA and SSP) on Millet Production", *African Journal of Agricultural Science and Food Research,* vol. 9, no. 1, pp. 1-10, 2023.

[11] P. Dutta, M. Majumder, and A. Kumar, "Parametric optimization of liquid flow process by ANOVA optimized DE, PSO & GA algorithms", *International Journal of Engineering and Manufacturing,* vol. 11, no. 5, pp. 14-24, 2021.
[http://dx.doi.org/10.5815/ijem.2021.05.02]

[12] P. Dutta, and A. Kumar, "Modelling of liquid flow control system using optimized genetic algorithm", *Stat. Optim. Inf. Comput.,* vol. 8, no. 2, pp. 565-582, 2020.
[http://dx.doi.org/10.19139/soic-2310-5070-618]

[13] S. Mandal, P. Dutta, and A. Kumar, "Modeling of liquid flow control process using improved versions of elephant swarm water search algorithm", *SN Appl. Sci.,* vol. 1, no. 8, p. 886, 2019.
[http://dx.doi.org/10.1007/s42452-019-0914-5]

[14] P. Dutta, S.K. Biswas, M. Majumder, and M. Majumder, "Parametric optimization of Solar Parabolic Collector using metaheuristic Optimization", *Computational Intelligence and Machine Learning,* vol. 2, no. 1, pp. 26-32, 2021.

[http://dx.doi.org/10.36647/CIML/02.01.A004]

[15] P. Dutta, M. Majumder, and A. Kumar, "An improved grey wolf optimization algorithm for liquid flow control system", *International Journal of Engineering and Manufacturing,* vol. 11, no. 4, pp. 10-21, 2021.
[http://dx.doi.org/10.5815/ijem.2021.04.02]

[16] P. Dutta, and M. Majumder, "Parametric optimization of drilling parameters in aluminum 6061T6 plate to minimize the burr", *International Journal of Engineering and Manufacturing,* vol. 11, no. 6, pp. 36-47, 2021.
[http://dx.doi.org/10.5815/ijem.2021.06.04]

[17] P. Dutta, S. Pal, A. Kumar, and K. Cengiz, *Artificial Intelligence for Cognitive Modeling: Theory and Practice.* Chapman and Hall/CRC, 2023.
[http://dx.doi.org/10.1201/9781003216001]

[18] M.F.W. Festing, "The completely randomised and the randomised block are the only experimental designs suitable for widespread use in pre-clinical research", *Sci. Rep.,* vol. 10, no. 1, p. 17577, 2020.
[http://dx.doi.org/10.1038/s41598-020-74538-3] [PMID: 33067494]

CHAPTER 3

Study on Intelligent WSN Localization Error Using Anova-based Optimization Technique

Sumanta Dey[1,*], **Gour Gopal Jana**[1] and **Anubrata Mondal**[2]

[1] *Department of Electronics and Communication Engineering, Greater Kolkata College of Engineering & Management, West Bengal 743387, India*

[2] *Department of Electrical Engineering, Greater Kolkata College of Engineering & Management, West Bengal 743387, India*

Abstract: In the realm of wireless communication engineering, the localization of unidentified nodes in wireless sensor networks (WSN) is crucial. The localization of unknown nodes in wireless sensor networks (WSN) is an important problem in wireless communication engineering. Improving localization performance while extending the lifespan of energy-limited sensor nodes remains a key objective. The coordinates of unidentified nodes can typically be found using sensors that have the anchor nodes' known coordinates. However, it takes a lot of time to use bio-inspired algorithms. Therefore, it remains a difficult problem to find the best network configuration for node localization within a short period. This article describes an effective method for utilising an Elephant Swarm Water Search Algorithm (ESWSA) model to assess the ideal network parameters that lead to a low Average Localisation Error (ALE). The average localisation error (ALE) and the input variables' transmission range (TR), node density (ND), anchor ratio (AR), and iterations (IT) are nonlinearly related in this study using an ANOVA-based model. In the experimental section, a metaheuristic optimization technique was applied to predict the ALE for a given set of input variables, producing an accuracy of about 97.843% and 98.109% for cross-validation and testing the dataset.

Keywords: ALE, ANOVA, ESWSA, Metaheuristic optimization technique, WSNs.

INTRODUCTION

A WSN is made up of several small, low-cost sensors that are dispersed around an area to measure physical characteristics or monitor habitat conditions. It may also be used in various real-world applications, including target tracking and precision farming [1]. These sensors must be able to accurately estimate their locations with

* **Corresponding author Sumanta Dey:** Department of Electronics and Communication Engineering, Greater Kolkata College of Engineering & Management, West Bengal 743387, India; E-mail: sumanta.dey2002@gmail.com

Pijush Dutta, Sudip Mondal, Korhan Cengiz and S. Balamurugan (Eds.)

fewer resources in most applications. These sensors can quickly determine their positions using GPS. GPS is too large and expensive to be practically integrated into every sensor; thus, another strategy is requiredto be implemented using the concept of localization algorithms [2]. Several localization techniques have been developed to handle different localization problems. To function well in a variety of indoor and outdoor environments and topologies, these algorithms need to be adaptive. Range-based methods use the distance between the anchor and unknown sensor nodes to calculate the position of the unknown nodes. They employ range metrics such as Received Signal Strength Indication (RSSI), Angle of Arrival, and Time of Arrival [3, 4]. The range-free techniques, in contrast, employ straightforward connectivity-related operations to locate the unknown node, such as the centroid [5] and ad-hoc positioning system [6]. They simply require the anchor node's beacon signal to be present in the medium. Range-based algorithms are utilized more frequently and are favored over range-free algorithms among the two [7]. In an attempt to develop a simpler algorithm, several bio-inspired algorithms were used for range-based approaches [8]. The localization error was minimized with observable outcomes. This is mostly due to the CS algorithm's tuning settings, which facilitate computation. Recently, a modified form of CS was developed, which increased the typical CS algorithm's rate of convergence [9]. To enhance the search process, the mutation probability and the random walk step size were changed. ALE metrics assessed the accuracy of these localization methods. The algorithm with the lowest ALE value was chosen. After choosing a BIA for node localization, the main issue that arises is the computing time. To determine the appropriate network characteristics and optimize the ALE below the threshold for the best case, the algorithm must be repeated several times during the network creation. We selected and retrieved four features from the improved ESWSA algorithm: the number of iterations, node density, anchor ratio, and transmission range. Finally, we used these data to train the ANOVA model, from which we were able to derive the predicted value of ALE using ESWSA. This article is divided into six sections. Relevant works are discussed in Section II. The system model for the node localization problem is covered in Section III. Additionally, Section IV describes the settings and simulated scenarios for the updated ESWSA. We have covered the ALE prediction findings in Section V. Lastly, the discussion and conclusion are provided in Section VI.

REVIEW WORKS

We have covered several techniques for increasing the node localization accuracy in this section. According to a method provided by Ghargan *et al.* in their paper published in the journal Science, artificial neural networks (ANN) are individually hybridized with PSO, backtracking search algorithms (BSA), and gravitational search algorithms (GSA) to improve localization accuracy [10]. From the results, it was observed that the GSA-ANN hybrid outperformed the other techniques. The Naive Bayes (NB) method, Decision Tree (DT), Support Vector Machine (SVM), and Artificial Neural Network (ANN) were among the methods whose cumulative localization error distribution curves were analyzed [10]. Based on cumulative localization error distributions, the experimental results showed that NB performed better than the other ML approaches [11].

SYSTEM MODEL

The proposed model mainly highlighted the node localization procedure that is covered initially in this part. Next, the method for figuring out how far the anchor is from unknown nodes is discussed. After that, how the improved ESWSA algorithm for node localization formed its goal functions and operated is elaborated inthe latter part of this section.

System architecture

The sensor nodes were dispersed at random throughout an X-Y square unit area. There were M anchor nodes, and N was an unknown node in the system that needed to be localized. Within the given TR, sensors could transmit and receive the data. All of the localizable unknown nodes' coordinates were evaluated using the anchor's positional data as a guide.

Problem Formulation

The unknown nodes utilize the RSSI to determine how far away they are from the anchor nodes. Shadowing and multipath fading lead sensors to lose power while exchanging information. Eq. (1) illustrates how log-normal shadowing [12] is used to describe this path loss.

$$\text{PL (d)} = \text{PL (0)} + 10 \times \eta \times log_{10}\frac{d}{d_0} + X_g \quad \textbf{(1)}$$

PL(d) and PL(0) are the path loss for the reference distance 0 and d. Several factors, including the propagation environment, antenna height, and signal frequency, affect the value of η. For an indoor environment, its values are greater than 4 and fall between 2 and 6 meters [13]. The attenuation brought on by fading is represented by the Gaussian random variable X_g. Equation (2) expresses its variance, σ^2.

$$\sigma^2 = \gamma^2 D_{ij}^2 \quad \textbf{(2)}$$

Where, y^2 represents the localization error

$$D_{ij} = \sqrt{(x_i - x_j)^2 + (y_i - y_j)^2} \tag{3}$$

The measured distance is represented by D'_{ij}

$$D'_{ij} = D_{ij} + N_{ij} \tag{4}$$

where N_{ij} range error between nodes i and j. There is always a range error while attempting to locate the unknown nodes [14]. This is achieved by constructing an Optimization Function (OF), which is the mean square of the error between the real distance of the assessed node coordinates and the estimated distance of the actual unknown node coordinates from the neighboring anchor nodes. This is accomplished by minimizing the objective function (OF), given by

$$\text{OF} = \frac{1}{M}\sum_{j=1}^{M}(D_{ij} - D'_{ij})^2 \tag{5}$$

The minimum value of M is 3, *i.e.*, for an unknown node to be deemed localizable, it must have a minimum of three anchor nodes within its transmission range.

MATHEMATICAL MODEL OF THE LOCALIZATION PROBLEM

As independent parameters such as TR, ND, AR, and IT vary, the average localization error (ALE) exhibits nonlinear features. Furthermore, there is a clear correlation between ND, AR, and TR. Every time a major input parameter is altered, recalibration of the average location error analysis is extremely time-consuming and challenging. An empirical technique, such as RSM or ANOVA, is used to create a mathematical model to improve calibration, and computational intelligence is used to determine the ideal values of the prevalent input parameters. These numerical models show a correlation between the output parameters, average localization error (ALE), and the input parameters, TR, ND, AR, and IT. Without recalibration, these models will help determine the optimal operating conditions and predict the average localization error under particular circumstances (for instance, for different estimations of input parameters TR, ND, AR, and IT). The mathematical model of ANOVA used in this study is represented by Eq. (6).

$$F = \mu_1 TR^{\mu_2} ND^{\mu_3} AR^{\mu_4} IT^{\mu_5} \tag{6}$$

Where, μ_1, μ_2, μ_3, μ_4 and μ_5 are the coefficients of the power series ANOVA model. ESWSA is currently used to extract the optimal. To minimize the error, we employed RMSE as an objective function in this study [15, 14]. The error function (TR, ND, AR, IT, X) and set of parameters *X* for ANOVA-based modeling can be expressed as

$$f(TR, ND, AR, IT, X) = = \mu_1 TR^{\mu_2} ND^{\mu_3} AR^{\mu_4} IT^{\mu_5} — F \quad (7)$$

X = {μ1, μ2, μ3, μ4, μ5} Where, F is the experimental data.

Elephant Swarm water Search algorithm ESWSA

ESWSA [16] was proposed with the aid of several correspondence techniques. This optimization was primarily based on the elephant swarm's water search mechanism during dry spells. Assume that the elephant group is randomly assigned to a d-dimensional optimization problem.

After the t-th iteration, the position of the i-th elephant group in a swarm is now given as

$$X_{id}^{t} = (x_{i1,} x_{i2,} x_{i3,} \ldots\ldots. x_{id,}) \text{ \& velocity is by } V_{id}^{t} = (v_{i1,} v_{i2,}, v_{i3,} \ldots\ldots\ldots\ldots v_{id}).$$

At the present iteration, the i-th elephant group's local best solution is denoted by

$p_{best\ id}^{t} = (p_{i1,}, p_{i2,}, p_{i3,} \ldots\ldots\ldots\ldots\ldots p_{id})$ and the global best solution is

denoted by $G_{best\ id}^{t} = (g_{i1}, g_{i2}, g_{i3}, \ldots\ldots\ldots\ldots g_{id})$.

The following equations are used to update these values based on the switching probability (p) [17].

$$V_{id}^{t+1} = V_{id}^{t} * \omega^{t} + \epsilon \odot (G_{best\ id}^{t} - X_{id}^{t}) \text{ if } rand > p \text{ [for global search]} \quad (8)$$

$$V_{id}^{t+1} = V_{id}^{t} * \omega^{t} + \epsilon \odot (p_{best\ id}^{t} - X_{id}^{t}) \text{ if } rand \le p \text{[for local search]} \quad (9)$$

To balance exploration and exploitation, ⊙ and wt represent element-wise multiplication and inertia weight. This equation describes how it changes.

$$\omega^{t} = \omega_{max} - \{ \frac{\omega_{max} - \omega_{min}}{t_{max}} \} \times t \quad (10)$$

The maximum iteration number and the range inertia weight (0.4, 0.6) are represented by the parameters tmax, wmax, and and wmin, respectively [18]. The following formula represents an elephant group's updated position:

$$X_{id}^{t+1} = V_{id}^{t+1} + X_{id}^{t} \tag{11}$$

It gives the optimum output derived from the algorithm's optimal position value. According to the paper [19], p=0.6 provides ESWSA with unparalleled performance. In this sense, we have also applied this incentive to our present problem.

Simulation Experiments and Performance Evaluation

MATLAB 2007B is used to conduct all of the simulation experiments in this section. To perform this research, overall, 107 datasets were taken, where 17 datasets were taken as testing datasets and 90 datasets were taken as training datasets. A number of variables, including AD, TR, and ND, in terms of average localization error and localization success ratio, were used to evaluate the performance of the modified PSO algorithm, or ESWSA. Using Equation (12), the average localization error is calculated.

$$\text{Average localization Error (ALE)} = \sum_{i=1}^{NL} \frac{\sqrt{(X_i - x_i)^2 + (Y_i - y_i)^2}}{NL} \tag{12}$$

Simulation Setup

The node density, or total number of sensor nodes, is fixed at 100, 200, and 300. Every sensor node is randomly distributed throughout a two-dimensional sensor area of 100 × 100 m^2. Ten to thirty percent of all sensor nodes are anchor nodes. Random anchor node deployment occurs. For anchor nodes, it is presumed that there is no localization problem. The communication range of each sensor node is between 10 and 25 meters. The parameters for the proposed ESWSA algorithm are determined through extensive experiments, and the findings show that the following parameter settings can result in greater localization precision with fewer iterations: t_max, ω_max, and andω_(min) are the values of the maximum iteration number 5000, upper boundary (0.9) and lower boundary (0.4) of the inertia weight, and switching probability (p) is set to 0.6. The range of □ inside [0,1] is represented by ω^tare, which stands for element-wise multiplication and inertia weight. The nest number is 100, according to the improved ESWSA algorithm. Every algorithm has an iteration threshold of 5000.

EXPERIMENTAL RESULTS

The Effect of Anchor Density

AD has a major impact on the cost and efficacy of WSN localization. The impact of anchor density on localization performance is evaluated in this subsection. The designated anchor ratios are 10%, 14%, 15%, 18%, 20%, 22%, 26%, 28%, 29%, and 30% of all sensor nodes. Localization accuracy is significantly improved when the network's anchor ratio rises from 15% to 30%, as shown in Fig. (**1**).

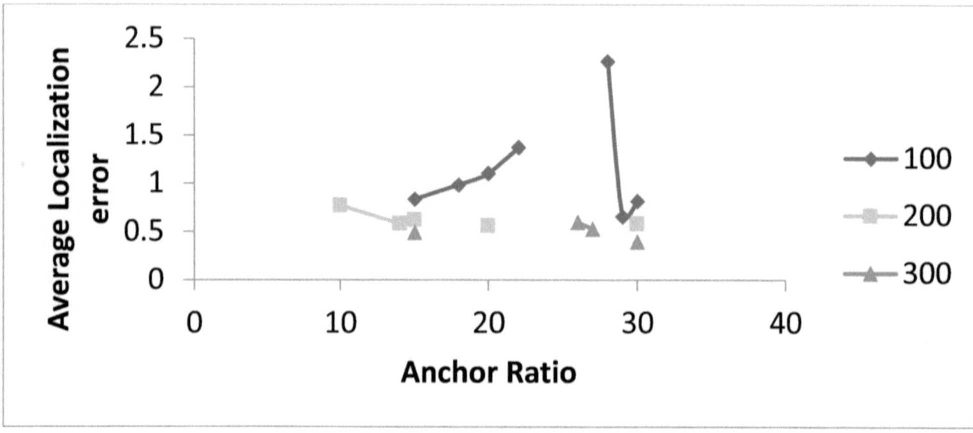

Fig. (1). The effect of anchor ratio on average localization error with different levels of node density.

Additionally, the average localization error falls in proportion to node density.

The Effect of Transmission Range

Another crucial factor influencing sensor node energy usage and localization performance is communication range. The communication range varies between 10 and 20 meters. Additionally, it is noted that the average localization error is marginally higher when the communication range is less than 20 meters. This is a result of numerous nodes in the network not being connected. Fig. (**2**) illustrates how the average localization error significantly drops as the communication range rises. The reason for this is that more anchor data is available to identify the location of unknown nodes. It is clear that the average localization error gradually drops as ND rises because more anchor nodes are within communication range and sensor nodes have a high degree of network connectivity.

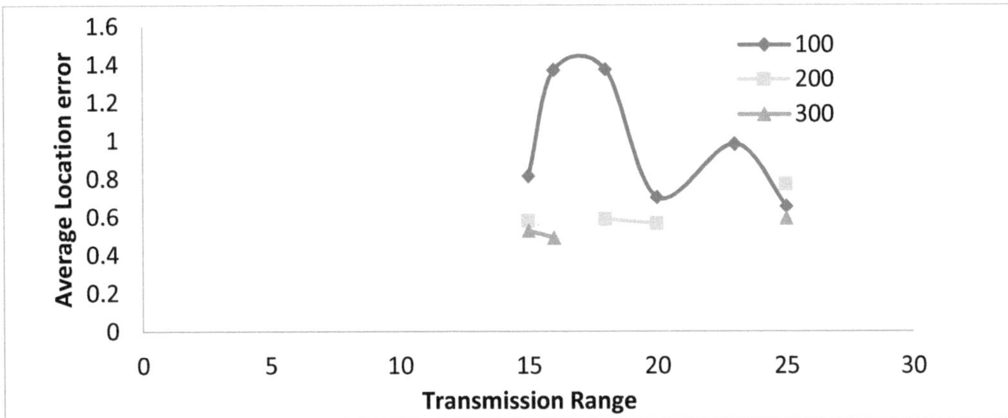

Fig. (2). The effect of communication range.

RESULT OBTAINED AFTER OPTIMIZATION

After the optimization of the power series nonlinear equation of the ANOVA model by the ESWSA algorithm, five coefficients were obtained, which have already been mentioned in section 2, to acquire minimum RMSE. Table **1** shows the coefficients of the present research on the ANOVA model.

Table 1. Coefficient obtained after optimization.

μ1	μ2	μ3	μ4	μ5
25	0.025287	0.124974	-0.50056	-0.3217

After optimization, the resulting objective functions are expressed by Eq.13.

$$OF = 25\ TR^{0.025287} ND^{0.124974} AR^{-0.50056} IT^{-0.3217} \qquad \textbf{(13)}$$

Overall accuracy of the present model is divided into two parts: accuracy for cross-validation and accuracy for the testing model. It is observed from Table **2** that the suggested model generates sufficient accuracy for both categorical datasets.

Table 2. Accuracy for Cross Validation and Testing dataset.

Nature of the dataset	Cross validation	Testing Dataset
Accuracy	97.843%	98.109%

Fig. (3)represents the characteristics graph between deviation (change in experimental and calculated output to the actual output) and the number of testing datasets. From the result, it is seen that deviation lies between 0.4 and -0.25, which is quite stable. Fig. (**4**) represents the convergence speed of the proposed model. From the graph, it is seen that it is quite stable after the number of iterations increases to 1000, which indicates that the output obtained from the proposed optimization is quite stable. Table **3**represents the computational time of the proposed model.

Fig. (3). Characteristics graph between deviation and number of testing datasets.

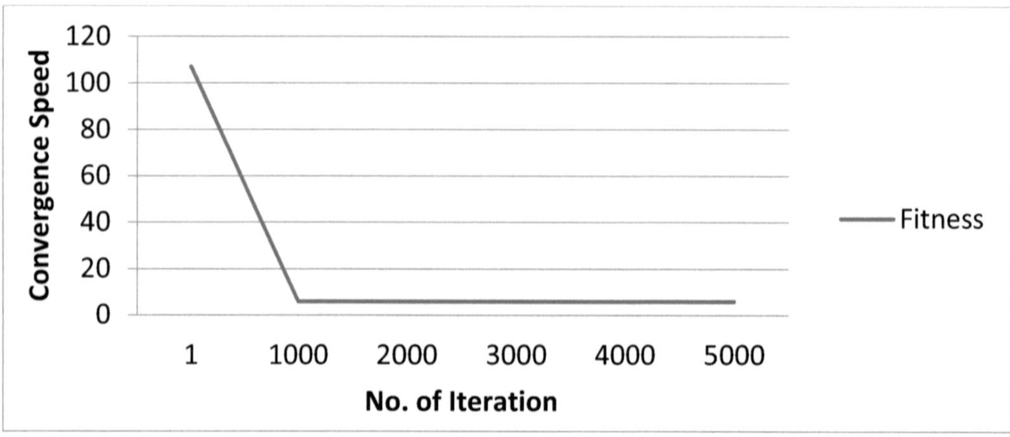

Fig. (4). Characteristics graph for convergence speed for different numbers of iterations.

Table 3. Runtime for ANOVA-based ESWSA Algorithm.

Process	Runtime
ANOVA-based ESWSA	36.4528Sec

CONCLUSION

Here, the goal was to create an algorithm by examining the characteristics of a basic wireless sensor network system and applying a power series nonlinear mathematical model based on an enhanced Elephant Swarm Water Search algorithm (ESWSA). This provides a basis for optimizing node location in practical WSN systems using the proposed method. Additionally, the proposed model enhances the rate of convergence and lowers the average localization error, both of which are advantageous for lowering processing costs and prolonging the life of sensor nodes.

REFERENCES

[1] K.S. Adu-Manu, J.D. Abdulai, F. Engmann, M. Akazue, K.A. Justice, G.E. Baiden, and G. Sarfo-Kantanka, "WSN Architectures for Environmental Monitoring Applications", *J. Sens.,* p. 2022, 2022.

[2] X. Huang, J. Yi, S. Chen, and X. Zhu, "A wireless sensor network-based approach with decision support for monitoring lake water quality", *Sensors (Basel),* vol. 15, no. 11, pp. 29273-29296, 2015. [http://dx.doi.org/10.3390/s151129273] [PMID: 26610496]

[3] N. Patwari, J.N. Ash, S. Kyperountas, A.O. Hero, R.L. Moses, and N.S. Correal, "Locating the nodes: cooperative localization in wireless sensor networks", *IEEE Signal Process. Mag.,* vol. 22, no. 4, pp. 54-69, 2005.
[http://dx.doi.org/10.1109/MSP.2005.1458287]

[4] N. Bulusu, J. Heidemann, and D. Estrin, "GPS-less low-cost outdoor localization for very small devices", *IEEE Pers. Commun.,* vol. 7, no. 5, pp. 28-34, 2000.

[5] M. Vecchio, R. López-Valcarce, and F. Marcelloni, "A two-objective evolutionary approach based on topological constraints for node localization in wireless sensor networks", *Appl. Soft Comput.,* vol. 12, no. 7, pp. 1891-1901, 2012.
[http://dx.doi.org/10.1016/j.asoc.2011.03.012]

[6] A. Boukerche, H.A. Oliveira, E.F. Nakamura, and A.A. Loureiro, "Localization in time and space for wireless sensor networks: A Mobile Beacon approach", *2008 International Symposium on a World of Wireless, Mobile and Multimedia Networks,* pp. 1-8, 2008.
[http://dx.doi.org/10.1109/WOWMOM.2008.4594838]

[7] G. Mao, B. Fidan, and B.D.O. Anderson, "Wireless sensor network localization techniques", *Comput. Netw.,* vol. 51, no. 10, pp. 2529-2553, 2007.
[http://dx.doi.org/10.1016/j.comnet.2006.11.018]

[8] A. Pal, "Localization algorithms in wireless sensor networks: Current approaches and future challenges", *Network Protocols and Algorithms,* vol. 2, no. 1, pp. 45-73, 2010.
[http://dx.doi.org/10.5296/npa.v2i1.279]

[9] A. Simonetto, and G. Leus, "Distributed maximum likelihood sensor network localization", *IEEE Trans. Signal Process.,* vol. 62, no. 6, pp. 1424-1437, 2014.
[http://dx.doi.org/10.1109/TSP.2014.2302746]

[10] Y. Shang, and W. Ruml, Improved MDS-based localization.*IEEE INFOCOM 2004.* vol. Vol. 4. IEEE, 2004, pp. 2640-2651.
[http://dx.doi.org/10.1109/INFCOM.2004.1354683]

[11] D. Simon, "Biogeography-Based Optimization", *IEEE Trans. Evol. Comput.,* vol. 12, no. 6, pp. 702-713, 2008.
[http://dx.doi.org/10.1109/TEVC.2008.919004]

[12] A. Kumar, A. Khosla, J.S. Saini, and S. Singh, "Meta-heuristic range based node localization algorithm for wireless sensor networks", *2012 International Conference on Localization and GNSS,* pp. 1-7, 2012.
[http://dx.doi.org/10.1109/ICL-GNSS.2012.6253135]

[13] S. Yun, J. Lee, W. Chung, E. Kim, and S. Kim, "A soft computing approach to localization in wireless sensor networks", *Expert Syst. Appl.,* vol. 36, no. 4, pp. 7552-7561, 2009.
[http://dx.doi.org/10.1016/j.eswa.2008.09.064]

[14] B. Pitchaimanickam, and G. Murugaboopathi, "A hybrid firefly algorithm with particle swarm optimization for energy efficient optimal cluster head selection in wireless sensor networks", *Neural Comput. Appl.,* vol. 32, no. 12, pp. 7709-7723, 2020.
[http://dx.doi.org/10.1007/s00521-019-04441-0]

[15] M. Chih, "Self-adaptive check and repair operator-based particle swarm optimization for the multidimensional knapsack problem", *Appl. Soft Comput.,* vol. 26, pp. 378-389, 2015.
[http://dx.doi.org/10.1016/j.asoc.2014.10.030]

[16] S. Singh, and E. Mittal, "Range based wireless sensor node localization using PSO and BBO and its variants", *2013 International conference on communication systems and network technologies,* pp. 309-315, 2013.
[http://dx.doi.org/10.1109/CSNT.2013.72]

[17] P. Dutta, and A. Kumar, "Intelligent calibration technique using optimized fuzzy logic controller for ultrasonic flow sensor", *MATHEMATICAL MODELLING OF ENGINEERING PROBLEMS,* vol. 4, no. 2, pp. 91-94, 2017.
[http://dx.doi.org/10.18280/mmep.040205]

[18] P. Dutta, M. Majumder, and A. Kumar, "Parametric optimization of liquid flow process by ANOVA optimized DE, PSO & GA algorithms", *International Journal of Engineering and Manufacturing,* vol. 11, no. 5, pp. 14-24, 2021.
[http://dx.doi.org/10.5815/ijem.2021.05.02]

[19] P. Dutta, and A. Kumar, "Modelling of liquid flow control system using optimized genetic algorithm. Statistics, Optimization &", *Inf. Comput.,* vol. 8, no. 2, pp. 565-582, 2020.

CHAPTER 4

Modeling and Optimization of Process Parameters of Grinding Using ANOVA Analysis for Industry 5.0

Sudip Mandal[1,*], **Abhishek Ghosh**[2] and **Sujit Majumdar**[3]

[1] *Department of Electronics and Communication Engineering, Jalpaiguri Government Engineering College, Jalpaiguri, India*

[2] *Department of Mechanical Engineering, Supreme Knowledge Foundation Group of Institutions, Mankundu, Chandannagar, West Bengal 712139, India*

[3] *Department of Mechanical Engineering, Kalyani Government. Engineering College, Kalyani, India,*

Abstract: Modeling and optimization of the corresponding parameters of grinding processesare fascinating tasks for mechanical engineers. This paper mainly investigates a suitable model of the grinding process using a very popular statistical analysis tool, ANOVA, and Regression Analysis to control the output parameters, such as tangential force and change in temperature during grinding, by controlling the coolant flow rate, infeed of wheel, and scraperboard positioning. The experiment is also conducted to examine the effect of using a scraperboard on changing the grinding temperature. A K-type thermocouple brazed beneath the workpiece surface and a force dynamometer are used for measuring the grinding temperature and tangential force during experimentation. Initially, a linear regression model is used to model force and change in temperature. Next, ANOVA is used for response optimization for the grinding process, where the objective is to minimize both output variables. From the optimization, it is found that the use of a scraper board is very effective in minimizing the tangential force and generated temperature during grinding.

Keywords: ANOVA, Grinding process, Industry 5.0, Modeling, Optimization, Scarper board.

INTRODUCTION

Grinding is a precise surface finishing process, performed on a final product, that faces the disadvantage of excessive heat production, which leads to the burning of the grinding contact surface, transformation in metallurgical phase, high residual

* **Corresponding author Sudip Mandal:** Department of Electronics and Communication Engineering, Jalpaiguri Government Engineering College, Jalpaiguri, India; E-mail: sudip.mandal007@gmail.com

Pijush Dutta, Sudip Mondal, Korhan Cengiz and S. Balamurugan (Eds.)

stress, surface and sub-surface cracks, loss of surface integrity, *etc*. These consequently lead to the refusal of a final workpiece at the last stage of production. A significant amount of mechanical energy, primarily the force needed for grinding, transforms into thermal energy [1 - 3]. It happens due to the elevated friction coefficient between the tiny grits of the wheel and the workpiece. Hence, a liquid called coolant is utilized in the workpiece-wheel interface to lower the temperature. However, the surrounding air layer of the revolving grinding wheel hinders the effective penetration of the fluid jet into the grinding zone [4 - 7]. Because of this potential limitation, impingement of the fluid jet through the workpiece-wheel junction becomes challenging, and controlling the air pressure around the wheel becomes imperative. Considering the airflow effect along with the other prevailing parameters for better prediction accuracy, the modeling of the grinding process becomes much more complex and demanding. This modeling and optimization not only lower the expenses and duration of experiments, but they also enhance comprehension of the process.

Unlike other machining operations, heat production in grinding is a critical event that is obligatory to be controlled to achieve better surface integrity of finished products. To regulate heat generation, the requirement of force for machining is to be checked, since a major portion of the force applied in the course of grinding is converted to heat [8]. Hence, both the force applied and heat generation are closely interrelated and are two important characteristics that need to be addressed for better process performance. The unavoidable circumstances of heat generation due to the interaction between the workpiece and the abrasive grits of varying rake angles are usually controlled by applying a stream of fluid into the grinding area. Previous studies indicate that the existence of a rotating air-ring around the wheel restricts the suitable entrance of the coolant stream in the interface between wheel and workpiece, resulting in a higher friction coefficient and heat development [9, 10]. So, the impact of the air boundary on heat generation needs to be investigated. Further, a relationship is required to be established between five important parameters that can be used to decide the optimal input conditions of grinding. Hybrid modeling is therefore needed, which may help in better decision making, choosing the best input settings. This study aimed to determine the best input parameters to reduce the need for force and the production of heat during the process of grinding.

Different models have been generated based on numerous parameters of grinding, including the texture of the grinding wheel's surface, the wear on the wheel, the value of the surface of the workpiece, the forces and energy involved in grinding, and the relationship between the workpiece and the wheel [11 - 13]. To predict the results of the grinding process, different modeling techniques, including experiential, logical, regression, finite element method (FEM), and heuristics, have been utilized. Cao *et al.* [14] developed a model for the topography of wheel-cutting-face based on various experiential correlations, demonstrating that this approach can greatly enhance the quality of the ground surface. Leonesio also utilized a z-buffer method to enhance the quality of the surface [15]. Salisbury [16] created a model of the wheel surface that can be combined with a model of the surface grinding process to simulate the texture of the workpiece's surface. Models [17] are developed to improve surface irregularity and metal removal rate by applying response surface methodology by controlling the depth of cut and the speed of the wheel and table. Mathematical models were developed by Janardhan *et al.* [18] to improve surface roughness and the rate of metal elimination. Temperature distribution was described using partial differential equations [19], and statistical or mathematical techniques like Laplace and Fourier transforms coupled with the Green's function method [20], as well as Finite Element Analysis [21], were employed.

However, very few researchers considered the airflow around the grinding wheel along with other parameters to forecast the alteration in workpiece temperature difference and the tangential grinding force. The influence of numerous factors, such as grinding cycles, force, wheel speed, cut-depth, and grinding fluid flow, on temperature was previously analyzed. Implementation of an air-deflector has been shown to enhance the grinding ratio, improve the quality of surface, also diminish the machining forces [22, 23]. Consequently, the modeling of various grinding parameters along with the scraper board, which authoritatively affects the grinding performance, is a new study. Further, the application of the ANOVA model equations to analyze the increase in the percentage of temperature and grinding force is based on experimental research, which accounts for the regulation of the rotating air. The remainder of the document is structured in the following way. Section II describes the experimental process and data of grinding. Next, the proposed methodology for modeling the grinding process has been described. The results are elaborated in Section IV, which is followed by the Conclusion and Reference Section. An ANOVA-based approach isusedto develop mathematical models for grinding processes, which helps identify optimal grinding conditions, contributing to human-machine interaction crucial for Industry 5.0.

INVESTIGATION INTO GRINDING

The empirical section of this study was carried out on a surface grinding machine with a conventional alumina wheel (specification: AA46/54K5V8). Experiments were carried out in up-grinding mode at different flow rates and infeeds of the grinding wheel, at a speed of 29.3 m/s, *i.e.*, wheel surface velocity in the presence or absence of the scraper board. The tangential force was noted from the grinding of the digital screen of the dynamometer, and the temperature was noted from the temperature gauge, while utilizing them for modeling the process. The experimental conditions are shown in Table **1**.

Table 1. Diverse grinding conditions for tests.

Environment of grinding (Input conditions)	Level of parameters
Flow rate of coolant	0.082 liter/s, 0.166 liter/s, 0.194 liter/s, 0.32 liter/s
Infeed	20 μm, 30 μm, 40 μm
Scraper board	Present (1), Absent (0)

Kohli *et al.* [2] conducted a study on energy distribution during the grinding process. They observed that at the 1.5 mm depth of AISI 1020 steel, a nearly 400°C temperature variation was there than the ground surface. In this study, a thermocouple was attached 2 mm below the grinding surface, and the variation in temperature *(ΔT)* with the change in input parameters was analyzed to establish a correlation between them.

The values of the variation in temperature percentage (ΔT) and the grinding tangential force (F) were recorded from the experiment under various conditions: infeed (S_i), coolant flowrate (*Q*), and the presence of Scraper Board (*SB*). The corresponding outputs are shown in Table **2**.

Table 2. Experimental data of the grinding process.

SL No	Infeed	Flowrate	Scraper Board	ΔT	F
1	20	0.082	1	31	19
2	30	0.082	1	31	16
3	40	0.082	1	31	16
4	20	0.166	1	30	15
5	30	0.166	1	30	16
6	40	0.166	1	31	18
7	20	0.194	1	28	14
8	30	0.194	1	29	15
9	40	0.194	1	29	15
10	20	0.32	1	25	14
11	30	0.32	1	26	14
12	40	0.32	1	27	15

(Table 2) cont.....

SL No	Infeed	Flowrate	Scraper Board	ΔT	F
13	20	0.082	0	36	17
14	30	0.082	0	38	18
15	40	0.082	0	39	20
16	20	0.166	0	35	16
17	30	0.166	0	37	16
18	40	0.166	0	39	19
19	20	0.194	0	35	15
20	30	0.194	0	36	16
21	40	0.194	0	36	16
22	20	0.32	0	29	15
23	30	0.32	0	33	15
24	40	0.32	0	34	16

METHOD AND RESULT ANALYSIS

In this study, the regression model for the outputs, *i.e.*, tangential force and change in temperature, was modeled initially using MINITAB 21 software. The adequacy of the developed mathematical model was tested using ANOVA. Surface plots and contour plots for responses were also given. Moreover, the output variables were optimized to find the best suitable conditions for grinding using ANOVA.

Regression Model for the Tangential Force

The regression equation expresses a mathematical model that defines a functional relationship between the input variables and the response. In the present study, a first-order model, *i.e.*, a linear regression model, was developed to express the responses in terms of process variables, *i.e.*, infeed, flow rate, and the presence of scrapper board. The regression equation for the tangential force can be expressed as

$$F = 17.00 + 0.0625\ \text{Infeed} - 12.04\ \text{Flowrate} - 1.000\ \text{Scraper Board}$$

Table **3** represents different coefficients of tangential force along with p-value and T-value, while Table **4** shows the model summary of tangential force.

Table 3. Coefficients for tangential force.

Term	Coef	SE Coef	T-Value	P-Value	VIF
Constant	17.00	1.02	16.73	0.000	-
Infeed	0.0625	0.0275	2.27	0.034	1.00
Flowrate	-12.04	2.63	-4.58	0.000	1.00
Scraper Board	-1.000	0.449	-2.23	0.038	1.00

Table 4. Model summary for tangential force.

S	R-sq	R-sq(adj)	R-sq(pred)
1.10011	60.85%	54.98%	41.29%

Table **5** shows the ANOVA analysis for the tangential force. R^2 is a determining factor that gives the goodness of model fitting. Here, the value of R^2 for tangential force is found to be 60.85%, which is far superior to 60%. It indicates that approximately 60.85% of the variability in the data for the output is explained by the model. It specifies that the proposed model is sufficient. The adjusted R^2 value of the model is 54.98%. Moreover, it is very well known that the terms whose P-value is much higher than the significance level (0.05) have no statistical significance on the response. From the above table, it can be seen that all input variables, *i.e.*, infeed, flow rate, and presence of scrapper board, are very significant. Among these process variables, flow rate is found to be the most crucial as its p-value is the least.

Table 5. Analysis of variance for tangential force.

Source	DF	Adj SS	Adj MS	F-Value	P-Value
Regression	3	37.628	12.543	10.36	0.000
Infeed	1	6.250	6.250	5.16	0.034
Flowrate	1	25.378	25.378	20.97	0.000
Scraper Board	1	6.000	6.000	4.96	0.038
Error	20	24.205	1.210	-	-
Total	23	61.833	-	-	-

The relationships between the response and the grinding parameters are demonstrated graphically using contour plots or surface plots. Surface plots (Fig. **1**) are 3-dimensional graphs, where a response is plotted against any two variables when the other variables are held at some constant level. Contour plots (Fig. **2**) are a 2-dimensional plot that illustrates contours of constant response, with the axis system being an explicit couple of the process parameters, while the other variables remain constant. These plots are mainly essential when the stationary point is a saddle point or is far from the desired operating area.

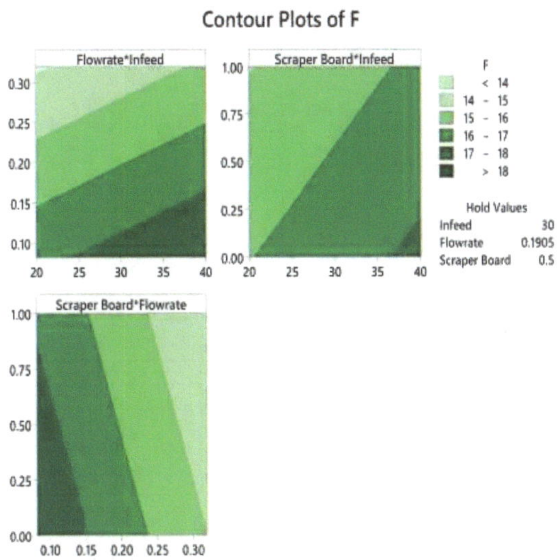

Fig. (1). Contour plots for tangential force.

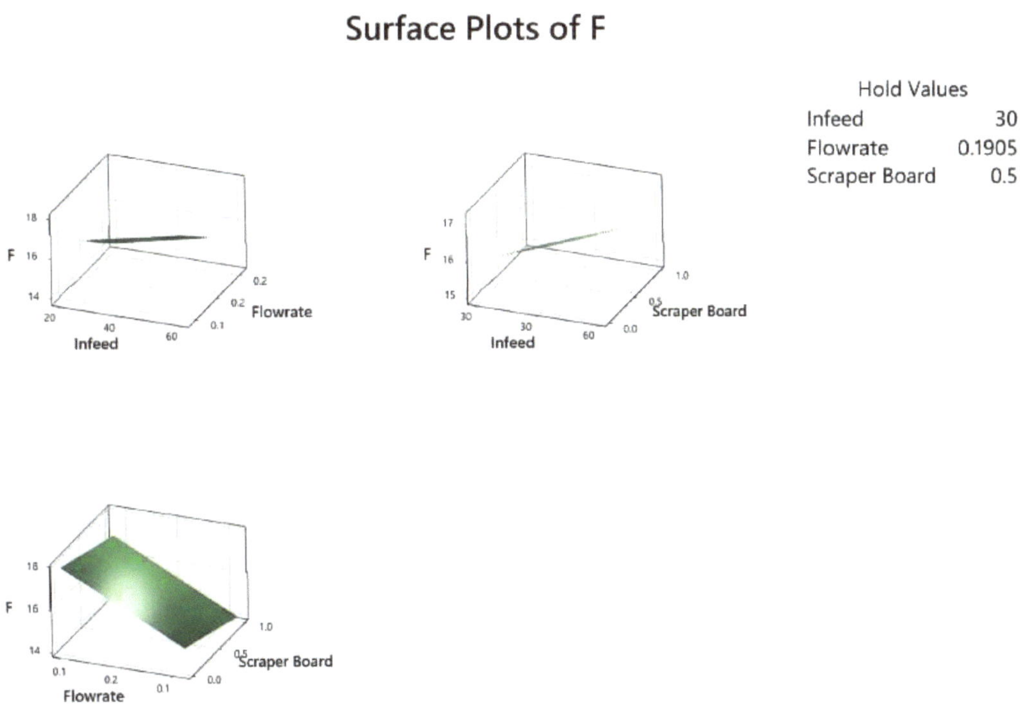

Fig. (2). Surface plots for tangential force.

Regression Model for the Change in Temperature

The regression equation (first-order linear model) for the change in temperature can be expressed as

$$\Delta T = 36.852 + 0.1063 \text{ Infeed} - 23.39 \text{ Flowrate} - 6.583 \text{ Scraper Board}$$

Table **6** shows the coefficient of each model parameter, while Table **7** represents the regression value for temperature change.

Table 6. Coefficients for change in temperature.

Term	Coef	SE Coef	T-Value	P-Value	VIF
Constant	36.852	0.904	40.76	0.000	-
Infeed	0.1063	0.0245	4.34	0.000	1.00
Flowrate	-23.39	2.34	-10.00	0.000	1.00
Scraper Board	-6.583	0.400	-16.48	0.000	1.00

Table 7. Model summary for change in temperature.

S	R-sq	R-sq (adj)	R-sq (pred)
0.978688	95.13%	94.39%	92.50%

The value of R^2 of this model for tangential force is 95.13%, which indicates how the model fits with the data efficiently. It indicates that the model can explain at least 95.13% of variability in the data for the response. It means that the proposed model is very ample and precise. The adjusted R^2 value of the model is also very satisfactory, *i.e.*, 94.39%. From Table **8**, it can be seen that all input variables, *i.e.*, infeed, flowrate, and presence of scrapper board, are very significant and equally responsible for the change in temperature as all of them have very low p-values. Figs. (**3** and **4**) indicate the contour plot and surface plot, respectively, for ΔT.

Table 8. Analysis of variance for change in temperature.

Source	DF	Adj SS	Adj MS	F-Value	P-Value
Regression	3	373.80	124.601	130.09	0.000
Infeed	1	18.06	18.063	18.86	0.000
Flowrate	1	95.70	95.698	99.91	0.000
Scraper Board	1	260.04	260.042	271.49	0.000
Error	20	19.16	0.958	-	-
Total	23	392.96	-	-	-

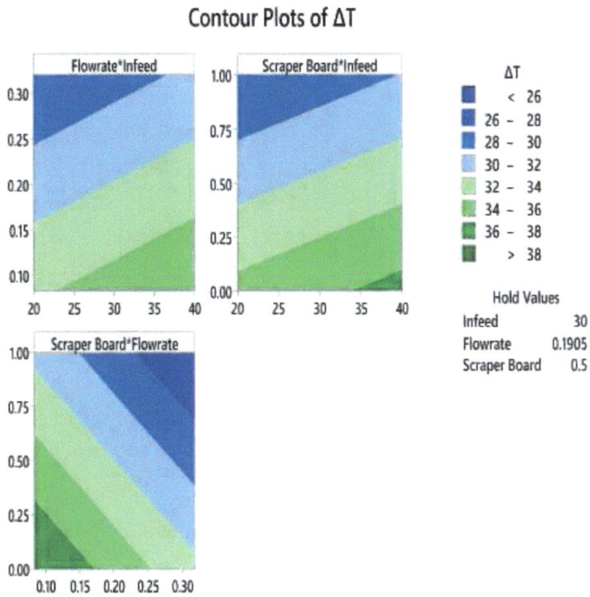

Fig. (3). Contour plots for change in temperature.

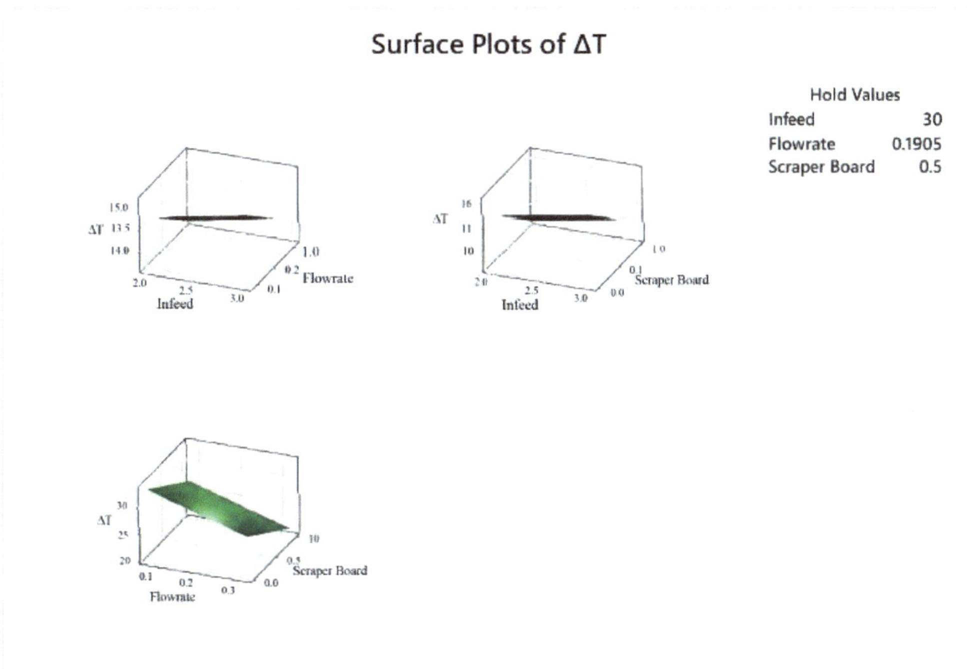

Fig. (4). Surface plots for change in temperature.

Response Optimization

In the next phase of the work, the multi-objective optimization of the response is applied using ANOVA. The aim is to find the optimized parametric conditions (*i.e.*, best set of values for infeed, flow rate, and presence of scrapper board) at which output variables will be minimized, *i.e.*, both tangential force and temperature change. From Tables **9** and Table **10**, it is observed that the optimized parametric combination is current Infeed = 20, Flow rate = 0.32, and scrapper board=1 (presence of it) with desirability = 1. The minimum value of ΔT=24.9086 and F=13.3985. A multi-objective optimization plot for grinding is shown in Fig. **5**.

Table 9. Parameter settings for optimization.

Response	Goal	Lower	Upper	Weight	Importance
ΔT	Minimum	25	39	1	1
F	Minimum	14	20	1	1

Table 10. Solution after optimization.

Solution	Infeed	Flowrate	Scraper Board	ΔT Fit	F Fit	Composite Desirability
1	20	0.32	1	24.9086	13.3985	1

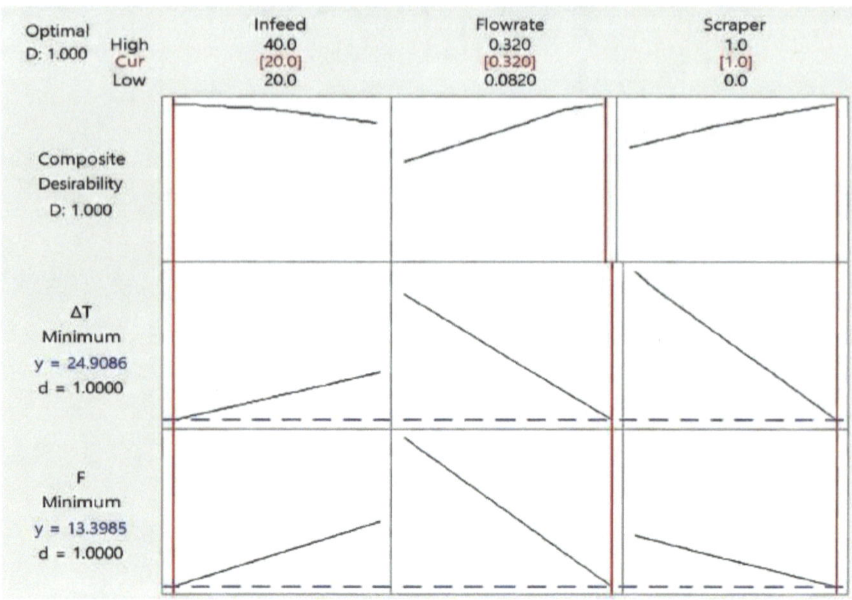

Fig. (5). Multi-objective optimization plots for grinding.

The minimum value of tangential force and change in temperature is obtained in the presence of a scrapper board (*i.e.*, optimized value is 1). It supports the technical theory behind the introduction of scrapper boards in grinding. The presence of a scrapper board prevents the airflow around the grinder and helps lower the generation of temperature.

CONCLUSION

In this work, the grinding process has been modelled based on the input parameters (*i.e.*, infeed, flow rate, and presence of scrapper board) using Regression Equations and ANOVA analysis. The introduction of a scraper board during grinding is a new technique that helps reduce the generated tangential force and temperature (created due to friction with air). Here, a first-order linear regression equation has been used for modeling from the experimental data. From the ANOVA analysis, it has been found that all variables are equally significant for this process. Next, the output variables are optimized to find out an optimal condition for grinding (*i.e.*, best set of values of infeed, flowrate, scrapper board) so that the generated temperature and tangential force are minimized. Using ANOVA, multiple objective function-based optimizations have been successfully achieved. In the future, other machine learning tools can be incorporated for better results. Using this ANOVA for mathematical modeling of grinding and to find out optimal welding conditions is a typical example of Industry 5.0.

REFERENCES

[1] S. Malkin, *Grinding Technology, Theory and Applications of Machining with Abrasives.* Soc. of Manuf. Eng.: Dearborn, MI, 1989.

[2] S. Kohli, C. Guo, and S. Malkin, "Energy partition to the workpiece for grinding with aluminum oxide and CBN abrasive wheels", *J. Eng. Ind.,* vol. 117, no. 2, pp. 160-168, 1995. [http://dx.doi.org/10.1115/1.2803290]

[3] C. Guo, Y. Wu, V. Varghese, and S. Malkin, "Temperatures and energy partition for grinding with vitrified CBN wheels", *CIRP Ann.,* vol. 48, no. 1, pp. 247-250, 1999. [http://dx.doi.org/10.1016/S0007-8506(07)63176-X]

[4] B. Mandal, S. Majumdar, S. Das, and S. Banerjee, "Formation of a significantly less stiff air-layer around a grinding wheel pasted with rexine leather", *International Journal of Precision Technology,* vol. 2, no. 1, pp. 12-20, 2011. [http://dx.doi.org/10.1504/IJPTECH.2011.038106]

[5] S. Majumdar, B. Mondal, S. Das, and S. Chakroborty, "Global Journal on Advancement in Engineering and Science (GJAES) Vol. 1 Issue 1: March-2015 (ISSN No: 2395-1001)," Global J. Adv. Eng. Sci., vol. 1, no. 1, Mar. 2015.

[6] B. Mandal, R. Singh, S. Das, and S. Banerjee, "Improving grinding performance by controlling air flow around a grinding wheel", *Int. J. Mach. Tools Manuf.,* vol. 51, no. 9, pp. 670-676, 2011. [http://dx.doi.org/10.1016/j.ijmachtools.2011.06.003]

[7] S. Mihić, R. Dražumerič, F. Pušavec, J. Badger, and P. Krajnik, "The use of computational fluid dynamics in the analysis of fluid flow and thermal aspects in grinding", *Proc. Inst. Mech. Eng., B J. Eng. Manuf.,* vol. 231, no. 12, pp. 2103-2111, 2017. [http://dx.doi.org/10.1177/0954405415624657]

[8] S. Malkin, and C. Guo, "Thermal analysis of grinding", *CIRP Ann.,* vol. 56, no. 2, pp. 760-782, 2007. [http://dx.doi.org/10.1016/j.cirp.2007.10.005]

[9] S. Majumdar, S. Kumar, S. Chakraborty, and D. Roy, "Effective application of scraper board in grinding", *Tribol. Int.,* vol. 116, pp. 120-128, 2017. [http://dx.doi.org/10.1016/j.triboint.2017.07.009]

[10] Z.L. Han, and C.H. Li, "Theoretical modeling and simulation of airflow field near grinding wheel", *Int. J. Control Autom.,* vol. 6, no. 4, pp. 145-156, 2013.

[11] X. Chen, W.B. Rowe, B. Mills, and D.R. Allanson, "Analysis and simulation of the grinding process. Part IV: Effects of wheel wear", *Int. J. Mach. Tools Manuf.,* vol. 38, no. 1-2, pp. 41-49, 1998. [http://dx.doi.org/10.1016/S0890-6955(97)00041-2]

[12] R.L. Hecker, S.Y. Liang, X.J. Wu, P. Xia, and D.G.W. Jin, "Grinding force and power modeling based on chip thickness analysis", *Int. J. Adv. Manuf. Technol.,* vol. 33, no. 5-6, pp. 449-459, 2007. [http://dx.doi.org/10.1007/s00170-006-0473-y]

[13] T.A. Nguyen, and D.L. Butler, "Simulation of surface grinding process, part 2: interaction of the abrasive grain with the workpiece", *Int. J. Mach. Tools Manuf.,* vol. 45, no. 11, pp. 1329-1336, 2005. [http://dx.doi.org/10.1016/j.ijmachtools.2005.01.006]

[14] Y. Cao, J. Guan, B. Li, X. Chen, J. Yang, and C. Gan, "Modeling and simulation of grinding surface topography considering wheel vibration", *Int. J. Adv. Manuf. Technol.,* vol. 66, no. 5-8, pp. 937-945, 2013. [http://dx.doi.org/10.1007/s00170-012-4378-7]

[15] M. Leonesio, P. Parenti, A. Cassinari, G. Bianchi, and M. Monno, "A time-domain surface grinding model for dynamic simulation", *Procedia CIRP,* vol. 4, pp. 166-171, 2012. [http://dx.doi.org/10.1016/j.procir.2012.10.030]

[16] E.J. Salisbury, K.V. Domala, K.S. Moon, M.H. Miller, and J.W. Sutherland, "A three-dimensional model for the surface texture in surface grinding, part 2: Grinding wheel surface texture model", *J. Manuf. Sci. Eng.,* vol. 123, no. 4, pp. 582-590, 2001. [http://dx.doi.org/10.1115/1.1391428]

[17] B. Dasthagiri, and E.V. Goud, "Optimization studies on surface grinding process parameters", *Int. J. Innov. Res. Sci. Eng. Technol.,* vol. 4, no. 7, pp. 6148-6156, 2015.

[18] M. Janardhan, A.G. Krishna, and D.V. Prasad, "Modeling and optimization of surface grinding process parameters using non-dominated sorting genetic algorithm (NSGA)", *Int. J. Manuf. Sci. Technol.,* vol. 5, no. 2, pp. 117-133, 2011.

[19] R.J. Gu, M. Shillor, G.C. Barber, and T. Jen, "Thermal analysis of the grinding process", *Math. Comput. Model.,* vol. 39, no. 9-10, pp. 991-1003, 2004. [http://dx.doi.org/10.1016/S0895-7177(04)90530-4]

[20] D.L. Skuratov, Y.L. Ratis, I.A. Selezneva, J. Pérez, P. Fernández de Córdoba, and J.F. Urchueguía, "Mathematical modelling and analytical solution for workpiece temperature in grinding", *Appl. Math. Model.,* vol. 31, no. 6, pp. 1039-1047, 2007. [http://dx.doi.org/10.1016/j.apm.2006.03.023]

[21] C. Sharma, S. Ghosh, and P. Talukdar, "Finite element analysis of workpiece temperature during surface grinding of Inconel 718 alloy", *Proc. 5th Int. & 26th All India Manuf. Technol. Design Res. Conf.,* pp. 12-14, 2014.

[22] B. Lin, K. Zhou, J. Guo, Q.Y. Liu, and W.J. Wang, "Influence of grinding parameters on surface temperature and burn behaviors of grinding rail", *Tribol. Int.,* vol. 122, pp. 151-162, 2018. [http://dx.doi.org/10.1016/j.triboint.2018.02.017]

[23] D.M. Babic, A. Torrance, and D.B. Murray, "Soap mist jet cooling of grinding processes", *Key Eng. Mater.,* vol. 291-292, pp. 239-244, 2005. [http://dx.doi.org/10.4028/www.scientific.net/KEM.291-292.239]

CHAPTER 5

An ANOVA-based Optimization Technique to Predict the Part Weight During Micro-powder Injection Molding of Alumina Feedstock

S. K. Tanbir Islam[1,*], **Peeraj Mazumder**[2], **Pijush Dutta**[3] and **Barun Haldar**[4]

[1] *Department of Mechanical Engineering, Greater Kolkata College of Engineering and Management, Baruipur-743387, India*

[2] *Department of Mechanical Engineering and Mining Machinery Engineering, Indian Institute of Technology, Jharkhand, Dhanbad, India*

[3] *Department of Computer Science and Engineering, Greater Kolkata College of Engineering and Management, Baruipur-743387, India*

[4] *Industrial Engineering Department, College of Engineering, Imam Mohammad Ibn Saud Islamic University (IMSIU), Riyadh-11432, Saudi Arabia*

Abstract: Micro-powder injection molding (μ-PIM) has significantly evolved as a technique for manufacturing micro-components. It is well established that injection parameters play a critical role in achieving proper mold filling. Injection molding parameters significantly affect performance in terms of cost, product quality, and sustainability. Choosing the most effective (optimal) combination of injection parameters is therefore essential for each PIM procedure. To address this optimization challenge, a novel algorithm is employed in this study. An optimization technique based on ANOVA is used to predict good mold filling utilizing part weights. The proposed model takes injection pressure, temperature, and actual injection shot size as input variables and predicts the weight of the injected sample. The model is validated using the experimental results. The ANOVA-based Jaya Algorithm achieved maximum accuracies of 95.73% and 96.04% for the training and testing datasets, respectively.

Keywords: ANOVA, Alumina feedstock, Micro-powder injection molding, Modeling, Optimization.

INTRODUCTION

Micro-parts are defined as components with a maximum size below 10 mm and features in the micron range. Powder injection molding (PIM) has emerged as a viable method for producing complex-shaped parts at a competitive cost since the

* **Corresponding author S. K. Tanbir Islam:** Department of Mechanical Engineering, Greater Kolkata College of Engineering and Management, Baruipur-743387, India; E-mail: tanbirislam@gmail.com

Pijush Dutta, Sudip Mondal, Korhan Cengiz and S. Balamurugan (Eds.)

early 1990s. The field of micro-powder injection molding (μ-PIM), which is only a miniature version of regular PIM, was explored by researchers after significant breakthroughs in conventional PIM [1, 2]. μ-PIM's high form intricacy and micron-level component dimension precision are two main benefits. Moreover, it becomes commercially viable when mass production is a primary requirement [3 - 5]. Using plastic injection molding technology and powder metallurgy, the PIM process creates net-shaped metal, ceramic, or hard material parts [1]. Additionally, a modified feedstock may be used for micro components (micro-PIM) using extremely tiny powders. The μ-PIM process consists of four steps, similar to conventional PIM. In the first step, a sigma-blade mixer is used to combine metal or ceramic powders with thermoplastic polymeric materials (binders) to create a uniform mixture called a feedstock. The required component's geometry is then created by feeding the feedstock in the form of pellets into the injection molding machine. According to the binder formulation, the binder is then extracted from the injection molded component using a solvent, catalyst, or heating technique. Finally, the debound specimens are sintered in a furnace with the temperature raised to a degree where the metal or ceramic powders fuse to create the component's shape [5]. The quality of the final product depends on efficient injection molding, as defects such as short shots, jetting, voids, weld lines, and powder-binder separation cannot be corrected in subsequent stages [5, 6]. Several commercial programs, including Moldflow, Moldex3D, PIMSolver, COMSOL, FLUENT, and others, are available to model mold-filling issues, mostly in plastic injection molding. Nonetheless, with some restrictions, researchers have previously employed these techniques for powder injection molding [7, 8]. High shear, the primary cause of powder-binder separation, is frequently observed in flow through micro-cavities, particularly during the micro-PIM process [9 - 11]. According to reports, powder-binder segregation may be detected more effectively using multiphase simulations than with a single-phase analysis [12]. The multiphase modeling technique has already been used by researchers [13 - 15], who have also noted that high temperatures and shear strain rates affect the alteration in drag force among phases, which causes powder-binder separation. The different types of defects lead to inappropriate mold filling that turns into a low part weight compared to the theoretical value. So, part weight can represent the quality of the injection molding component.

AN ARTIFICIAL NEURAL NETWORK'S (ANN) PRELIMINARY DETAILS

To solve the nonlinearity issue between data input and output, one AI model that draws inspiration from the structure of human neurons is the artificial neural network (ANN) [16]. This model is used to predict outcomes for unknown input parameters within a defined domain. This model builds a complicated structure.

Compared to conventional techniques, an ANN has a significant amount of potential to forecast and decide more useful outcomes. An ANN's only objective is to teach a computer anything so that its network can adjust to a certain dataset. Artificial neural networks (ANNs) are appropriate for pattern identification, speech detection, and data classification challenges because, like humans, they can learn by example and use this information for training [17]. A neural network typically uses a feed-forward architecture consisting of three layers, which is one of the most widely adopted designs. This network's input layer consists of a collection of input units that take in input feature vector items. Together with the hidden units, the input units (neurons) are completely linked to the hidden layer. Additionally, the output layer is entirely coupled to the hidden units or neurons. The output layer processes the activation signals propagated from the input layer. A neural network may use one or more hidden layers to transport the input layer's data to its final layer. The magnitude offset is the node's interval or threshold F. It has the following effects on node output *O*'s activation:

$$O = f(I) = f\ (\textstyle\sum_{i=1}^{n} I_i w_i - \phi_k\ ) \quad \textbf{(1)}$$

For the networks to generate the intended input-output mapping for the classification job, the ANN must be trained. A learning algorithm adjusts the connection weights, also known as synaptic weights. This adjustment occurs as the network is trained using a set of instances or data. The NN system's goal is to respond to certain input signals with the desired output. The system is set up to its standard or random values before NN training. The weights that establish the link between the nodes can be altered during training, and certain traditional learning methods, such as the backpropagation algorithm, can also alter the structure based on input data and hidden values [18]. This suggests that by altering the solution's structure and the weights' computation, the NNs may be made more efficient. Recently, several metaheuristic and evolutionary optimization approaches have been effectively used to learn an NN's weights [19 - 21].

JAYA ALGORITHM

Assume that the goal is to minimize (or maximize) a function y(x). If there are "m" design variables and "n" candidate solutions (k = 1, 2, …, n) at any given iteration I, the best candidate solution is the one that offers the most favorable objective function value (*i.e.*, y(x) best) within all the candidate solutions, and the worst candidate solution is the one that offers the most unsuccessful objective function value (*i.e.*, y(x) worst) within all the candidate solutions [22]. In the ith iteration, the jth variable for the kth candidate is changed following Eqn.

$$x_{new}^{j,k,i} = x^{j,k,i} + r_1^{j,i}\ (x^{j,best,i} - \text{abs}\ (x^{j,k,i}\ )) - r_2^{j,i}\ (x^{j,worst,i} - \text{abs}\ (x^{j,k,i}\ )) \quad \textbf{(2)}$$

Where, $x^{j,best,i}$ denotes the value of the jth variable for the best candidate; $x^{j,worst,i}$ denotes the value of the jth variable for the worst candidate; $x^{newj.k,i}$ reflects the altered $x^{j,k,i}$; $r_1^{j,i}$ and $r_2^{j,i}$ are the two random values for the jth variables at the ith iteration in the interval (0, 1).

The term $r_2^{j,i}$ ($x^{j,best,i}$ – abs $x^{j,k,i}$) represents the solution's tendency to approach the optimal value, while the tendency to avoid the worst solution is indicated by the term - $r_2^{j,i}$ and $r_2^{j,i}$ ($x^{j,worst,i}$) – abs ($x^{j,k,i}$)). It is updated if the value of the function provided by $x^{newj.k,i}$ is superior to the value provided by $x^{newj.k,i}$ [22, 23]. All of the function values that are approved after one iteration are supplied as input for the subsequent one. The algorithm constantly seeks to prevent failure (*i.e.*, veering away from the worst option) and succeed (*i.e.*, arriving at the optimal solution) [24–26].

MATHEMATICAL MODEL

In this study, an analytical framework is developed to model part weight (g) in micro-powder injection molding using alumina feedstock. The cost of production is taken into account while formulating the optimization issue. Temperature (°C), pressure (Bar), and actual shot size (mm) are the key parameters taken into account in this work. Table **1** represents the optimum values of weights for the linear model equation 1

$$w = w_1 * T^\circ + w_2 * p + w_3 * l + w_4 \quad \textbf{(3)}$$

$$w = -0.0008611 * T - 0.00011299 * p + 0.0010741 * l + 0.400496 \quad \textbf{(4)}$$

Table 1. Optimum value of the coefficient for different weights

Techniques	W_1	W_2	W_3	W_4	f_{min}	Computational Time
Jaya Algorithm	-0.000861	-0.0001129	0.0010741	0.400496	2.40819e-13	20.9770 s

The Jaya algorithm's convergence graph is displayed in Fig. (**1**). Until it approaches the combined goal function's minimal value, the convergence graph is shown to constantly decrease without being stuck in local optima. This demonstrates that the Jaya algorithm is reliable, capable of strong exploration and exploitation, and successful in resolving multi-objective optimization issues. Fig. (**2**) shows the characteristics graph of the Jaya algorithm for deviation versus the number of training datasets.

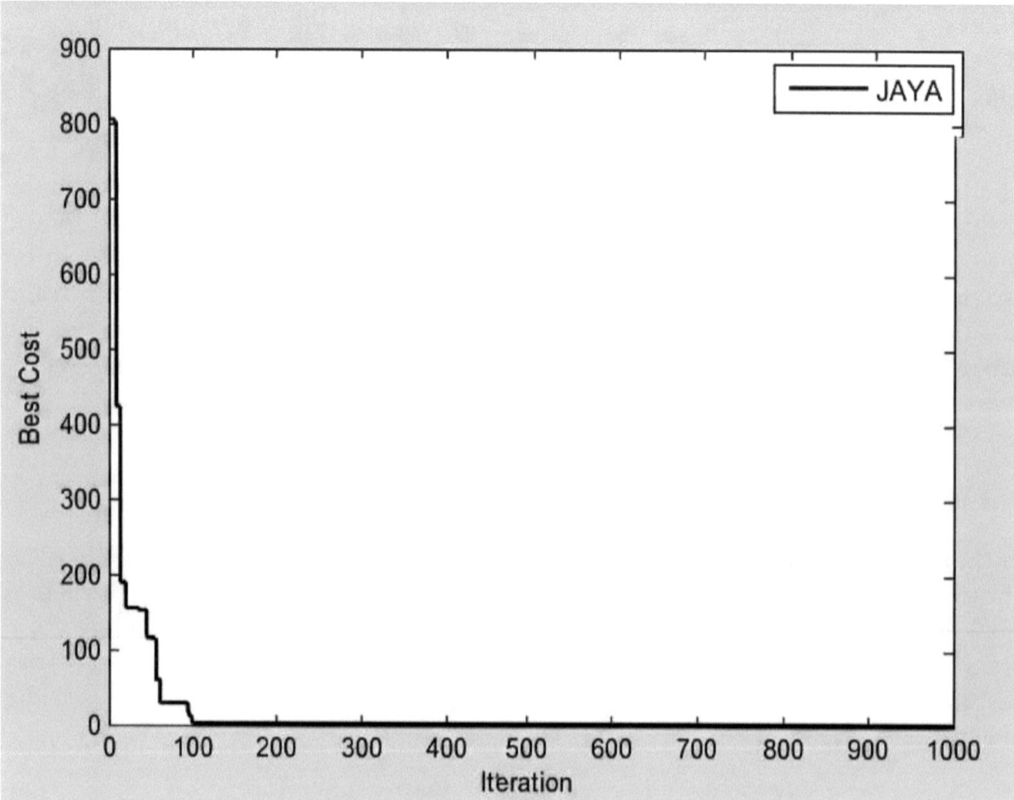

Fig. (1). Convergence speed of jaya algorithm.

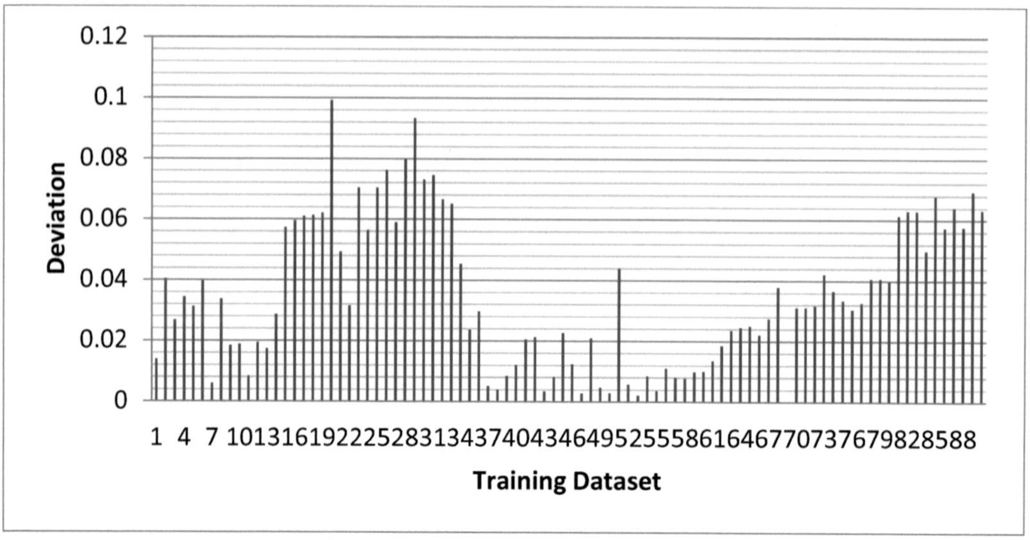

Fig. (2). Deviation characteristics for the training dataset.

RESULT ANALYSIS

The boundary conditions for the independent variables—temperature (°C), pressure (bar), and actual shot size (mm)—are given below:

$135° \leq T° \leq 155°$

$60 \leq p \leq 80$

$2.2 \leq l \leq 8.7$

In this subsection, the ANN nonlinear equation is optimized by the Jaya algorithm to obtain the minimum fitness function for optimum input variables. In this study, the Jaya algorithm is selected with an initial population of 20 and a maximum number of generations equal to 100. Based on thorough experimental trials, this set of standard control parameters is selected, keeping the number of function evaluations constant for each experimental trial while taking into account beginning population sizes of 10, 20, 30, 40, 50, 70, and 100. Then, the set of standard control settings that produces the best outcome in fewer generations is selected. Fig. (**3**) shows the characteristics curve of the proposed algorithm between the deviation curve and the number of test datasets. This result is compared with solutions obtained by previous researchers using other advanced optimization algorithms; the Jaya algorithm's solution is presented in Table **2**. In the last stage, we find out the optimal input parameters for the proposed algorithm that achieve the minimum fitness value shown in Table 3.

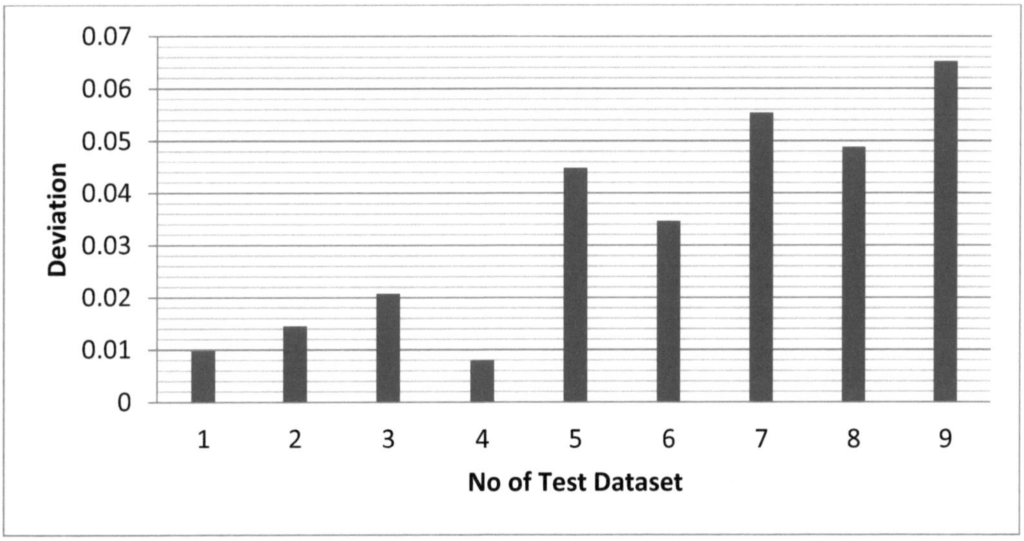

Fig. (3). Deviation characteristics for the testing dataset.

Table 2. Accuracy and RMSE for training and testing datasets.

Types of Datasets	Accuracy (%)	RMSE (%)
Training Dataset	95.7334	4.2666
Testing Dataset	96.0764	3.9206

Table 3. Results of the Jaya algorithm for part weight and its parameters

Techniques	Temperature *T*(°C)	Pressure p (Bar)	Actual shot size L (mm)	Part weight W (gm)	Minimum fitness
Jaya Algorithm	145	70	7	0.2476	1.2359e-17

CONCLUSION

This paper employed the Jaya algorithm to optimize injection parameters in a mold-filling problem. With a high rate of convergence, the Jaya algorithm yielded superior outcomes in terms of the COF value. The nonlinear model was implemented with the help of ANOVA based on input and response variables. Overall, research was performed in two stages. In the first stage, accuracy and RMSE were calculated for the training and testing datasets. In the last stage, the optimum process parameters were obtained, which showed a satisfactory output. Future research should focus on developing an a posteriori version of the Jaya algorithm, which can then be used to tackle optimization issues for various conventional and contemporary machining processes while taking into account several goals at once. The optimization issues of other manufacturing processes, such as casting, welding, shaping, *etc*., may also be resolved using the Jaya algorithm.

ACKNOWLEDGEMENTS

The authors express their gratitude to the members of the Foundry Group, CSIR-CMERI, for their valuable support. They also sincerely thank the CSIR-CMERI for carrying out the experimental work.

REFERENCES

[1] R. German, and A. Bose, *Injection molding of metals and ceramics.* Metal Powder Industries Federation: Princeton, NJ, 1997.

[2] V. Piotter, E. Honza, T. Mueller, and K. Plewa, "Recent Developments in Metal and Ceramic Micro Injection Moulding", *European Congress and Exhibition on Powder Metallurgy. European PM Conference Proceedings,* p. 1, 2012.

[3] V. Piotter, W. Bauer, R. Knitter, M. Mueller, T. Mueller, and K. Plewa, "Powder injection moulding of metallic and ceramic micro parts", *Microsyst. Technol.,* vol. 17, no. 2, pp. 251-263, 2011. [http://dx.doi.org/10.1007/s00542-011-1274-2]

[4] F. Petzoldt, "Micro powder injection moulding - challenges and opportunities", *Powder Injection Moulding International,* vol. 2, no. 1, pp. 37-42, 2008.

[5] U.M. Attia, and J.R. Alcock, "A review of micro-powder injection moulding as a microfabrication technique", *J. Micromech. Microeng.,* vol. 21, no. 4, p. 043001, 2011. [http://dx.doi.org/10.1088/0960-1317/21/4/043001]

[6] S.T. Islam, S.K. Samanta, A.K. Lohar, and A. Bandyopadhyay, "Rheological study of alumina feedstock for a micro-powder injection moulding application", *Mater. Res. Express,* vol. 6, no. 9, p. 095204, 2019. [http://dx.doi.org/10.1088/2053-1591/ab2ce6]

[7] S.G. Laddha, C. Wu, S.J. Park, S. Lee, S. Ahn, R.M. German, and S.V. Atre, "Characterization and simulation of macroscale moldfilling defects in microminiature powder injection molding", *Int. J. Powder Metall.,* vol. 46, no. 3, pp. 49-57, 2010.

[8] S. T. Islam, S. K. Samanta, S. Das, and H. Chattopadhyay, "Simulation of Micro-Powder Injection Molding Using a Dynamic Mesh Approach," J Micro Nanomanuf, vol. 10, no. 3, Sep. 2022. [http://dx.doi.org/10.1115/1.4062717]

[9] F. Ilinca, and J.F. Hétu, "Three-Dimensional Numerical Simulation of Segregation in Powder Injection Molding", *Int. Polym. Process.,* vol. 23, no. 2, pp. 208-215, 2008. [http://dx.doi.org/10.3139/217.2123]

[10] R. Heldele, S. Rath, L. Merz, R. Butzbach, M. Hagelstein, and J. Haußelt, "X-ray tomography of powder injection moulded micro parts using synchrotron radiation", *Nucl. Instrum. Methods Phys. Res. B,* vol. 246, no. 1, pp. 211-216, 2006. [http://dx.doi.org/10.1016/j.nimb.2005.12.030]

[11] S.T. Islam, S.K. Samanta, S. Das, and H. Chattopadhyay, "A numerical model to predict the powder–binder separation during micro□powder injection molding", *J. Am. Ceram. Soc.,* vol. 105, no. 7, pp. 4608-4620, 2022. [http://dx.doi.org/10.1111/jace.18401]

[12] S.K. Samanta, H. Chattopadhyay, B. Pustal, R. Berger, M.M. Godkhindi, and A. Bührig-Polaczek, "A numerical study of solidification in powder injection molding process", *Int. J. Heat Mass Transf.,* vol. 51, no. 3-4, pp. 672-682, 2008. [http://dx.doi.org/10.1016/j.ijheatmasstransfer.2007.04.033]

[13] A. Greiner, D. Kauzlarić, J.G. Korvink, R. Heldele, M. Schulz, V. Piotter, T. Hanemann, O. Weber, and J. Haußelt, "Simulation of micro powder injection moulding: Powder segregation and yield stress effects during form filling", *J. Eur. Ceram. Soc.,* vol. 31, no. 14, pp. 2525-2534, 2011. [http://dx.doi.org/10.1016/j.jeurceramsoc.2011.02.008]

[14] S.K. Samanta, H. Chattopadhyay, and M.M. Godkhindi, "Modelling the powder binder separation in injection stage of PIM", *Prog. Comput. Fluid Dyn.,* vol. 11, no. 5, pp. 292-304, 2011. [http://dx.doi.org/10.1504/PCFD.2011.042181]

[15] F. Shang, B. Qiao, Y. Dong, Z. Cao, W. Sun, and Y. He, "Simulation on the two-phase separation of powder injection molding 316L stainless steel", *Medziagotyra,* vol. 25, no. 3, pp. 246-251, 2019. [http://dx.doi.org/10.5755/j01.ms.25.3.19137]

[16] S. Asadi, E. Hadavandi, F. Mehmanpazir, and M.M. Nakhostin, *Hybridization of evolutionary Levenberg-Marquardt neural networks and data pre-processing for stock market prediction.* vol. 35. Knowl Based Syst, 2012.

[17] J.K. Basu, D. Bhattacharyya, and T. Kim, "Use of Artificial Neural Network in Pattern Recognition", *Int. J. Softw. Eng. Appl.,* vol. 4, no. 2, 2010.

[18] Mirza Cilimkovic, "Neural Networks and Back Propagation Algorithm," *Institute of Technology Blanchardstown, Blanchardstown Road North Dublin,* vol. 15, 2015.

[19] P. Dutta, K. Cengiz, and A. Kumar, “Study of bio-inspired neural networks for the prediction of liquid flow in a process control system,” in *Cognitive Big Data Intelligence with a Metaheuristic Approach*, 2021.

[20] P. Dutta, S. Pal, A. Kumar, and K. Cengiz, Artificial Intelligence for Cognitive Modeling. 2023. [http://dx.doi.org/10.1201/9781003216001]

[21] S. Bellubbi, B. Mallick, A.S. Hameed, P. Dutta, M.K. Sarkar, and S. Nanjundaswamy, "Neural Network (NN)-Based RSM-PSO Multiresponse Parametric Optimization of the Electro Chemical Discharge Micromachining Process During Microchannel Cutting on Silica Glass", *J. Adv. Manuf. Syst.,* vol. 21, no. 4, pp. 869-897, 2022. [http://dx.doi.org/10.1142/S0219686722500330]

[22] E. H. Houssein, A. G. Gad, and Y. M. Wazery, “Jaya Algorithm and Applications: A Comprehensive Review,” in Lecture Notes in Electrical Engineering, vol. 696, 2021. [http://dx.doi.org/10.1007/978-3-030-56689-0_2]

[23] R.A. Zitar, M.A. Al-Betar, M.A. Awadallah, I.A. Doush, and K. Assaleh, "An Intensive and Comprehensive Overview of JAYA Algorithm, its Versions and Applications", *Arch. Comput. Methods Eng.,* vol. 29, no. 2, pp. 763-792, 2022. [http://dx.doi.org/10.1007/s11831-021-09585-8] [PMID: 34075292]

[24] S. Khatir, D. Boutchicha, C. Le Thanh, H. Tran-Ngoc, T.N. Nguyen, and M. Abdel-Wahab, *Improved ANN technique combined with Jaya algorithm for crack identification in plates using XIGA and experimental analysis.* vol. 107. Theoretical and Applied Fracture Mechanics, 2020.

[25] Y. Zhang, A. Chi, and S. Mirjalili, *Enhanced Jaya algorithm: A simple but efficient optimization method for constrained engineering design problems.* vol. 233. Knowl Based Syst, 2021.

[26] K. Yu, B. Qu, C. Yue, S. Ge, X. Chen, and J. Liang, *A performance-guided JAYA algorithm for parameters identification of photovoltaic cell and module.* vol. 237. Appl Energy, 2019.

CHAPTER 6

ANOVA-based Analysis and Optimization of Micro-performances during Blend Hole Generation on Glass

Bijan Mallick[1,*] and **Azzam S. Hameed**[2]

[1] *Faculty of ME Department, Global Institute of Management and Technology, Krishnanagar, MAKAUT, West Bengal, India*

[2] *Faculty of ME Department, Wasit University, Kut, Iraq*

Abstract: Electrochemical discharge machining (ECDM) performance enhancement is challenging when applied in the industrial field. The book chapter shows the second-order correlating mathematical models with pulse on-time, electrolyte concentration, duty ratio, inter-electrode gap, and applied voltage for diametric over cut (DOC) and tool wear rate (TWR) when a mixture of potassium hydroxide (KOH) and sodium hydroxide (NaOH) is used as an electrolyte during blind hole generation on glass. ANOVA is used to analyze the fitness of models, as well as the effects of and process parameters. Desirability function analysis is performed in this chapter for the minimization of DOC and TWR for blind hole formation on glass and contour diagrams. Multi-objective optimization also represents the better results of micro-hole fabrication by the ECDM process. It is found that 50V/30mm IEG/20wt%/45 µs/.50 duty ratio/50Hz pulse frequency provides a minimum TWR of tungsten carbide tool and DOC of micro-hole.

Keywords: DOC, Glass, Micro-ECDM, Micro-blind hole, NaOH+KOH, TWR.

INTRODUCTION

Fizeau (1819-1896) and Foucault (1819-1868) made the ECDM system, and Kurafuji and Suda (1968) applied it for machining performances. Some fundamentals and material removal aspects of the ECDM process have been propounded [1]. A better accuracy and quality improvement in ECDM performances are described [2]. Several applications of ECDM in the field of micro-drilling of advanced ceramics are also discussed [3, 4]. Mixed graphite dust is added to the electrolyte to increase conductivity in ECDM [5]. A certain

* **Corresponding author Sudip Mandal:** Faculty of ME Department, Global Institute of Management and Technology, Krishnanagar, MAKAUT, West Bengal, India; E-mail: bijan.ju@gmail.com

Pijush Dutta, Sudip Mondal, Korhan Cengiz and S. Balamurugan (Eds.)

application of glass in ECDM is described [6]. Mixed electrolytes and GRA are used for micro-machining analysis [7]. Different shapes of profiles and parameter effects are analyzed using PSO-RSM, GA-ANN, and ANOVA-RSM during micro-channeling on brittle materials [8 - 14]. Taguchi-GRA proposes to find better results of the ECDM process during the micro-fabrication of glass [15]. To fulfill the objectives of the book chapter, the lineup of experimentations and analysis is performed to achieve the target results during micro-hole generation on glass by micro-ECDM. This chapter aims to achieve the target results of the work and control the process parameters, such as machining voltage, pulse frequency (fixed 50Hz), pulse on-time inter-electrode gap (IEG), duty ratio, electrolyte concentration, etc. A tungsten micro-tool with a diameter of 250 μm is used, and a 1:1 mixture of NaOH and KOH is employed for micro-hole generation on glass. Fig. (**1**) shows the micro-ECDM system, which is used for the experimental work of micro-hole generation on glass.

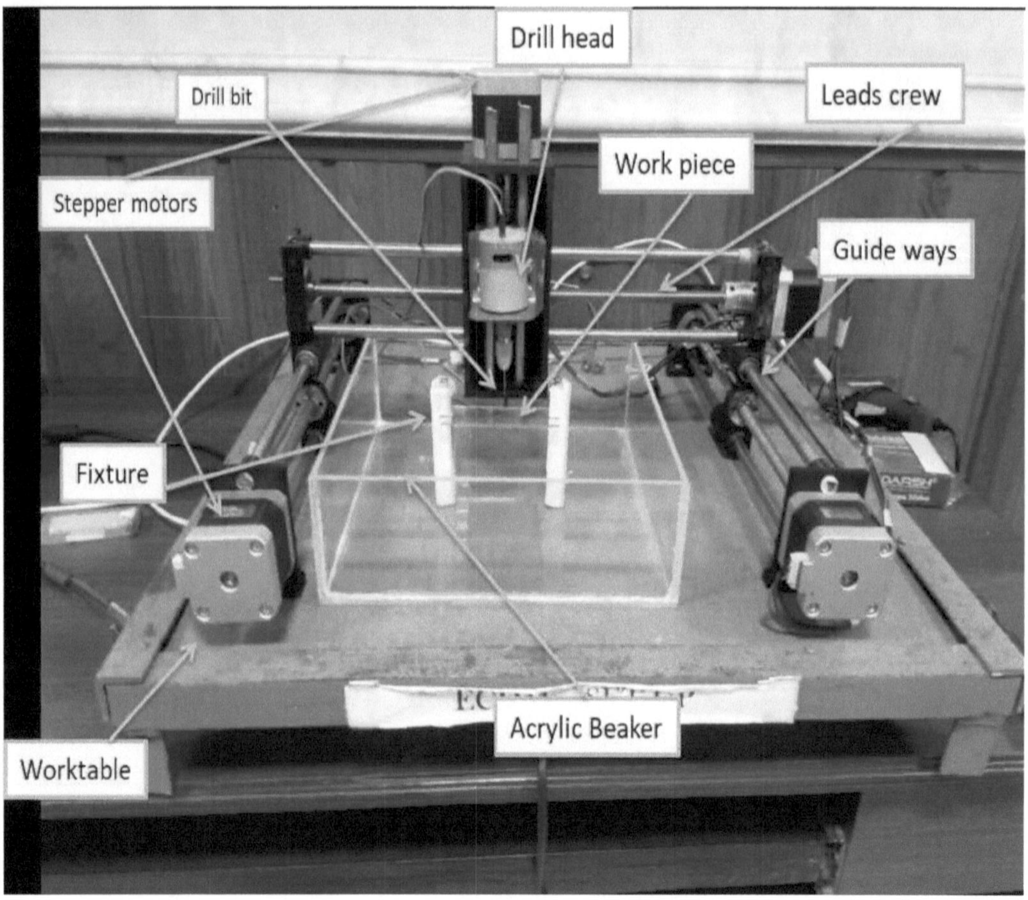

Fig. (1). The Micro-ECDM setup.

EXPERIMENTAL PLANNING AND RESULT ANALYSIS BASED ON ANOVA AND DESIRABILITY FUNCTION

Table **1** represents the levels and ranges of the process parameters. A face-centered design (-1 to +1) of experiments is chosen for experimentation. Every combination of parameters is set properly, and 1 tungsten carbide tool is used only once using a mixed electrolyte of 1:1 NaOH and KOH. Table **2** shows the experimental results for various parametric combinations. An optical microscope is used to measure diametric overcut, and a weighing machine is used to measure tool wear rate.

Table 1. Range of variables

Process Parameters (Variables)	Range		
	-1	0	+1
Voltage(V)	50	55	60
Pulse on-time(μs)	45	50	55
IEG(mm)	30	35	40
Duty ratio	0.45	0.50	0.55
Electrolyte Con.(wt%)	20	25	30

Table 2. Experimental results.

StdOrder	VOLTAGE(V) (x1)	PULSE ON TIME(μs) (x2)	IEG(mm) (x3)	DUTY RATIO(x4)	ELECTROLYTE CON.(wt%)(x5)	DOC(μm)	TWR(mg/hr)
1	50	45	30	0.45	30	230	0.030
2	60	45	30	0.45	20	432	0.039
3	50	55	30	0.45	20	292	0.038
4	60	55	30	0.45	30	522	0.042
5	50	45	40	0.45	20	320	0.033
6	60	45	40	0.45	30	412	0.033
7	50	55	40	0.45	30	230	0.031
8	60	55	40	0.45	20	372	0.033
9	50	45	30	0.55	20	218	0.017
10	60	45	30	0.55	30	370	0.039
11	50	55	30	0.55	30	202	0.038
12	60	55	30	0.55	20	540	0.033
13	50	45	40	0.55	30	228	0.031
14	60	45	40	0.55	20	374	0.033

StdOrder	VOLTAGE(V) (x1)	PULSE ON TIME(μs) (x2)	IEG(mm) (x3)	DUTY RATIO(x4)	ELECTROLYTE CON.(wt%)(x5)	DOC(μm)	TWR(mg/hr)
15	50	55	40	0.55	20	370	0.030
16	60	55	40	0.55	30	594	0.039
17	50	50	35	0.50	25	212	0.033
18	60	50	35	0.50	25	430	0.037
19	55	45	35	0.50	25	396	0.028
20	55	55	35	0.50	25	470	0.036
21	55	50	30	0.50	25	260	0.023
22	55	50	40	0.50	25	336	0.019
23	55	50	35	0.45	25	416	0.037
24	55	50	35	0.55	25	458	0.038
25	55	50	35	0.50	20	408	0.025
26	55	50	35	0.50	30	414	0.026
27	55	50	35	0.50	25	404	0.026
28	55	50	35	0.50	25	400	0.027
29	55	50	35	0.50	25	402	0.027
30	55	50	35	0.50	25	404	0.027
31	55	50	35	0.50	25	402	0.027
32	55	50	35	0.50	25	404	0.027

ANOVA ANALYSIS FOR MATHEMATICAL MODEL VALIDATION

Non-linear second-order mathematical models are shown as equations 1 and 2, which are fitted with R-Sq = 98.6% and R-Sq(adj) = 96.50% for DOC. For TWR, R-Sq = 96.61% and R-Sq(adj) = 94.9%, which represent the fitness level above 95%. F ratio and p-value for lack of fit at standard DOF is 4.6, or approximately zero p-value, and ANOVA. Tables **3** and **4** indicate the actual fitness values for Adj.SS and MSS, as well as the F ratio and p-value.

Table 3. ANOVA of Adj.SS and MSS for DOC and TWR.

Source	DF	Adj.SS DOC	Adj.SS TWR	Adj.MSS DOC	Adj.MSS TWR
Regression	20	295308	0.001120	14765	0.000056
Linear	5	193152	0.000276	38630	0.000055
Square	5	43637	0.000577	8727	0.000115

Source	DF	Adj.SS DOC	Adj.SS TWR	Adj.MSS DOC	Adj.MSS TWR
Interaction	10	58519	0.000267	5852	0.000027
Lack-of-Fit	06	3705	0.000038	617	0.000006
Pure Error	06	-	-	-	-
Total	31	-	-	-	-

Table 4. ANOVA of F ratio and P value for DOC and TWR.

Source	DF	F of DOC	F of TWR	P of DOC	P of TWR
Regression	20	43.68	15.67	0.000	0.000
Linear	5	114.28	15.47	0.000	0.000
Square	5	25.82	32.27	0.000	0.000
Interaction	10	17.31	7.46	0.000	0.001
Lack-of-Fit	06	231.56	38.47	0.001	0.001
Pure Error	06	-	-	-	-
Total	31	-	-	-	-

$$\text{Min\_DOC}(x)=Y(\text{DOC})= 394.08 +96.889*x(1)+ 34.000*x(2)+ 9.444*x(3) + 7.111*x(4) -6.889*x(5)-66.653 *(x(1))^2+45.347*(x(2))^289.653*(x(3))^2+ 49.347*(x(4))^2+34.23*(x(5))^2+23.347*x(1)*x(2)+21.375*x(1)*x(3)-19.875* x(1)*x(4)+12.125*x(1)*x(5)+30.625*x(2)*x(3)+4.875*x(2)*x(4)+23.625*x(3)*x(4)+11.625*x(3)*x(5) -5.375 *x(4)*x(5) \tag{1}$$

$$\text{Min\_TWR}(x)=Y(\text{TWR})= 0.028106+0.002611 *x(1)+ 0.002056 *x(2) -0.000944 *x(3) -0.001000 *x(4) +0.001556 *x(5) +0.005940 *(x(1))^2+0.002940 *(x(2))^2-0.008060 *(x(3))^2+0.008440 *(x(4))^2-0.003560*(x(5))^2 -0.001437 *x(1)*x(2) -0.001063 *x(1)*x(3)- 0.000812 *x(1)*x(4)+ 0.000188 *x(1)*x(5)- 0.001438 *x(2)*x(3)+ 0.000687 *x(2)*x(4)+ 0.000313 *x(3)*x(4)+ 0.001562 *x(2)*x(5) -0.001063 *x(3)*x(5)+ 0.002562 *x(4)*x(5); \tag{2}$$

Analysis of Process Parameters' Effects on DOC

Fig. (**2**) explains the effects of voltage, duty ratio, electrolyte concentration, pulse on time, and IEG (inter-electrode gap) on DOC. From Fig. (**2**), it is clear that DOC mainly depends on critical voltage, as well as on all the other parameters; also, tool diameter plays a great role in it. From Fig. (**2**), it is also observed that pulse on time and voltage play a vital role in increasing the DOC. Duty ratio initially increases from 0.45 to 0.50 and then decreases. A 30 wt% electrolyte concentration provides a lower DOC, but a lower IEG is more beneficial for minimizing DOC. Fig. (**3**) shows the contour effects plot of voltage-pulse-on time, IEG-duty ratio, and electrolyte concentration-duty ratio for DOC. By graphical analysis, it can be assumed that the minimum DOC is found at 55 volt/25wt%/0.55 duty ratio/40 mm IEG/55 micro-sec pulse on time.

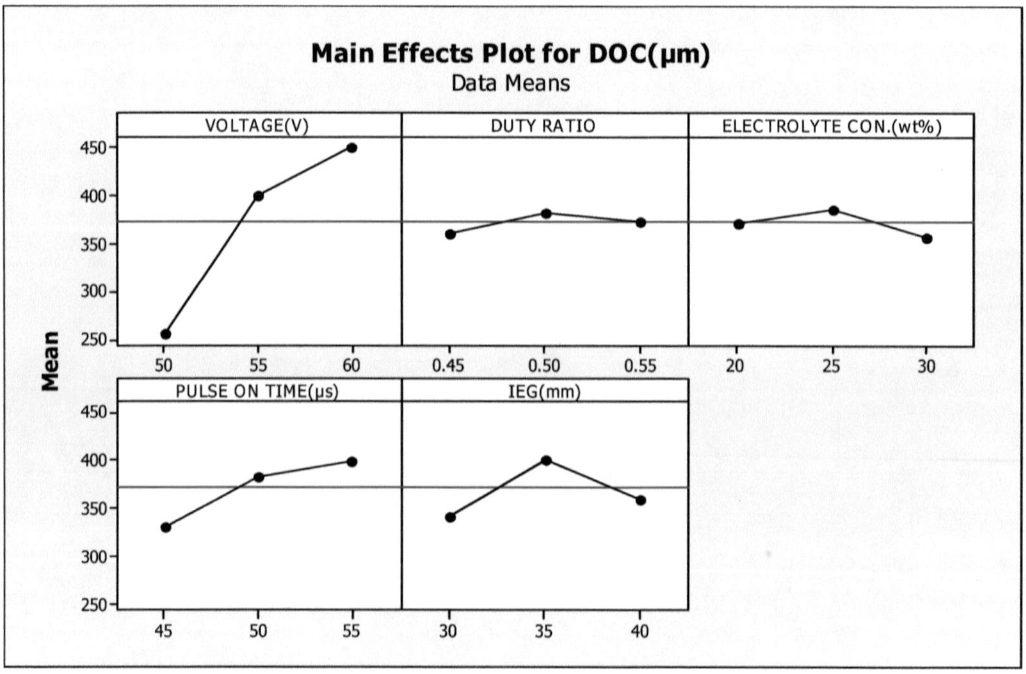

Fig. (2). Effects of voltage, duty ratio, electrolyte concentration, pulse on time, and IEG of DOC.

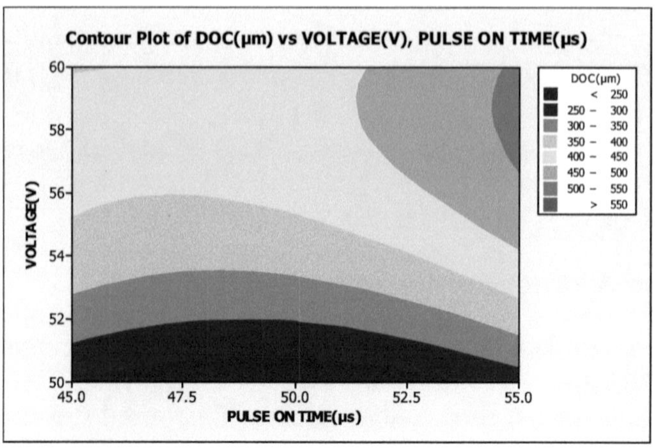

Fig. (3a). Contour effects plot of voltage-pulse on time for DOC.

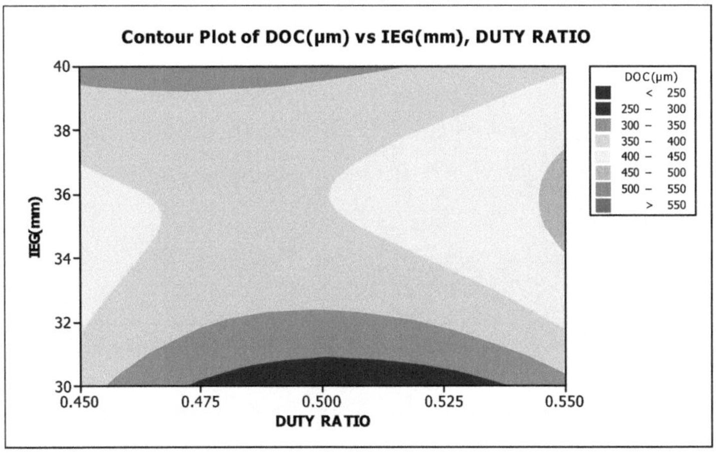

Fig. (3b). Contour effects plot of IEG-duty ratio for DOC.

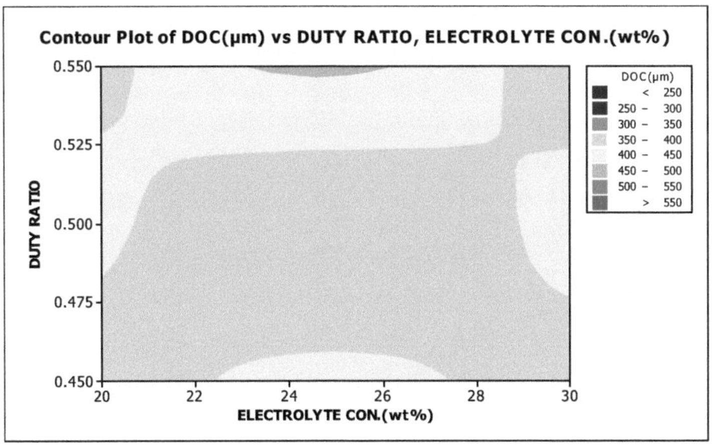

Fig. (3c). Contour effects plot of electrolyte concentration-duty ratio for DOC.

Analysis of Process Parameters' Effects on TWR

Fig. (**4**) elucidates the effects of voltage, duty ratio, electrolyte concentration, pulse on time, and IEG (inter-electrode gap) on TWR. From Fig. (**4**), it is clear that TWR mainly depends on the critical voltage, which leads to higher temperatures during machining. From Figs. (**3a-3c**), it is also clear that a 50-microsecond pulse on-time and 55-volt voltage play a vital role in minimizing TWR. A moderate duty ratio of 0.50 is best for achieving the minimum TWR; after that, TWR increases, and a 30 wt% electrolyte concentration provides higher TWR, but a 35 mm IEG assists in achieving the minimum TWR. Fig. (**4**) shows the contour effects plot of voltage-pulse-on time, IEG-duty ratio, and electrolyte concentration-duty ratio for TWR. By graphical analysis, it can be assumed that the minimum TWR is found at 55 volt/25wt%/0.5 duty ratio/35 mm IEG/50 micro-sec pulse on time. Figs. (**5a-5c**) represents the contour effects plot of voltage-pulse-on time, IEG-duty ratio, and electrolyte concentration-duty ratio for TWR. Fig. (**6**) presents the multi-objective minimization graphical presentation for minimum DOC and TWR. Fig. (**7**) shows an optical microscopic view of through-hole generation on silica at optimal conditions.

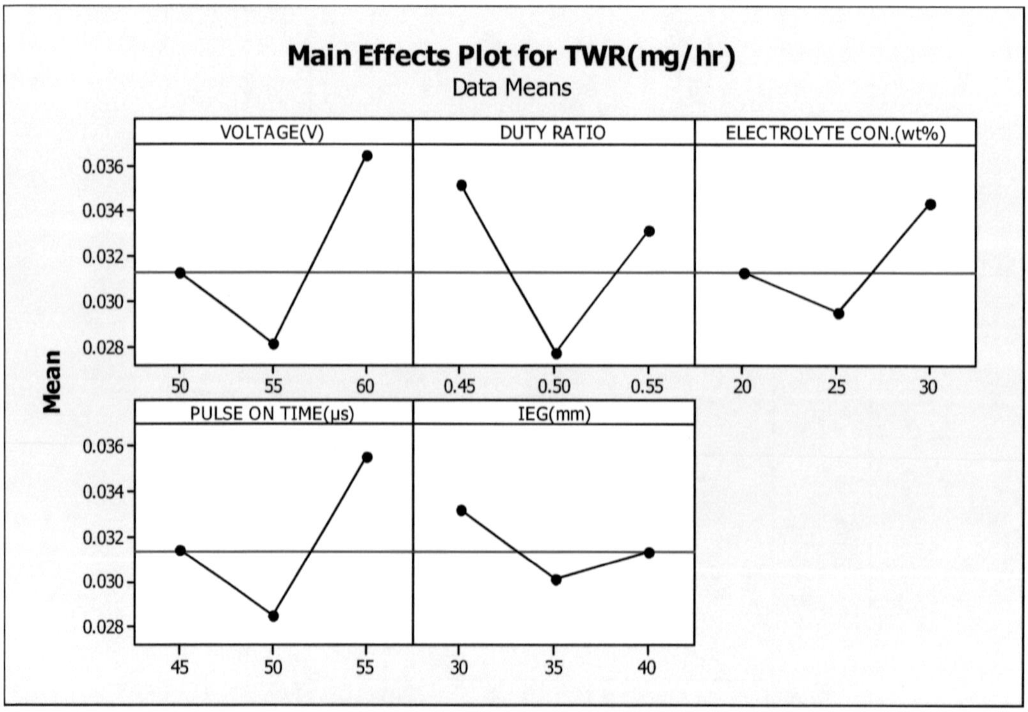

Fig. (4). Effects of voltage, duty ratio, electrolyte concentration, pulse on time, and IEG of TWR.

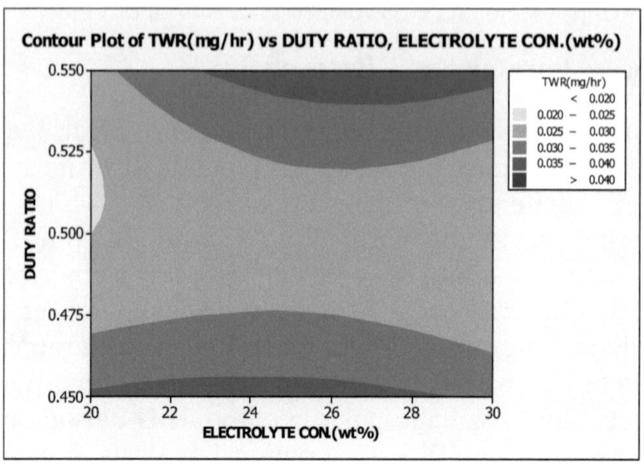

Fig. (5a). Contour effects plot of voltage-pulse on time.

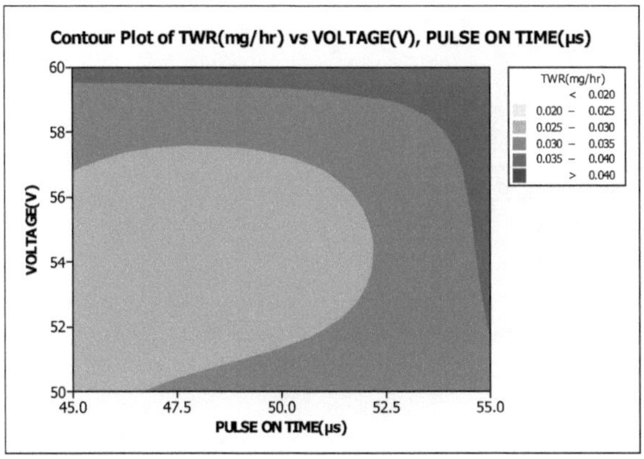

Fig. (5b). Contour effects plot of IEG-duty ratio.

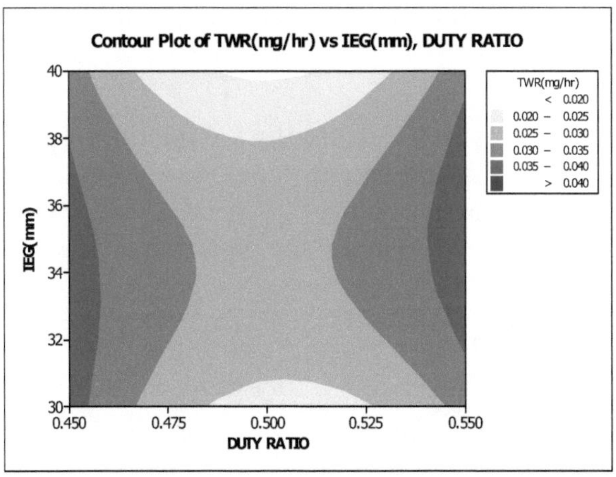

Fig. (5c). Contour effects plot of electrolyte concentration-duty ratio for TWR.

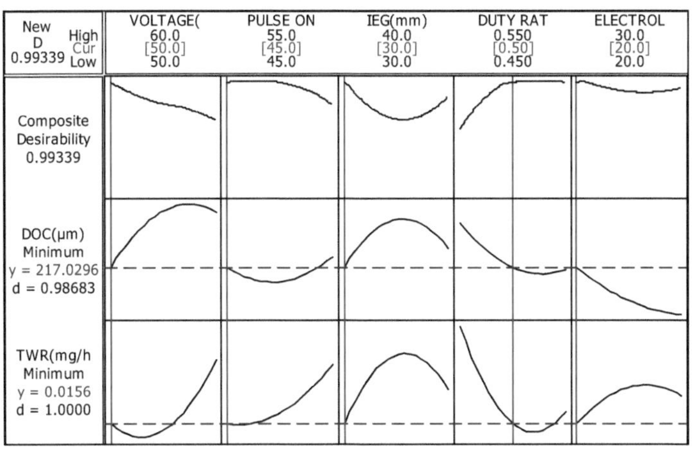

Fig. (6). Multi-objective optimization plot of DOC and TWR for minimization.

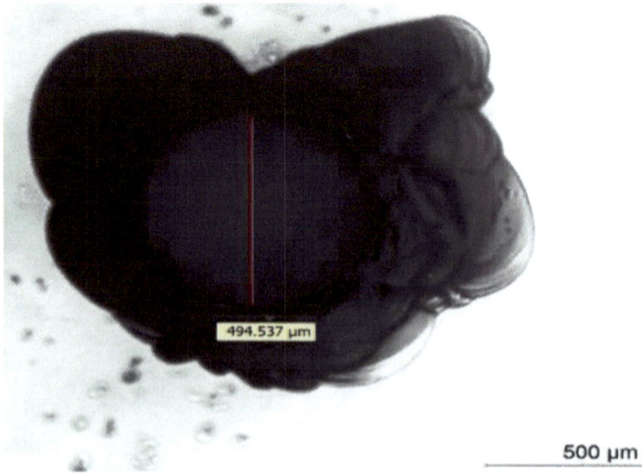

Fig. (7). Microscopic view of micro-blind hole cutting on glass at optimal conditions.

CONCLUSION

From the ANOVA analysis and desirability of function-based optimization for micro-hole generation on silica, it can be concluded that the applied voltage leads to a critical voltage that takes action mainly on DOC and TWR during the micro-ECDM process. It directly influences the pulse on time to reach the critical voltage.

In this study, ANOVA analysis predicted the best fitness of models. Minimum DOC was found at 55 volt/25wt%/0.55 duty ratio/40mmIEG/55 micro-sec pulse on time, while minimum TWR was found at 55 volt/25wt%/0.5 duty ratio/35 mm IEG/50 micro-sec pulse on time during micro-hole generation on silica by ECDM. Minimization of DOC and TWR was achieved at 50 volt/20wt%/0.5 duty ratio/30 mm IEG/45 μs pulse on time.

The achieved results have been successfully utilized for micro-blind hole generation on silica.

REFERENCES

[1] I. Basak, and A. Ghosh, "Mechanism of spark generation during electrochemical discharge machining: a theoretical model and experimental verification", *J. Mater. Process. Technol.,* vol. 62, no. 1-3, pp. 46-53, 1996.
[http://dx.doi.org/10.1016/0924-0136(95)02202-3]

[2] B. Bhattacharyya, B.N. Doloi, and S.K. Sorkhel, "Experimental investigations into electrochemical discharge machining (ECDM) of non-conductive ceramic materials", *J. Mater. Process. Technol.,* vol. 95, no. 1-3, pp. 145-154, 1999.
[http://dx.doi.org/10.1016/S0924-0136(99)00318-0]

[3] B.R. Sarkar, B. Doloi, and B. Bhattacharyya, "Parametric analysis on electrochemical discharge machining of silicon nitride ceramics", *Int. J. Adv. Manuf. Technol.,* vol. 28, no. 9-10, pp. 873-881, 2006.

[http://dx.doi.org/10.1007/s00170-004-2448-1]

[4] B.R. Sarkar, B. Doloi, and B. Bhattacharyya, "Non-traditional Micromachining Processes Fundamentals and Applications, 10. Electrochemical Discharge Micro-machining of Engineering Materials", *Springer Int. Publishing,* 2017.

[5] M.S. Han, B.K. Min, and S.J. Lee, "Improvement of surface integrity of electro-chemical discharge machining process using powder-mixed electrolyte", *J. Mater. Process. Technol.,* vol. 191, no. 1-3, pp. 224-227, 2007.
[http://dx.doi.org/10.1016/j.jmatprotec.2007.03.004]

[6] R. Wüthrich, V. Fascio, and H. Langen, "Machining of non-conducting materials using electrochemical discharge phenomenon—an overview", *Int. J. Mach. Tools Manuf.,* vol. 45, no. 9, pp. 1095-1108, 2005.
[http://dx.doi.org/10.1016/j.ijmachtools.2004.11.011]

[7] A.D. Oza, A. Kumar, V. Badheka, and A. Arora, "Traveling Wire Electrochemical Discharge Machining (TW-ECDM) of Quartz Using Zinc Coated Brass Wire: Investigations on Material Removal Rate and Kerf Width Characteristics", *Silicon,* pp. 1-2, 2019.

[8] B. Mallick, S. Biswas, B.R. Sarkar, B. Doloi, and B. Bhattacharyya, "On Performance of Electrochemical Discharge Micro-Machining Process Using Different Electrolytes and Tool Shapes", *Int. J. Manuf. Mater. Mech. Eng.,* vol. 10, no. 2, pp. 49-63, 2020.
[http://dx.doi.org/10.4018/IJMMME.2020040103]

[9] B. Mallick, B.R. Sarkar, B. Doloi, and B. Bhattacharyya, "Analysis on the effect of ECDM process parameters during micro-machining of glass using genetic algorithm", *J. Mech. Eng. Sci.,* vol. 12, no. 3, pp. 3942-3960, 2018.
[http://dx.doi.org/10.15282/jmes.12.3.2018.13.0344]

[10] B. Mallick, B.R. Sarkar, B. Doloi, and B. Bhattacharyya, "Analysis on electrochemical discharge machining during micro-channel cutting on glass", *International Journal of Precision Technology,* vol. 7, no. 1, pp. 32-50, 2017.
[http://dx.doi.org/10.1504/IJPTECH.2017.084554]

[11] B. Mallick, B. R. Sarkar, B. Doloi, and B. Bhattacharyya, "Modelling and analysis on Performance of ECDM Process for the Fabrication of μ-Channels on Glass through Response Surface Methodology", *Manuf. Technol. Today (MTT),* vol. 18, no. 9, 2019.

[12] B. Mallick, B.R. Sarkar, B. Doloi, and B. Bhattacharyya, "Multi Criteria Optimization of Electrochemical Discharge Micro-Machining Process during Micro-Channel Generation on Glass", *Appl. Mech. Mater.,* vol. 592-594, pp. 525-529, 2014.
[http://dx.doi.org/10.4028/www.scientific.net/AMM.592-594.525]

[13] B. Mallick, A. S. Hameed, B. R. Sarkar, B. Doloi, and B. Bhattacharyya, "Experimental Investigation for Improvement of Micro-Machining Performances of μ-ECDM Process", *Mater. Today,* 2019.

[14] B. Mallick, B. R. Sarkar, B. Doloi, and B. Bhattacharyya, "Improvement of Surface Quality and Machining Depth of μ-ECDM Performances Using Mixed Electrolyte at Different Polarity", *Silicon,* 2021.
[http://dx.doi.org/10.21203/rs.3.rs-854051/v1]

[15] S. Bellubbi, N. S., and B. Mallick, "Multi Response Optimization of ECDM Process Parameters for Machining of Microchannel in Silica Glass Using Taguchi–GRA Technique," *Silicon*, 2021.
[http://dx.doi.org/10.1007/s12633-021-01167-4]

CHAPTER 7

Micro-ECDM Performance Analysis Based on ANOVA

Bijan Mallick[1,*], **S. K. Hikmat**[1], **Krishnendu Mondal**[2] and **Pijush Dutta**[3]

[1] *Faculty of ME Department, Global Institute of Management and Technology, Krishnanagar, MAKAUT, West Bengal, India*

[2] *Faculty of ME Department, Future Institute of Engineering and Management, MAKAUT, West Bengal, India*

[3] *Faculty of CSE Department, Greater Kolkata College of Engineering and Management, West Bengal, India*

Abstract: The augmentation of the characteristics of micro-ECDM during micro-drilling on borosilicate glass is a challenging task. The book chapter indicates the ANOVA-based second-order mathematical models by correlating with voltage and conductivity of the electrolyte for radial over cut (ROC) and material removal rate (MRR) when NaOH is used as electrolyte during drilling on borosilicate glass. ANOVA is used to find the best fitness models for MRR and ROC. In this chapter, root mean square error (RMSE) for ROC and MRR is proposed during the drilling of glass by the ECDM process. It is found that optimized parametric combinations are 51 V/172 mmho-cm / 40mm, which achieve minimum ROC and MRR using stainless steel (SS) micro-tool.

Keywords: Drilling, Glass, Micro-ECDM, MRR, NaOH, ROC.

INTRODUCTION

According to modern developments, electrical, optical, and medical equipment must integrate and reduce the size of high-strength performance devices. Often, brittle materials are used to make these parts (non-conductive). Advanced materials, such as ceramics and composites, are used increasingly for applications in various advanced industries like automobile, aeronautics, and nuclear because of their exceptional qualities, which include high compressive strength, high hardness, high strength-to-weight ratio, high corrosion resistance, high-temperature resistance, high wear resistance, and good thermal shock resistance. Engineering ceramics are often processed using traditional powder metallurgy

* **Corresponding author Bijan Mallick:** Faculty of ME Department, Global Institute of Management and Technology, Krishnanagar, MAKAUT, West Bengal, India; E-mail: bijan.ju@gmail.com

Pijush Dutta, Sudip Mondal, Korhan Cengiz and S. Balamurugan (Eds.)

sintering and compacting processes. It is very difficult to generate complex shapes with a higher degree of accuracy than the conventional technique. Therefore, there is an urgent need for an alternative manufacturing process, which will be a resurgence of conventional machining processes for creating products with hard, brittle, and advanced materials such as glass, ceramics, *etc*. Some non-conventional machining processes have great potential to manufacture a product with the above-mentioned materials. Arndt and Probst (1922) examined the significance of the electrodes' wettability in the anode effect and noted that the development of "larger and larger growing" bubbles preceded the anode effect. However, since Kellogg's breakthrough in 1950, electrode effects have been the subject of more thorough research. Electrochemical discharges were extensively researched and applied in a wide range of fields, from wireless telegraphy to X-ray imaging, in the late 19th and early 20th centuries. These were frequently referred to as "anode or cathode effects" in the literature, depending on which electrode phenomenon occurred. The physical and chemical causes of the electrode effects, or the electrochemical discharge machining process, have been attempted to be explained by several writers in the past few decades. A brief discussion of previous research investigations is given below. It has been observed that a large number of bubbles would cover the tool surface area at a critical applied voltage, leading to isolation between the tool and electrolyte, and an insulating layer would be formed in the surroundings of the tool [1]. A semi-empirical model was developed to predict the material removal rate during an idealized electrochemical discharge machining operation [2]. A spark generation mechanism was experimented with in the electrochemical discharge machining (ECDM) process [3]. Gautam and Jain [4] investigated the spark electrochemical spark machining process for the enhancement of process capability with the help of various tool kinematics, such as machining with eccentricity, machining without eccentricity, and rotation of the tool. The effect of various predominant process parameters of the ECDM process was experimented on different machining criteria, such as material removal rate and the overcut phenomenon [5]. The machining of non-conducting zirconia was investigated with an electrochemical discharge machining process [6]. A 3D model developed for an unsteady state heat condition problem using the finite element method (FEM) to predict the material removal rate during electrochemical spark machining (ECSM) machining of non-conducting materials [7]. A 3D-micro structuring of glass machining characteristics was investigated by the spark-assisted chemical engraving (SACE) process [8]. The limitations of machining depth associated with the electrochemical spark machining process were studied [9]. A time-varying current during ECDM of non-conducting material was investigated to reveal the basic mechanism of temperature rise and material removal [10]. The machining operation of optical glass, quartz, and engineering ceramics was studied with the traveling wire-ECDM process [11]. A spark-assisted chemical engraving process was investigated in the light ofelectrochemistry [12]. A reversible interconnection for a glass-based microfluidic system was developed using the ECDM process [13]. A theoretical model for electrode effects was established with the help of percolation theory in the spark-assisted chemical engraving process [14]. Different types of channels and parameter influences were experimented using RSM, GA, PSO, etc [15 - 21]. An optimized process parameter based on GRA-Taguchi analysis was determined during the micro-machining of glass [22].

This chapter mainly focuses on ANOVA-based modeling as well as multi-response optimization for the minimization of ROC as well as MRR. Fig. (**1**) represents the micro-ECDM setup for micro-drilling operation on glass.

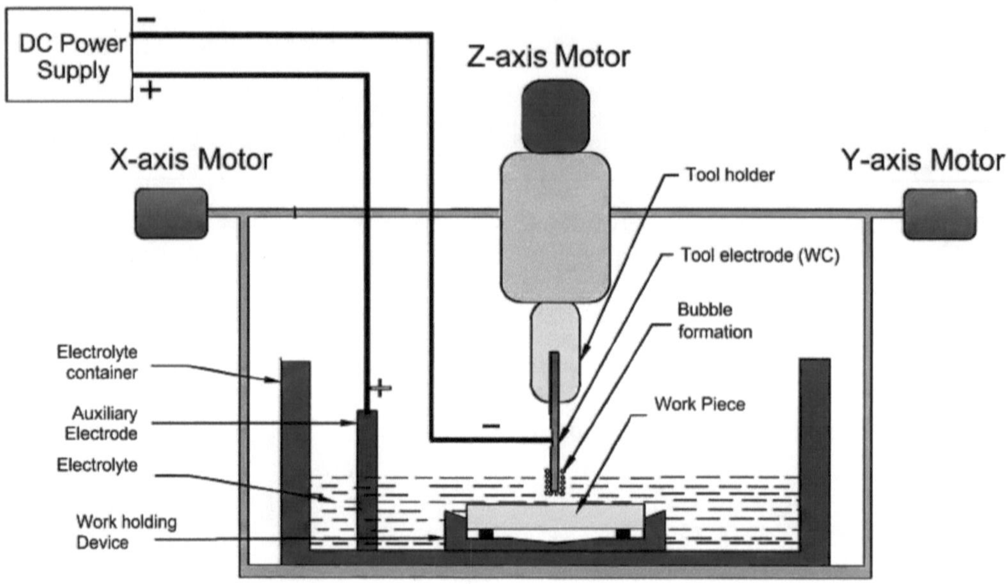

Fig. (1). The Micro-ECDM setup

EXPERIMENTAL DESIGN BASED ON THE FACTORIAL METHOD

A complete factorial design is one in which every setting of each component appears alongside every setting of every other factor. All input components are specified at two levels, each in a simple complete factorial experimental design. “High” and “low,” or “+1” and “-1,” are the names given to these levels, respectively. A two-level complete factorial design includes every conceivable high/low combination of all the input elements. A factorial experiment in which just a suitably selected percentage of the treatment combinations needed for the full factorial experiment is chosen to be conducted is known as a fractional factorial design. The 2k required for a full factorial can easily grow to be quite big, even if the number of variables in a design is tiny. This problem can be solved by running only a portion of the runs that the complete factorial design specifies; the topic of concern here is which runs to perform and which to omit. Typically, we choose a subset of the runs that the complete factorial requires, *etc*. Balance and orthogonality are desired characteristics of well-chosen fractional factorial designs for 2-level studies. A factor's measuring scale is rearranged in such a way that the low value becomes -1 and the high value becomes +1. The design matrix contains all orthogonal columns after the coding of every component in a two-level complete factorial experiment. But in experiment three, their factorial design is followed during experimentation, where an intermediate value indicated by '0' is introduced. The functional relationship between the radial overcut (ROC) or material removal rate (MRR) and the investigated independent variables, *i.e.*, applied voltage and electrolyte type, can be represented by the following equation:

$$\text{MRR or ROC} = KV^{\alpha}C^{\beta}G^{\gamma}D^{\lambda} \quad \textbf{(1)}$$

Where K is the constant of proportionality and and are exponents.

Equation 1 may be written in logarithmic form as

$$\log \text{MRR or} \log \text{ROC} = \log \text{K} + \alpha \ \log \text{V} + \beta \ \log \text{C} + \gamma \ \log \text{G} + \lambda \log \text{D} \quad \textbf{(2)}$$

This may represent a linear mathematical model as

$$\text{MRR' or ROC'} = \alpha_0 X_0 + \alpha_1 X_1 + \alpha_2 X_2 + \alpha_3 X_3 + \alpha_4 X_4 \quad \textbf{(3)}$$

Where MRR' or ROC is the true response of MRR or ROC on a logarithmic scale. Xo = Dummy variable and X_1, X_2, X_3, X_4 = Logarithmic transformations of voltage, electrolyte conductivity, inter-electrode gap, and duty factor. While are parameters to be estimated. Equation 3 can be written as

$$Y' = Y - \varepsilon = a_0X_0 + a_1X_1 + a_2X_2 + a_3X_3 + a_4X_4 \quad \textbf{(4)}$$

Where Y' = Estimated response and Y =measured response on a log scale, ε = Experimental error, a_1, a_2, a_3, a_4 values are the estimates ofparameters, respectively. The null hypothesis can be considered.

Ho (a_o=a_1=a_2= a_3 = a_4 =0)

This is to say that none of the factors, *viz.* voltage, electrolyte, inter-electrode gap, or duty factor, has a significant effect on the MRR or ROC. The design of the experiment is based on 2^k factorial regressions with extreme values of each independent input parameter. There are four more experiments with a midpoint value of each parameter, making the total number of experiments eight. The levels of ECDM process parameters are shown in Table **1**, and the matrix form of these arrays is shown in Table **2**.

Table 1. Process parameters and their levels.

Parameters	Symbols	Codes		
		-1	0	+1
Applied Voltage	V	50	55	60
Electrolyte Conductivity	C	170	210	250

Table 2. Combinations of control parameters based on factorial design

Expt. No	Col. No &Factor Assignment		Actual Values of Parameters	
	LogV X_1	LogC X_2	Voltage (volt)	Electrolyte Conductivity (mho-cm^1)
1	-1	-1	50	170
2	+1	-1	60	170
3	-1	+1	50	250
4	+1	+1	60	250
5	0	0	55	210
6	0	0	55	210
7	0	0	55	210
8	0	0	55	210

To determine which machining parameters had a significant impact on the observed values, the decomposition of the variance, also referred to as analysis of variance (ANOVA), can provide a better sense of the relative effect of the various factors. In this investigation, the experimentally obtained data were analyzed using ANOVA and the F-test to support their significant impact on various machining characteristics. The associated meaning and equations are displayed in Table **3**.

Table 3. Basic analysis of variance (ANOVA).

Source of Varition	**Sum of Squares**	**Degrees of Freedom**	**Mean Square**	**F_0**
BETWEEN TREATMENT	$SS_{Treatment} = \sum_{i=1}^{a}\sum_{j=1}^{n}\left(y_i - \bar{y}_{..}\right)^2$	a-1	$MSS_{Treatment}$	$F_0 = \frac{MS_{Treatme}}{MS_E}$
ERROR (WITHIN TREATMENT)	$SS_E = SS_T - S_{Treatment}$	N-1	MSS_E	-
TOTAL	$\sum_{i=1}^{a}\sum_{j=1}^{n}\left(y_i - \bar{y}_{..}\right)^2$	N-1	-	-

Where the total number of observations under the ith treatment is denoted by□□. The average of the observations under the ith treatment is denoted by y_i. Likewise, $y.$ stands for the grand average of every observation, which can be symbolically expressed as:

$$y_i = \sum_{j=1}^{n} y_{ij} \ , \bar{y}_i = \frac{y_i}{n} \qquad i=1,2,\ldots\ldots\ldots\ldots a$$

$$y_{..} = \sum_{i=1}^{a}\sum_{j=1}^{n} y_{ij}$$

$$y.. = y../N$$

Where N is the total number of observations. The mean sum of the square of each factor is calculated by dividing the sum of the square of each parameter/ factor by its degree of freedom, and then the P-value of each parameter/ factor is calculated as a ratio of the mean sum of the square of each parameter/ factor to the mean sum of the square of error. F, n_1, n_2 is as quoted from the Tables for Statisticians, where (1-a) is the percentage of confidence level. The contribution of the input parameters is defined as significant at the confidence level of (1-a) if the calculated F-values are greater than the standard F, n_1, n_2. Also, the coefficient of multiple determinations R^2 is a measure of the amount of reduction in the variability of 'Y' obtained by using the variables X_1, X_2............................X_N in the model and calculated as below.

$$R^2 = \frac{SS_R}{SS_T} = 1 - \frac{SS_E}{SS_T} \quad (5)$$

A high R^2 score, however, does not always indicate that the regression model is sound. Whether or not the extra variable is statistically significant, it will always raise R^2 when it is included in the model. As a result, models with higher R^2 values may produce subpar forecasts for fresh data or mean response estimates. Consequently, some model builders favor using a modified R^2 static, which is defined as

$$R^2_{adj} = 1 - \left(\frac{N-1}{N-P}\right)\left(1 - R^2\right) \quad (6)$$

Where, N= Total no. of experiments, p= degree of freedom of the model. If R^2 and differ significantly, there is a good chance of the presence of insignificant terms in the model. Equations 1-6 present the basic formulation of modeling.

RESULT AND DISCUSSION

The responses of the ECDM process are the material removal rate (MRR) and radial over-cut (ROC) during micro-drilling of non-conductive glass materials. Generally, applied voltage, type and concentration of electrolyte, inter-electrode gap (IEG), and temperature of the electrolyte have a great influence on the above-mentioned responses of the electro-chemical discharge machining (ECDM) process. Besides these responses, the ECDM process is also influenced by some power circuit parameters, *i.e.*, resistance, capacitance, and inductance, in the ECDM system for achieving the micromachining performance domain. Electrolyte conductivity (at three different levels) and pulsed DC supply voltage, two important process factors, were assessed for their impact on the weight of material removed during glass drilling for the fixed inter-electrode gap at 40 mm. The drilling operation was carried out by a 350 μm stainless steel tool. Here, the coded values were used as '-1' +1', and '0' according to the levels of applied voltage and electrolyte conductivity during the experimentation in the ECDM process. The experimental results are given in Table **4**.

Table 4. Experimental Results and their Log Values.

Expt.No	MRR (mg/h)	ROC ()	Log of MRR	Log of ROC
1	13.627	106.41	1.1344	2.0270
2	90.44	206.5	1.9564	2.3150
3	16.03	133.04	1.2050	2.1240
4	231.20	650.27	2.3640	2.8131
5	29.99	183.23	1.4682	2.2630
6	31.99	176.19	1.5051	2.2460
7	38.94	219.28	1.5904	2.3410
8	77.83	204.17	1.8912	2.3100

Development of a Mathematical Model for Material Removal Rate (MRR)

To explore the multi-parametric mixes, factorial regression was used to conduct the experiments at three different levels of each of the two parameters. To study the effect of the two parameters, *i.e.*, pulsed DC supply voltage (V) and electrolyte conductivity (C), on the total material removed from glass, MINITAB software was used. The coefficients of the mathematical model based on the factorial regression model were estimated. The results obtained from this study, as shown in Table **4**, were used to formulate a mathematical model for MRR. Equation 7 represents the mathematical link between the material removal rate and the parameters of the machining process under consideration.

$$Y(MRR) = 43.5852V^{0.49525}C^{0.11955} \quad \textbf{(7)}$$

The sensitivity analysis of the model for material removal rate was done to identify certain errors depending on the error contribution in the measurement of applied voltage and electrolyte conductivity. Using partial derivatives in Equation 7, Equation 8 is achieved.

$$\begin{aligned} \Delta MRR &= \left(\frac{\partial MRR}{\partial V}\right) \times \Delta V + \left(\frac{\Delta MRR}{\partial C}\right) \times \Delta C \\ \frac{\Delta MRR}{MRR} &= 0.49525\left(\frac{\Delta V}{V}\right) + 0.11955\left(\frac{\Delta C}{C}\right) \end{aligned} \quad \textbf{(8)}$$

Where, $\frac{\Delta MRR}{MRR}$ = Sensitivity of MRR in percentage, expressed as decimal

$\frac{\Delta V}{V}$ = Sensitivity of voltage

$\frac{\Delta C}{C}$ = Sensitivity of conductivity

Equation 8 gives a sensitivity analysis of MRR. Assuming a 5% variation in each variable, a percentage error in the material removal rate of 43% was found. Assuming an error in the output response can be found.

Development of a Mathematical Model for Radial Overcut (ROC)

The coefficients of mathematical modeling based on the factorial design in the regression model were found using the Design of Experiment (DOE) tools of MINITAB software. The radial overcut on glass material at three-level parameter values was obtained using the experimental findings. A mathematical model was developed during the micro-drilling of glass by electrochemical discharge machining using 350 µm stainless steel as below:

$$Y(ROC) = 201.7855V^{0.24427}C^{0.14877} \quad \textbf{(9)}$$

To determine certain errors depending on the error contribution in the measurement of applied voltage and electrolyte conductivity, the sensitivity analysis of the model for material removal rate was performed. Using partial derivatives on equation 9, equation 10 is achieved.

$$\Delta ROC = \left(\frac{\partial ROC}{\partial V}\right) \times \Delta V + \left(\frac{\partial ROC}{\partial C}\right) \times \nabla C \quad \textbf{(10)}$$

$$\left(\frac{\Delta ROC}{ROC}\right) = 0.2447\left(\frac{\nabla V}{V}\right) + 0.14877\left(\frac{\nabla C}{C}\right)$$

Where, $\left(\frac{\Delta ROC}{ROC}\right)$ = Sensitivity of ROC in percentage, expressed as a decimal.

$\frac{\nabla V}{V}$ = Sensitivity of voltage.

$\frac{\nabla C}{C}$ = Sensitivity of conductivity.

Equation 5 gives a sensitivity analysis of MRR. Assuming a 5% variation in each variable, a percentage error in radial overcut of 42% was calculated. Assuming an error in the output response can be found.

Analysis of Variance Test for MRR

To identify the machining parameters that significantly impact machining performances and to ascertain the significant impact of the machining parameters in regulating the responses of the micro-drilling on glass by the electrochemical discharge machining process, the analysis of variance (ANOVA) was conducted in this study. Table **5** shows the ANOVA results utilizing the experimentally obtained data according to a factorial design.

Table 5. ANOVA results for MRR.

Input Factor	DOF	Sum of Squares	Mean Sum of Squares	F- value
REGRESSION	2	1.03826	0.51913	18.01
ERROR	5	0.14415	0.02883	-
TOTAL	7	1.18241	-	-

$F_{0.25}$, 2,5 = 1.85; $F_{0.1}$, 2,5 =3.78; $F_{0.05}$, 2,5 =5.79; $F_{0.025}$, 2,5 = 8.43; $F_{0.01}$, 2,5=13.27

$F_{0.25}$, 2,7 = 1.70; $F_{0.1}$, 2,7 =3.26; $F_{0.05}$, 2,7 =4.74; $F_{0.025}$, 2,7 =6.54; $F_{0..01}$, 2,7 =9.55

Multiple R = 0.93; R^2 = 0.87 and R^2_{adj} = 0.86

Since there is only one possible alternative hypothesis, the null hypothesis, Ho, is always rejected in this experiment due to the calculated F being greater than the standard F, and the voltage and electrolyte conductivity have a significant effect on the material removal rate at a 95% confidence level.

Analysis of Variance Test for ROC

Based on the factorial design method, the analysis of variance (ANOVA) was performed to find out the significant process parameters for radial overcut during the micro-machining of glass by electrochemical discharge machining technology. The results thus obtained are listed in Table **6**.

Table 6. ANOVA results for ROC.

Input Factor	DOF	Sum of Squares	Mean Sum of Squares	F- value
REGRESSION	2	0.327217	0.163609	17.16
ERROR	5	0.047659	0.009532	-
TOTAL	7	0.374877	-	-

F_{025}, 2,5=1.85; $F_{0.1}$, 2,5 =3.78; $F_{0..05}$, 2,5=5.79; $F_{0.025}$, 2,5 = 8.43; $F_{0.01}$, 2,5=13.27

$F_{0..25}$, 2,7 = 1.70; $F_{0..1}$, 2,7 =3.26; $F_{0.05}$, 2,7 =4.74; $F_{0.025}$, 2,7 =6.54; $F_{0.01}$, 2,7 =9.55

Multiple R = 0.93; R^2 = 0.87 and R^2_{adj} = 0.852

Here, standard F is much lower than the calculated F, so the null hypothesis Ho is rejected in this investigation, and both voltage and electrolyte conductivity have a significant effect on radial overcut.

Determination of Optimal Machining Parametric Combinations

An optimality search of the machining parametric combinations was performed to maximize the material removal rate and minimize the radial overcut with the help of factorial design during the micro-drilling of glass by the ECDM process. During the experimentations, the inter-electrode gap was kept fixed at 40 mm. Table **6** shows the Pareto optimality results. Here, population size and boundary conditions were considered as 150 and -1 to +1, respectively. Also, the third parameter was held at zero. From Table **7**, it is clear that 51 V/ 172 mmho-cm^1/ 40 mm is the optimum condition for maximized MRR and minimized ROC. After the selection of the optimal level of design parameters, the final step was to predict and verify the optimum condition for the abovementioned criteria of the micro-ECDM process. It is observed that predicted results are quite close to the experimental observations, and a comparison between experimentally obtained data and predicted results gave optimal parametric combinations for maximized MRR and minimized ROC. Prediction error is calculated using the following formula:

Table 7. Optimum parametric combinations.

Sl. No	Function 1	Function 2	Variable 1	Variable 2
1	-17.0536	-3.19351	-0.9908	-0.50160
2	-18.01194	-2.99460	-0.99083	-0.09250
3	-19.9999	1.738420	6.38357	1.992163
4	-16.10273	-5.25370	-0.99159	-0.86304
5	-15.83187	-6.07491	-0.99211	-0.96314
6	-16.4146	-4.35446	-0.98691	-0.74875
7	-18.5363	-1.23404	-0.75597	-0.02982
8	-18.49218	-1.57233	-0.79924	-0.01517
9	-18.7512	-0.59841	-0.64782	-0.01662
10	-16.813	-3.47209	-0.98068	-0.60054
11	-15.97924	-5.34940	-0.93025	-0.93374
12	-16.18920	-4.70531	-0.92687	-0.85861
13	-18.25502	-2.42249	-0.91045	-0.03955

(Table 7) cont.....

Sl. No	Function 1	Function 2	Variable 1	Variable 2
14	-16.57253	-3.94215	-0.97981	-0.69274
15	-15.73068	-6.36699	-0.99359	-0.99993
16	-18.93242	-0.11270	-537099	-0.02410

Microscopic views of micro-tools (before and after machining) and micro-holes drilled at optimized parametric combinations, *i.e.*, 51 V/172 mmho-cm / 40mm with RC circuit configuration, have been depicted.

CONCLUSION

After proper investigations, several conclusions were drawn for the analysis of the chapter on ANOVA-based micro-ECDM process optimization during the drilling of borosilicate glass.

The experimentations based on the factorial design method will not only help in analyzing the influence of the different process parameters on the various criteria but also help in searching out the optimal machining parameter combinations to meet the maximum fulfillment of the objective requirement of ECDM in glass part manufacturing practice, as highlighted in the present research investigations.

By applying the experimental data, the developed models for material removal rate and radial overcut have been proven to be accurate, and the effects of two process parameters, namely applied voltage and electrolyte conductivity, on respective machining criteria have been justified through ANOVA results and experimental analyses.

From the present investigation, it is found that MRR and ROC increase with the increase in applied voltage at a fixed electrolyte conductivity inter-electrode gap. Also, it is observed that MRR and ROC increase with the increase in electrolyte conductivity at the fixed applied voltage and inter-electrode gap. The multi-objective optimal parametric combination based on developed models for maximized MRR and minimized ROC is found at 51 V/ 172 mmho-cm / 40 mm.

REFERENCES

[1] I. Basak, and A. Ghosh, "Mechanism of spark generation during electrochemical discharge machining: a theoretical model and experimental verification", *J. Mater. Process. Technol.*, vol. 62, no. 1-3, pp. 46-53, 1996.
[http://dx.doi.org/10.1016/0924-0136(95)02202-3]

[2] I. Basak, and A. Ghosh, "Mechanism of material removal in electrochemical discharge machining: a theoretical model and experimental verification", *J. Mater. Process. Technol.*, vol. 71, no. 3, pp. 350-359, 1997.
[http://dx.doi.org/10.1016/S0924-0136(97)00097-6]

[3] A. Ghosh, "Electrochemical discharge machining: Principle and possibilities", *Sadhana,* vol. 22, no. 3, pp. 435-447, 1997. [http://dx.doi.org/10.1007/BF02744482]

[4] N. Gautam, and V.K. Jain, "Experimental investigation into ECSD process using various tool kinematics", *Int. J. Adv. Manuf. Technol.,* vol. 38, pp. 15-27, 1998.

[5] B. Bhattacharyya, B.N. Doloi, and S.K. Sorkhel, "Experimental investigations into electrochemical discharge machining (ECDM) of non-conductive ceramic materials", *J. Mater. Process. Technol.,* vol. 95, no. 1-3, pp. 145-154, 1999. [http://dx.doi.org/10.1016/S0924-0136(99)00318-0]

[6] B. Doloi, B. Bhattacharyya, and S.K. Sorkhel, "Electrochemical discharge machining (ECDM) of non-conductive ceramics", *Def. Sci. J.,* vol. 49, no. 4, pp. 331-338, 1999. [http://dx.doi.org/10.14429/dsj.49.3846]

[7] V.K. Jain, P.M. Dixit, and P.M. Pandey, "On the analysis of the electrochemical spark machining process", *Int. J. Mach. Tools Manuf.,* vol. 39, no. 1, pp. 165-186, 1999. [http://dx.doi.org/10.1016/S0890-6955(98)00010-8]

[8] V. Fascio, R. Wuthrich, D. Viquerat, and H. Lange, “3D microstructuring of glass using electrochemical discharge machining,” *Int. Symp. Micro Mechatronics Human Sci.*, Swice, 1999. [http://dx.doi.org/10.1109/MHS.1999.820003]

[9] V.K. Jain, and S.K. Chak, "Electrochemical spark trepanning of alumina and quartz,” *", *Mach. Sci. Technol.,* vol. 4, no. 2, pp. 277-290, 2000. [http://dx.doi.org/10.1080/10940340008945710]

[10] A. Kulkarni, R. Sharan, and G.K. Lal, "An experimental study of discharge mechanism in electrochemical discharge machining", *Int. J. Mach. Tools Manuf.,* vol. 42, no. 10, pp. 1121-1127, 2002. [http://dx.doi.org/10.1016/S0890-6955(02)00058-5]

[11] W.Y. Peng, and Y.S. Liao, "Study of electrochemical discharge machining technology for slicing non-conductive brittle materials", *J. Mater. Process. Technol.,* vol. 149, no. 1-3, pp. 363-369, 2004. [http://dx.doi.org/10.1016/j.jmatprotec.2003.11.054]

[12] V. Fascio, R. Wüthrich, and H. Bleuler, "Spark assisted chemical engraving in the light of electrochemistry", *Electrochim. Acta,* vol. 49, no. 22-23, pp. 3997-4003, 2004. [http://dx.doi.org/10.1016/j.electacta.2003.12.062]

[13] E.S. Lee, D. Howard, E. Liang, S.D. Collins, and R.L. Smith, "Removable tubing interconnects for glass-based micro-fluidic systems made using ECDM", *J. Micromech. Microeng.,* vol. 14, no. 4, pp. 535-541, 2004. [http://dx.doi.org/10.1088/0960-1317/14/4/014]

[14] R. Wüthrich, and H. Bleuler, "A model for electrode effects using percolation theory", *Electrochim. Acta,* vol. 49, no. 9-10, pp. 1547-1554, 2004. [http://dx.doi.org/10.1016/j.electacta.2003.11.014]

[15] B. Mallick, S. Biswas, B.R. Sarkar, B. Doloi, and B. Bhattacharyya, "On Performance of Electrochemical Discharge Micro-Machining Process Using Different Electrolytes and Tool Shapes", *Int. J. Manuf. Mater. Mech. Eng.,* vol. 10, no. 2, pp. 49-63, 2020. [http://dx.doi.org/10.4018/IJMMME.2020040103]

[16] B. Mallick, B.R. Sarkar, B. Doloi, and B. Bhattacharyya, "Analysis on the effect of ECDM process parameters during micro-machining of glass using genetic algorithm", *J. Mech. Eng. Sci.,* vol. 12, no. 3, pp. 3942-3960, 2018. [http://dx.doi.org/10.15282/jmes.12.3.2018.13.0344]

[17] B. Mallick, B.R. Sarkar, B. Doloi, and B. Bhattacharyya, "Analysis on electrochemical discharge machining during micro-channel cutting on glass", *International Journal of Precision Technology,* vol.

7, no. 1, pp. 32-50, 2017.
[http://dx.doi.org/10.1504/IJPTECH.2017.084554]

[18] B. Mallick, B. R. Sarkar, B. Doloi, and B. Bhattacharyya, "Modelling and analysis on Performance of ECDM Process for the Fabrication of μ-Channels on Glass through Response Surface Methodology," *Manuf. Technol. Today (MTT)*, vol. 18, no. 9, 2019.

[19] B. Mallick, B.R. Sarkar, B. Doloi, and B. Bhattacharyya, "Multi Criteria Optimization of Electrochemical Discharge Micro-Machining Process during Micro-Channel Generation on Glass", *Appl. Mech. Mater.,* vol. 592-594, pp. 525-529, 2014.
[http://dx.doi.org/10.4028/www.scientific.net/AMM.592-594.525]

[20] B. Mallick, A. S. Hameed, B. R. Sarkar, B. Doloi, and B. Bhattacharyya, "Experimental Investigation for Improvement of Micro-Machining Performances of μ-ECDM Process," *Mater. Today*, 2019.

[21] B. Mallick, B. R. Sarkar, B. Doloi, and B. Bhattacharyya, "Improvement of Surface Quality and Machining Depth of μ-ECDM Performances Using Mixed Electrolyte at Different Polarity," *Silicon*, 2021.
[http://dx.doi.org/10.21203/rs.3.rs-854051/v1]

[22] S. Bellubbi, N. S., and B. Mallick, "Multi Response Optimization of ECDM Process Parameters for Machining of Microchannel in Silica Glass Using Taguchi–GRA Technique," *Silicon*, 2021.
[http://dx.doi.org/10.1007/s12633-021-01167-4]

CHAPTER 8

Metaheuristics-based Parametric Optimization of Semi-automatic MIG Welded Austenitic AISI 304 Stainless Steel for Industry 5.0

Abhishek Ghosh[1] and **Sudip Mandal**[2,*]

[1] *Department of Mechanical Engineering, SKFGI Mankundu, West Bengal, India*

[2] *Department of Electronics and Communication Engineering, Jalpaiguri Government Engineering College, Jalpaiguri, India*

Abstract: Austenitic stainless steels are readily weldable, but sensitization and solidification cracks are common defects in the welding of such steels. It is found that the problem of solidification cracking remains under control if the weld pool solidifies in FA mode. 6-8% delta ferrite in the fusion zone can promote the FA mode of solidification. The effects of different semi-automatic MIG welding parameters, like welding current, gas flow rate, and welding speed, on solidification behavior and microstructure of the weldment are not clear. In this present work, an attempt has been made to optimize MIG welding input parameters to achieve 7% delta ferrite in the fusion zone. Initially, ANOVA-based analysis and optimization was performed. A new metaheuristic, namely the Elephant Swarm Water Search Algorithm (ESWSA), was used for optimization purposes to get the optimal condition of grinding.

Keywords: AISI304 austenitic stainless steel, ANOVA, ESWSA, Industry 5.0, Metaheuristics optimization, Semi-automatic MIG welding.

INTRODUCTION

Gas Metal Arc Welding (MIG welding) creates a bond between metals by heating them with an arc formed between a continuous, consumable electrode and the workpiece in a protective gas-shielded environment [1]. MIG welding is frequently used to weld austenitic stainless steels when quality, cost, and productivity are areas of concern [2]. Austenitic stainless steels are interstitial solid solutions of carbon with an FCC crystal structure [3]. They are non-magnetic, cannot be treated with heat, and offer toughness, ductility, and corrosion resistance [4]. Their superior properties have made them an automatic

* **Corresponding author Sudip Mandal:** Department of Electronics and Communication Engineering, Jalpaiguri Government Engineering College, Jalpaiguri, India; E-mail: sudip.mandal007@gmail.com

Pijush Dutta, Sudip Mondal, Korhan Cengiz and S. Balamurugan (Eds.)

choice to be used in nuclear, chemical, power, and aviation industries, as well as other critical areas [3]. The present work deals with the optimization of MIG welding parameters to achieve the FA mode of solidification during welding. RSM-based modeling and optimizations have already been successfully implemented by Ghosh *et al.* [5, 6] for TIG welding. Hence, in this work, ANOVA and metaheuristic-based parameters optimization of MIG welding have been considered for research. A machine learning-based approach for mathematical modeling of MIG welding and finding out optimal welding conditions helps in human-machine interaction, which can be used in Industry 5.0.

Sensitization and Solidification Cracking in Austenitic Stainless-steel Welds

Although austenitic stainless steels are weldable, sensitization and solidification cracking are common defects of their weldment [3, 4]. Solidification cracking is thought to occur because the solidifying weldment cannot withstand the strain during the freezing process [7]. Solidification cracking tendency in austenitic stainless steel is enhanced by impurities such as sulfur and phosphorus, forming low-melting sulfide and phosphide films, respectively, which segregate during solidification, causing more shrinkage stress [4].

Role of δ-ferrite on Solidification Mode and Weld Quality

Around 5 - 10% retained δ-ferrite in microstructure is beneficial to resistance against hot cracking and can minimize the detrimental effects of sulfur and phosphorus [4, 8]. Sulfur and phosphorus are not soluble in iron, chromium, and nickel, but their solubility is higher in δ-ferrite [9]. The ductility of ferrite at high temperatures is higher than that of austenite, which enables the relaxation of thermal stresses [10]. Additionally, the lower thermal expansion coefficient of δ-ferrite compared to austenite leads to reduced contraction stresses during solidification [10]. But the presence of too much δ-ferrite (>10 vol. %) in the weld zone tends to reduce the ductility, toughness, and corrosion resistance of the weldment, and extremely less quantity of δ-ferrite (<5 vol. %) cannot provide enough resistance to hot cracking [11]. But if the percentage volume of δ-ferrite reaches beyond 8-10%, a continuous network of δ-ferrite is formed, which can be beneficial for stress corrosion cracks (SCC) to propagate along the continuous path [12]. Kathak *et al.* [13] concluded that the corrosion rate at different atmospheres increased with an increase in δ-ferrite in microstructure from 3 vol. % to 8 vol. % and the corrosion rate increased rapidly beyond 8 vol. % δ-ferrite in weld microstructure [14 - 17]. Considering all the factors, it is concluded that 7% δ-ferrite in the as-welded condition in an austenitic stainless steel weld metal zone is suitable, and this value has been taken as a target during optimization.

EXPERIMENTAL PLAN AND PROCEDURE

An austenitic stainless-steel plate of type AISI 304 (100 mm length × 50 mm width × 3 mm thickness) is used as base metal (BM) for the present experiments. The chemical composition of the base metal is shown in Table **1**.

Table 1. Chemical composition of base metal.

	% C	% Mn	%Si	% S	% P	% Cr	% Ni	% Mo
AISI 304	0.08	1.52	0.61	0.02	0.035	18.45	8.12	0.05

ER 308L MIG welding electrode is used in the present work. The chemical composition of the electrode wire is shown in Table **2**.

Table 2. Chemical composition of electrode wire.

	% C	% Mn	%Si	% S	% P	% Cr	% Ni	% Mo
ER 304L	0.02	1.74	0.45	0.03	0.025	19.05	8.28	0.02

The CPT-400 semi-automatic MIG welding set-up was used for welding. 99% pure argon gas shielding was supplied for welding. Welding was completed in a single pass, square butt joint. The diameter of the electrode rod was taken as 1.2 mm. The XXQ-2005 (130 KV, 5 mA) radiographic testing machine was used for radiographic tests. Tensile test specimens were prepared according to the ASTM E8 standard, and the tests were conducted using a strong universal testing machine. The microstructural evaluation was performed with a Leica metallurgical microscope (model no. DMLM/11888605), adhering to the AWS D1.1 codes. After welding, the samples were cut transversely from the welds, followed by mechanical grinding, polishing, and etching with an aqua regia solution (HCl: HNO_3 = 3:1). The micro-hardness of the base metal, HAZ, and weld zone was measured using a LECO LM 248AT micro-hardness tester (Vickers scale). Ferrite content in the weld zone and HAZ was determined using a ferrite scope. The input parameters considered for the study were welding current (I), gas flow rate (F), and welding speed (S). The levels of these parameters are presented in Table **3**. A total of twenty welded specimens were fabricated under varying parametric conditions using the Response Surface Methodology (RSM) with a face-centered central composite design (CCD). Six center runs were chosen, and the axial points were selected with α = 1.682.

Table 3. Input parameters and their levels.

Input Parameters	Level 1	Level 2	Level 3
Welding current, A	100	115	130
Gas flow rate, lpm	10	12	14
Travel speed, mm/s	4.5	5	5.5

RESULTS AND DISCUSSIONS

Visual Inspection and Radiography Test

In visual observation, just after welding, no significant defect is found in any of the weldments. No significant defect is found in the X-ray radiography test of the welded samples. An X-ray photograph of the welded specimen 3 is shown in Fig. (**1**). The photograph indicates sound welding.

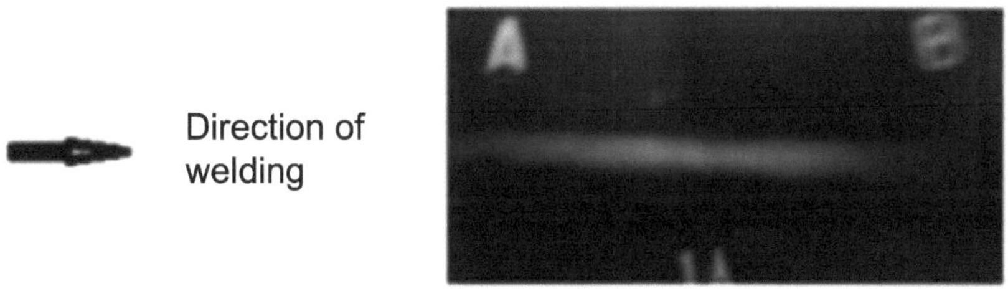

Fig. (1). X-ray photograph.

Tensile Test and Measurement of δ-ferrite

A tensile test of welded samples was carried out. Measured UTS of the samples is listed in Table **4**. Tensile test results of specimens show that the tensile strength of the specimens was retained after welding, and most of the samples failed from outside the joint. FN of the weld zone was measured using a ferrite-scope, which was calibrated to the FN scale. Three readings of FN for all three samples were taken, and their averages are listed in Table **4**.

Table 4. Measured UTS and FN values at different parametric conditions.

Sl. No.	Input conditions			UTS (MPa)	Zone of failure	Measured FN
	I	F	S			
1	100	14	5.5	561.39	Outside weld zone	10
2	115	14	5.0	565.25	Outside weld zone	8
3	100	14	4.5	568.06	Outside weld zone	7

(Table 4) cont.....

Sl. No.	Input conditions			UTS (MPa)	Zone of failure	Measured FN
	I	F	S			
4	130	10	4.5	543.83	From weld region	7
5	115	10	5.0	529.84	From weld region	9
6	130	10	5.5	555.60	Outside weld zone	8
7	115	12	5.0	539.34	From weld region	10
8	115	12	5.0	589.06	Outside weld zone	8
9	130	12	5.0	558.53	Outside weld zone	9
10	130	14	5.5	573.71	Outside weld zone	8
11	115	12	5.0	573.16	Outside weld zone	9
12	130	14	4.5	568.12	Outside weld zone	7
13	100	10	4.5	586.09	Outside weld zone	8
14	100	12	5.0	577.31	Outside weld zone	9
15	115	12	5.0	560.28	From weld region	9
16	115	12	5.5	560.36	From weld region	8
17	115	12	4.5	571.03	Outside weld zone	6
18	115	12	5.0	554.67	From weld region	9
19	100	10	5.5	571.40	Outside weld zone	9
20	115	12	5.0	577.92	Outside weld zone	9

Microstructural Analysis

The microstructure of the base metal (Fig. **2**) shows equiaxed austenitic grains with dispersed δ-ferrite. No carbide is found in the microstructure.

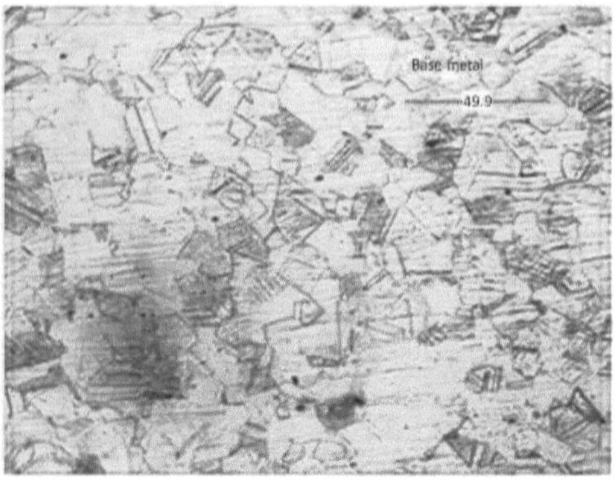

Fig. (2). Base metal microstructure.

Figs. (**3** - **5**) show microstructural photographs of specimen no.1, 8, and 15, respectively. Fig. (**3a**) shows the microstructure containing both the base metal and HAZ region. Grain coarsening of HAZ is observed, but no carbide is found. Fig. (**3b**) shows a HAZ-weld zone boundary region. Completely different types of microstructures of HAZ and the weld zone are found. Columnar grain growth is observed in the weld zone. Fig. (**3c**) shows lathy ferrite morphology in the austenitic grain in the weld zone. Fig. (**3d**) shows Widmanstatten ferrite in the weld zone microstructure. In both Figs. (**3c** and **3d**), a continuous chain of δ-ferrite is observed in the weld zone. But no solidification crack is observed in any specimen. Figs. (**4a** and **5a**) show the microstructure containing both the WM and HAZ regions. Grain coarsening of HAZ is observed, but no carbide is found. In Fig. (**5b**), a continuous chain of δ-ferrite is observed in the weld zone; grain growth is columnar. Skeletal δ-ferrite is observed in the weld zone of specimen 2 (Fig. **4b**). Lathy ferrite is present (Fig. **5b**) in the weld zone microstructure. HAZ microstructures of all three samples are almost the same.

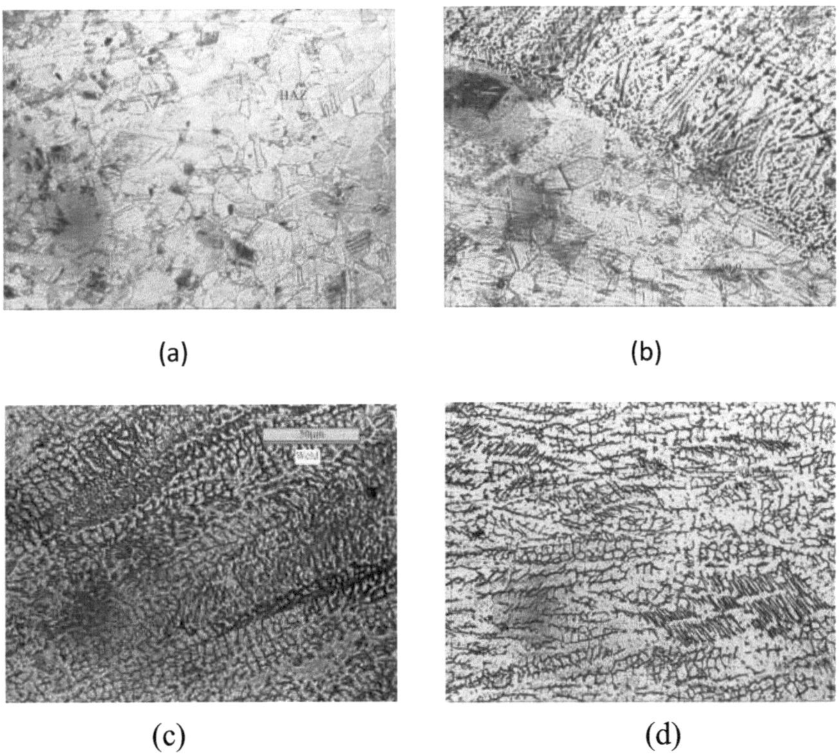

Fig. (3). Microstructure of sp. 1 **a**) Base metal -HAZ boundary, **b**) Weld-HAZ boundary, **c**) Weld zone, **d**) Widmanstatten ferrite in weld zone..

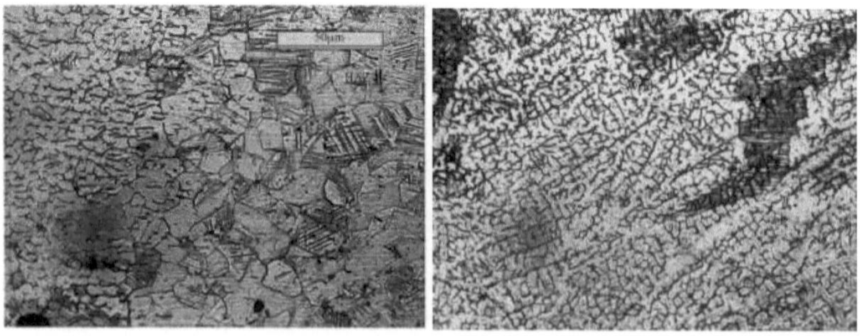

(a) (b)

Fig. (4). Microstructure of sp. 8 **a**) WM-HAZ boundary **b**) WM zone.

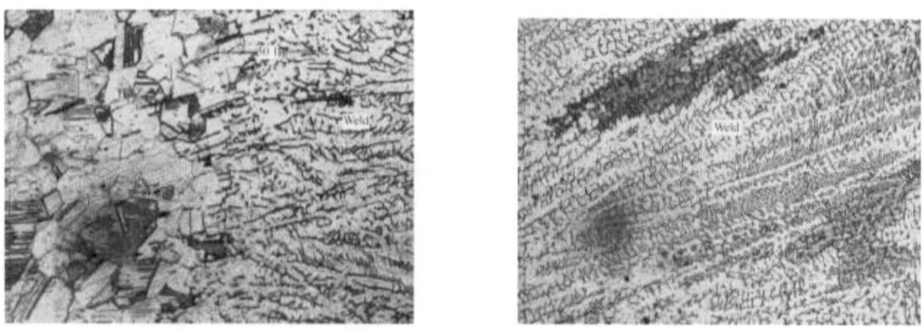

(a) (b)

Fig. (5). Microstructure of sp. 15 **a**) WM-HAZ boundary, **b**) WM zone.

Hardness Measurement

Different types of microstructures result in changes in hardness at different zones (base metal, HAZ, and weld zone) of a welded specimen. The Vickers micro-hardness test is selected in this study to measure hardness at selected locations. In Figs. (**6** - **8**), hardness profiles of specimen 5, specimen 13, and specimen 16 at different zones of the weldment are shown, respectively.

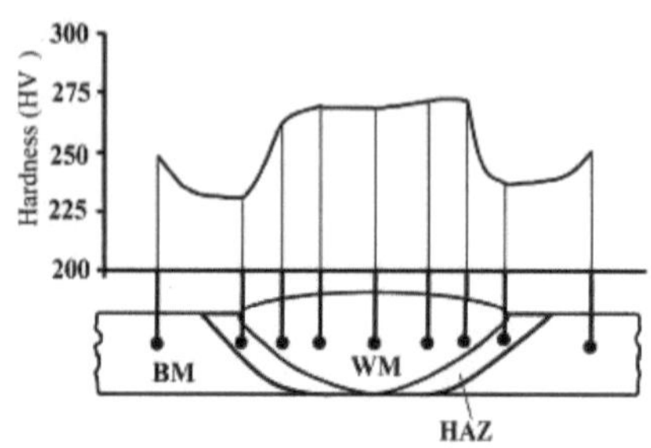

Fig. (6). Hardness profile of specimen 5.

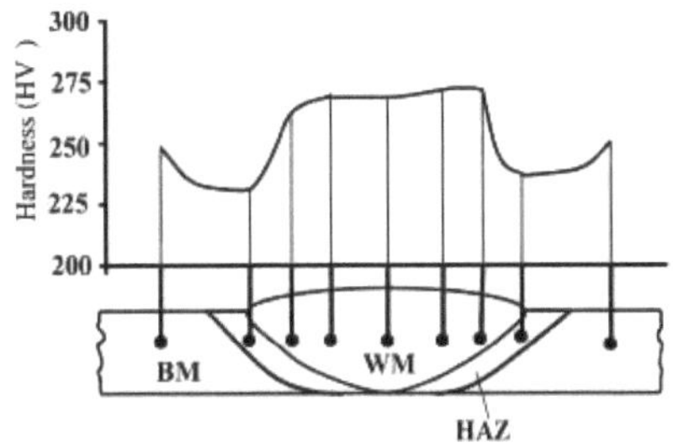

Fig. (7). Hardness profile of specimen 13.

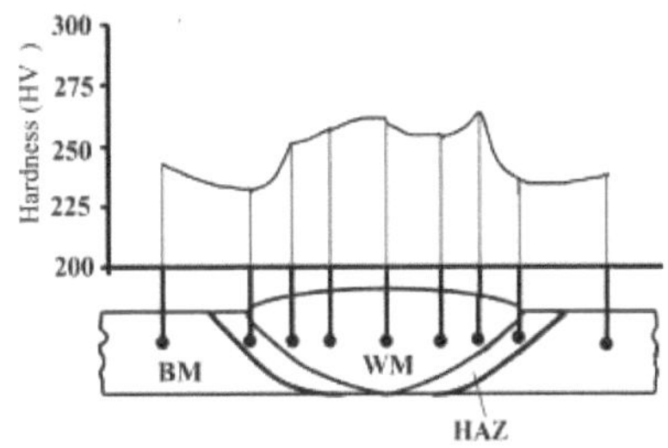

Fig. (8). Hardness profile of specimen 16.

For specimens 1 and speimen 2, it is observed that the hardness values of weld zones at different locations are almost equal, but in the case of specimen 3, the hardness values of weld zones at different points change sharply. The presence of δ-ferrite and other precipitations may change the hardness in different locations. But the effect of different parametric conditions on the hardness of the weldment is not clear. The hardness profile is almost the same in different parametric conditions.

SEM Analysis

SEM micrographs (Fig. **9**) of the fractured tensile surface of specimen 1 indicate, in general, ductile fracture. Fig. (**9a**) shows a complete ductile fracture. A more magnified view (900×1500) in Fig. (**9b**) shows a few dispersed carbide precipitations. Brittle fracture (slip) is found in a few small regions in Fig. (**9c**), possibly in the carbide precipitated area. A larger view of a carbide precipitated area is shown in Fig. (**9d**).

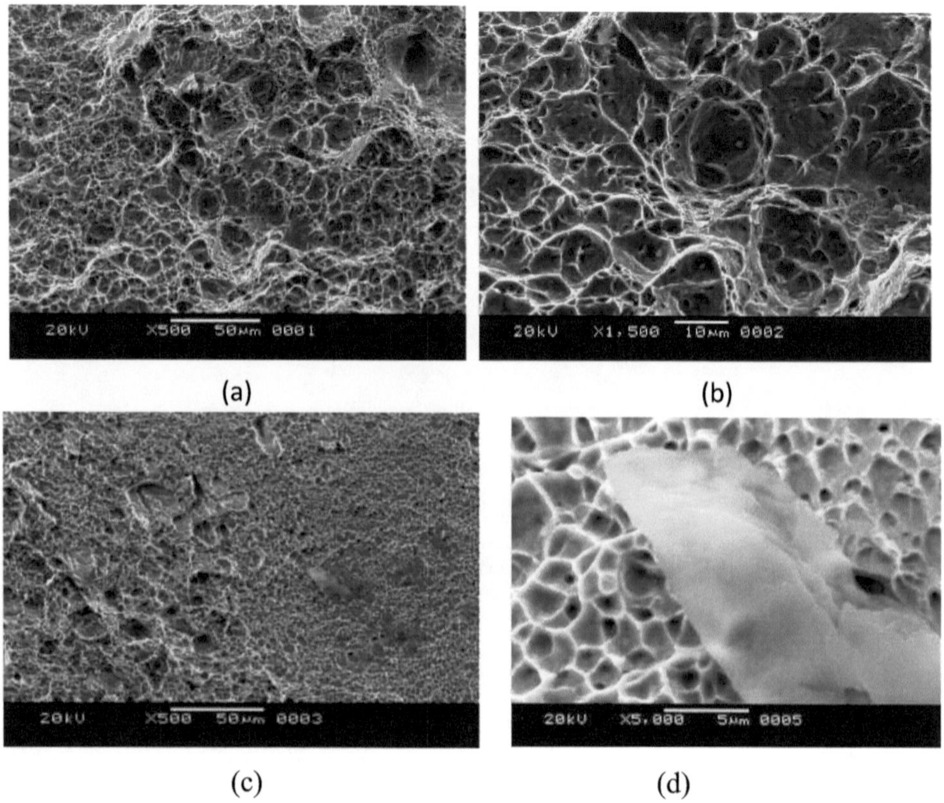

Fig. (9). Different view SEM micrograph of the welded sample.

ANALYSIS OF EXPERIMENTAL DATA

In this section, response surface analysis of the response FN was performed using MINITAB 21 software. Initially, a mathematical model was developed, and its adequacy was assessed through ANOVA. Additionally, surface and contour plots for the response are presented.

Numerical Modeling

RSM represents a mathematical model that defines the functional relationship between input variables and the response. In this study, a second-order model was developed to represent the responses in terms of the process variables, including welding current (I), gas flow rate (F), and welding speed (S), as shown in Equation 1.

FN = - 109.2 - 0.429*I - 1.64*F + 60.2*S + 0.00247 I*I + 0.014 F*F - 5.77 S*S + 0.000001 I*F - 0.0333 I*S + 0.250 F*S **(1)**

From Table **5**, it can be observed that the P-value of the model is 0.041, indicating that the model is statistically significant. Among the factors, welding speed (S) is the most influential variable affecting the response FN, with the lowest P-value of 0.007. Welding current (I) (P = 0.217) and gas flow rate (F) (P = 0.895) do not significantly impact the response, as their P-values are much higher than the significance level of 0.05. In terms of interaction terms, I-I (P = 0.217) and F-F (P = 0.895) are not statistically significant, while S-S (P = 0.007) is found to have a significant effect on the response. The interaction terms I-F (P = 1.000), F-S (P = 0.334), and I-S (P = 0.334) are not significant. The coefficient of determination (R^2) of the model is 78.94%, which is significantly above the 60% threshold, indicating that the model explains 78.94% of the variability in the data for the response. This suggests that the model is a good fit. The adjusted R^2 value is 55.54%.

Table 5. Estimated regression coefficient of the model.

Term	SE Coef.	F-Value	P-Value
Model	16.22	3.37	0.041
Linear	8.10	5.61	0.019
I	1.60	3.33	0.101
F	0.10	0.21	0.659
S	6.40	13.31	0.005
Square	6.67	4.63	0.032
I*I	0.84	1.76	0.217
F*F	0.01	0.02	0.895
S*S	5.69	11.84	0.007
2-way interaction	1.00	0.69	0.579
I*F	0.00	0.00	1.000
I*S	0.50	1.04	0.334
F*S	0.50	1.04	0.334
Lack of fit	2.3278	0.93	0.543
R2 = 78.94% R2 (adj) = 55.54%			

The relationships between the response and welding parameters are depicted graphically using contour plots and surface plots. Surface plots (Fig. **10**) are three-dimensional graphs that display the response against two variables while keeping the other variables constant. Contour plots (Fig. **11**) are two-dimensional graphs that illustrate contours of constant response, where the axes represent a specific pair of process variables, and the other variables are fixed. These plots are especially useful when the stationary point is a saddle point or far from the design region.

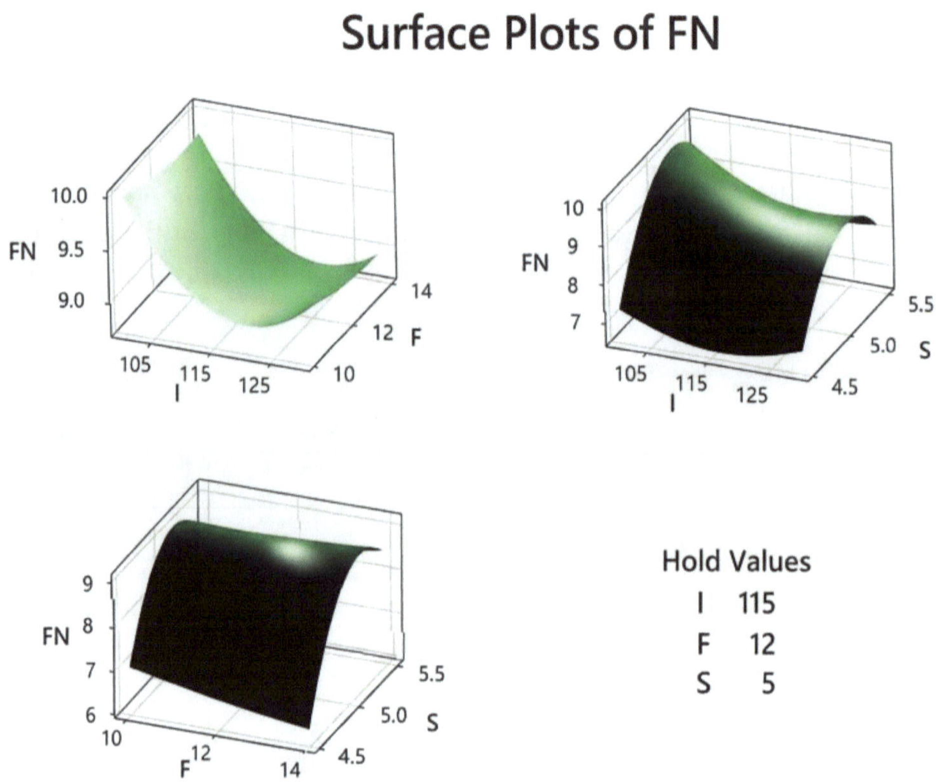

Fig. (10). Surface plots showing the combined effects of input parameters on the response.

Optimization using ANOVA

In Fig. (**12**), the single-objective optimization of the response is shown. The aim is to find the optimized parametric condition at which the target value of response (FN) would be 7 under operating ranges of input parameters. The optimized parametric combination is current I = 115.0 A, gas flow rate F = 12LPM, and travel speed S = 4.55 mm/s with desirability = 1

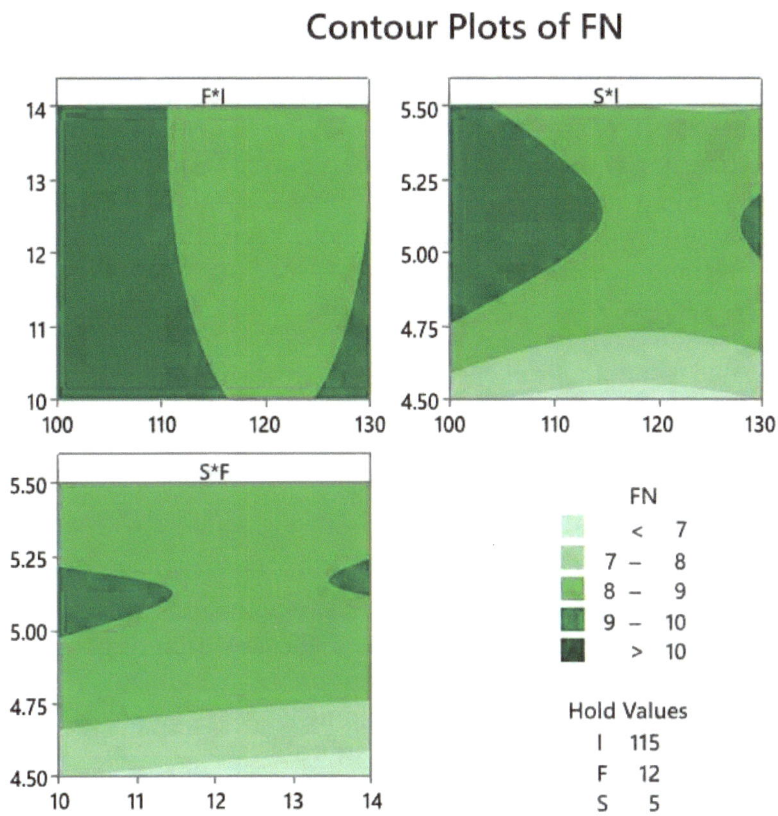

Fig. (11). Contour plots showing the combined effects of input parameters on the response.

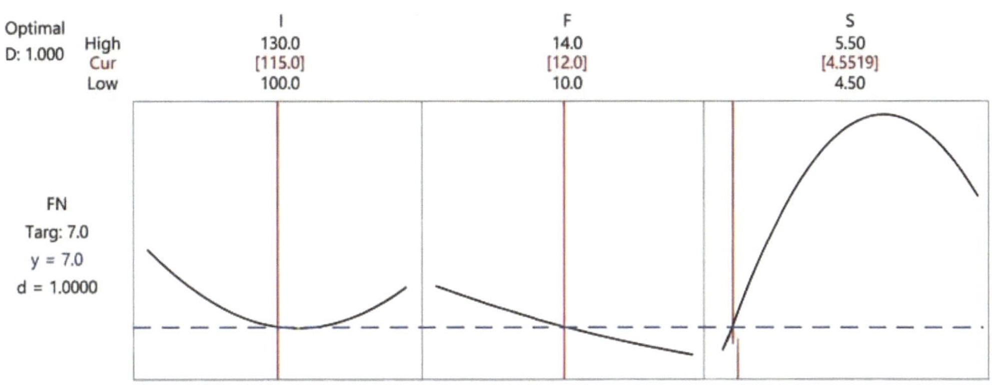

Fig. (12). Single-objective response optimization plot.

OPTIMIZATION USING ELEPHANT SWARM WATER SEARCH ALGORITHM (ESWSA)

Next, the goal was to determine the optimal point for MIG welding where the response value (FN) is minimized, representing the most favorable welding conditions. Three input parameters—welding current (I), gas flow rate (F), and welding speed (S)—were selected, and different FN values were obtained based on these conditions. The proposed method used the ESWSA [18 - 21] optimization technique. ESWSA is primarily based on the water search strategy, which mimics the behavior of intelligent and social elephants during drought conditions. The objective function for the ESWSA is the prediction error, which can be calculated using the Root Mean Square Error (RMSE), defined as follows:

$$RMSE = \sqrt{\frac{1}{m}\sum_{i=1}^{m}\left(\frac{X_{exp}-X_{Cal}}{X_{exp}}\right)^2} * 100\% \quad \textbf{(2)}$$

where X_{exp} is the experimental value of FN, X_{cal} is the calculated value of FN, and m is the number of training data. Here, RSM-based equation was used to calculate the value of FN during optimization. Table **6** shows different parameter settings for ESWSA for finding optimal conditions of welding. After successful optimization, the best conditions for welding can be given as I=117.1733A, F=14.00lpm, and S=4.50mm/s, as shown in Table **7**.

Table 6. Parameter setting for eswsa for finding the optimal condition of mig welding.

Parameters of ESWSA	Value
No of parameters to be optimized	3
Search Range of I	100 to 130
Search Range of F	10 to 14
Search Range of S	4.4 to 5.5
Number of initial solutions	20
Maximum Iteration	1000
probability switch	0.6

Table 7. Optimal conditions of MIG welding using ESWSA.

Model	I	F	S
RSM	117.17	14.000	4.5

Using the ESWSA metaheuristic, for the above-mentioned optimal conditions, the best value of FN was found to be 6.4794 for MIG welding

CONCLUSION

Based on the experimental works done and the interpretation of the results, several conclusions can be drawn for MIG-welded AISI 304 austenitic stainless steel.

Visual observation and radiography test show that austenitic stainless steel AISI 304 can be welded without any major defects by the MIG welding process at proper combinations of the input parameters. Results of the tensile test show that welded joints are ductile in nature; the ultimate tensile strength of the joints is satisfactory. Hardness is not uniform across different zones of the weldment. That may lead to different wear rates in different zones. A small amount of carbide is precipitated but dispersedly, not along the grain boundary. So, sensitization is not severe.

Sound weld quality can be achieved in MIG welding of austenitic stainless steel AISI 304 using ER 308L electrode and 99% pure Argon gas shielding at suitable combinations of input parameters.

ANOVA and ESWSA metaheuristic can both be applied for the optimization of the welding process, *i.e.*, to find out the optimal condition for MIG welding.

Using this machine learning-based approach for mathematical modeling of MIG welding and finding out optimal welding conditions is a typical example of Industry 5.0. In the future, other machine learning tools like Artificial Neural Networks, Fuzzy Logic, and other superior optimization techniques can be employed for the improvement in the results in terms of optimization and prediction of outputs.

ACKNOWLEDGEMENTS

The authors are greatly in debt to NITTTR, Kolkata, for their valuable help.

REFERENCES

[1] S. Kittichai, N. Santirat, and P. Sompong, World Academy of Science, Engineering and Technology, vol. 61, 2012.

[2] M.T. Liao, and W.J. Chen, "The effect of shielding-gas compositions on the microstructure and mechanical properties of stainless steel weldments", *Mater. Chem. Phys.,* vol. 55, no. 2, pp. 145-151, 1998.
[http://dx.doi.org/10.1016/S0254-0584(98)00134-5]

[3] D. B. Miracle, S. L. Donaldson, S. D. Henry, C. Moosbrugger, G. J. Anton, B. R. Sanders, *et al.*, "ASM Handbook," vol. 21, pp. 107–119, ASM International, Materials Park, OH, USA, 2001.

[4] J. C. Lippold and D. J. Kotecki, Welding Metallurgy and Weldability of Stainless Steels. Mar. 2005.

[5] A. Ghosh, S. Mandal, G. Nandi, and P.K. Pal, "Metaheuristic-based parametric optimization of TIG welded joint", *Trans. Indian Inst. Met.,* vol. 71, no. 8, pp. 1963-1973, 2018. [http://dx.doi.org/10.1007/s12666-018-1330-z]

[6] A. Ghosh, S. Mandal, G. Nandi, and P.K. Pal, *RSM Based Modeling and Optimization of TIG Welded Joint.* vol. XIX. REASON - A Tech. J., 2020.

[7] E. Zumelzu, J. Sepúlveda, and M. Ibarra, "Study on stainless steel properties", *J. Mater. Process. Technol.,* vol. 94, pp. 36-40, 1999. [http://dx.doi.org/10.1016/S0924-0136(98)00450-6]

[8] N. Suutala, T. Takalo, and T. Moisio, "The relationship between solidification and microstructure in austenitic and austenitic-ferritic stainless steel welds", *Metall. Trans., A, Phys. Metall. Mater. Sci.,* vol. 10, no. 4, pp. 512-514, 1979. [http://dx.doi.org/10.1007/BF02697081]

[9] B.T. Lu, Z.K. Chen, J.L. Luo, B.M. Patchett, and Z.H. Xu, "Pitting and stress corrosion cracking behavior in welded austenitic stainless steel", *Electrochim. Acta,* vol. 50, no. 6, pp. 1391-1403, 2005. [http://dx.doi.org/10.1016/j.electacta.2004.08.036]

[10] H. Cerjak, H. Bhadeshia, and E. Kozeschnik, *Mathematical Modelling of Weld Phenomena 7.* Verlag der Technischen Universität Graz, 2005.

[11] D.L. Olson, "Prediction of austenitic weld metal microstructure and properties", *Weld. J.,* vol. 64, no. 10, pp. 281s-295s, 1985.

[12] K.V.D. Rajesh, T. Buddi, P.R. Kanth, and K. Satyanarayana, "Microstructural and corrosion resistance study on plasma arc welded joints of AISI 304 and AISI 316", *Advances in Materials and Processing Technologies,* vol. 6, no. 2, pp. 189-205, 2020. [http://dx.doi.org/10.1080/2374068X.2020.1732158]

[13] H. Khatak, B. Raj, Ed., *Corrosion of Austenitic Stainless Steels: Mechanism, Mitigation and Monitoring.* Woodhead Publishing, 2002. [http://dx.doi.org/10.1533/9780857094018]

[14] R.Y. Chen, and W.Y.D. Yeun, "Review of the high-temperature oxidation of iron and carbon steels in air or oxygen", *Oxid. Met.,* vol. 59, no. 5-6, pp. 433-468, 2003. [http://dx.doi.org/10.1023/A:1023685905159]

[15] T.A. Siewert, C.N. McCowan, and D.L. Olson, "Ferrite number prediction to 100 FN in stainless steel weld metal", *Weld. J.,* vol. 67, no. 12, pp. 289-298, 1988.

[16] D.J. Kotecki, and T.A. Siewert, "WRC-1992 constitution diagram for stainless steel weld metals: A modification of the WRC-1988 diagram", *Weld. J.,* vol. 71, no. 5, pp. 171-178, 1992.

[17] C. A. Kot, H. C. Lin, J. B. van Erp, T. V. Eichler, and A. H. Wiedermann, *Evaluation of Aircraft Crash Hazards Analyses for Nuclear Power Plants*, NUREG/CR-2859, Argonne National Laboratory, Washington, DC, USA, 1982.

[18] S. Mandal, "Elephant swarm water search algorithm for global optimization", *Sadhana,* vol. 43, no. 1, p. 2, 2018. [http://dx.doi.org/10.1007/s12046-017-0780-z]

[19] S. Mandal, G. Saha, and R. K. Pal, "Recurrent neural network-based modeling of gene regulatory network using elephant swarm water search algorithm," J. Bioinform. Comput. Biol., vol. 15, no. 4, pp. 1750016(1–23), 2017. [http://dx.doi.org/10.1142/S0219720017500160]

[20] S. Mandal, "Modeling of photovoltaic systems using modified elephant swarm water search algorithm", *International Journal of Modelling and Simulation,* vol. 40, no. 6, pp. 436-455, 2020. [http://dx.doi.org/10.1080/02286203.2019.1650488]

[21] S. Mandal, "Identification of severity of infection for COVID-19 affected lungs images using elephant swarm water search algorithm", *International Journal of Modelling and Simulation,* vol. 42, no. 3, pp. 518-532, 2022. [http://dx.doi.org/10.1080/02286203.2021.1934797]

CHAPTER 9

Bio-Inspired Algorithm-based Performance Enhancement of Solar-powered SR Motor for Sustainable Marine Propulsion

G. Jegadeeswari[1,*] and **B. Kirubadurai**[2]

[1] *Department of Electrical and Electronics Engineering, Saveetha Engineering College, Chennai, India*

[2] *Aeronautical Engg, VelTech Dr. Rangarajan Dr. Sagunthala R&D Institute of Science and Tech, Chennai, India*

Abstract: Marine propulsion systems are evolving towards energy-efficient and environmentally friendly solutions, with solar-powered Switched Reluctance Motors (SRMs) emerging as a promising alternative. Despite SRM's inherent advantages, such as robust design, high efficiency, and fault tolerance, it suffers from torque ripples and non-linearity, which hinder its optimal performance in marine applications. This chapter investigates the performance enhancement of solar-fed SRMs in ship propulsion systems through the application of metaheuristic algorithms for intelligent control. Specifically, metaheuristic techniques such as Particle Swarm Optimization are employed to fine-tune controller parameters for minimizing torque ripple and improving speed control under varying load conditions. A solar-fed SEPIC converter is integrated into the system, providing a stable and renewable energy source while maintaining system's efficiency. The proposed approach leverages metaheuristic algorithms to optimize the performance of the SRM drive by adjusting the control gains, thus ensuring smooth and efficient propulsion. Simulation results demonstrate a significant reduction in torque ripples, enhanced speed response, and improved overall system efficiency compared to traditional PI controllers. The findings highlight the potential of metaheuristic algorithms to transform SRM technology into a viable solution for sustainable marine propulsion systems.

Keywords: Metaheuristic algorithms, Particle swarm optimization (PSO), Switched Reluctance Motor (SRM), Sustainable marine propulsion, Solar-powered propulsion, Torque ripple reduction.

* **Corresponding author G. Jegadeeswari:** Electrical and Electronics Engineering, Saveetha Engineering College, Chennai, India; E-mail: Jegadeeswari.dharan@gmail.com

Pijush Dutta, Sudip Mondal, Korhan Cengiz and S. Balamurugan (Eds.)

INTRODUCTION

As the maritime industry moves towards greener technologies, integrating solar power into ship propulsion systems is crucial for reducing carbon emissions and dependence on fossil fuels. The use of solar-fed Switched Reluctance Motors (SRMs), developed by *G. Jegadeeswari et al., in 2024,* aligns with global efforts to adopt renewable energy in transportation for reducing environmental impact while maintaining propulsion efficiency [1, 2].

SRMs, despite their advantages, face issues like torque ripple and non-linear control challenges. Metaheuristic algorithms, proposed by *G. Jegadeeswari et al., in 2023,* such as Particle Swarm Optimization, offer powerful solutions for tuning controller parameters [5, 3]. These algorithms can optimize motor performance, reduce torque ripple, and enhance speed control, which is critical for ensuring smooth and efficient marine propulsion. Ships operate in dynamic environments with varying load conditions, speed demands, and power fluctuations. *G. Jegadeeswari et al in 2020* [4] developed metaheuristic algorithms that are adaptive and can fine-tune controllers in real time, improving the SRM's ability to respond to these unpredictable conditions. This enhances the system's overall reliability, ensuring stable and efficient propulsion in both shallow and deep-water operations.

Harnessing solar energy and optimizing SRM performance, the system proposed by *M. Das et al., in 2015* can significantly lower operational costs related to fuel consumption and maintenance [6]. Solar-fed systems reduce the need for frequent refuelling and extend the ship's range, contributing to the economic sustainability of maritime operations. Furthermore, the robustness and fault tolerance of SRMs, combined with optimized control, can lower maintenance costs by minimizing wear and tear on mechanical components. *R. Errouissi et al., in 2018* [7] introduce advanced control methodologies through metaheuristic algorithms, which can be further expanded to other renewable energy-based propulsion systems. The success of this approach can inspire the development of more intelligent, adaptive, and eco-friendly propulsion technologies, making it a vital step toward the next generation of marine propulsion systems. *R. Prabhu et al., in 2019* [8] suggested that the solutions proposed in this chapter can be adapted not only to large commercial ships but also to smaller vessels such as autonomous underwater vehicles (AUVs) and drones, opening possibilities for wider applications in exploration, defense, and ocean research. The metaheuristic approach can also be extended to other motor types and renewable energy systems, demonstrating the scalability of the research. *H. Len et al., in 2015* [9] suggested a revolutionary high-performance converter among non-conventional energy sources. The Solar Photovoltaic (SPV) source has received a lot of interest because of its low environmental impact and low installation and maintenance costs. *J.F. Hansen et al., in 2015* [10] discussed that the atmospheric conditions have an important role in the power conversion efficiency of SPV systems. *K. Kavitha et al., in 2012* [11] developed an innovative speed control design of a PI controller for AC motor drives, taking input saturation into account. *G. Jegadeeswari in 2017* [12], showcased the development of a Proportional-Integral (PI) controller using an innovative technique that enables the approximate restoration of nominal tracking performance while mitigating the adverse effects induced by input saturation that allowed the bridgeless SEPIC converter to employ connected inductors, resulting in a reduced overall component count and lower inductance demand when compared to the regular SEPIC converter. OCC is a nonlinear control method used to regulate the voltage loops and improve behavior and transient state reactivity. *R. Vinifa et al., in 2024 and 2022* [13, 14] suggested THD reduction for a three-phase power multilevel inverter.

METHODOLOGY

The proposed study explains how a 4-phase, 8/6 switched reluctance motor (SRM) powered by photovoltaic is used to power the ship's propeller. Chapters four, five, and six include specifics on the proposed method, including its behavior and working principles. Switched Reluctance Motors use a variety of metaheuristic optimization techniques and intelligent controllers to minimize torque ripples and smooth control operation. The sudden increase in the speed and torque observed in the conventional induction motors is effectively addressed in maritime propulsion systems by replacing them with SR motors. Because hysteresis current control technology is used, the motor's speed will not drop when a load is changed. Photovoltaic systems will produce a low-level DC voltage with fluctuations that can be boosted by the use of a high-gain Single-Ended Primary Inductance Converter. With the help of a high-gain converter, the output of the solar system has been effectively controlled. Additionally, the high-gain converter is controlled by using a Maximum Power Point Tracking technique by implementing an Adaptive Neuro-Fuzzy Inference System. By effectively removing errors, the ANFIS-MPPT algorithm generates a control signal and maximizes the efficiency of photovoltaic (PV) systems using input voltage (VPV) and current (IPV). The PWM generator is controlled by this control signal, which produces PWM pulses that regulate the operation of the SEPIC Converter by energizing the switching processes, thereby controlling the output voltage of the converter.

The BR converter is also called an (n+1) semiconductor, and the (n+1) diode converter powers the motor phase windings and sends the Sepic Converter output to the motor. In addition, a PI and an optimization algorithm for fine-tuning the parameters of PI result in regulating the speed of SRM. The controller produces an error signal after it receives the motor's reference speed (N_{ref}) and its actual speed (N_{act}). With the help of the error elimination method, the controllers receive the control signal and provide an error-free signal. The PWM generator generates pulses by sending a control signal to activate the switching operations of the BR converter or the (n+1) semiconductor and (n+1) diode converter. Suggested systems are illustrated in Fig. (**1**).

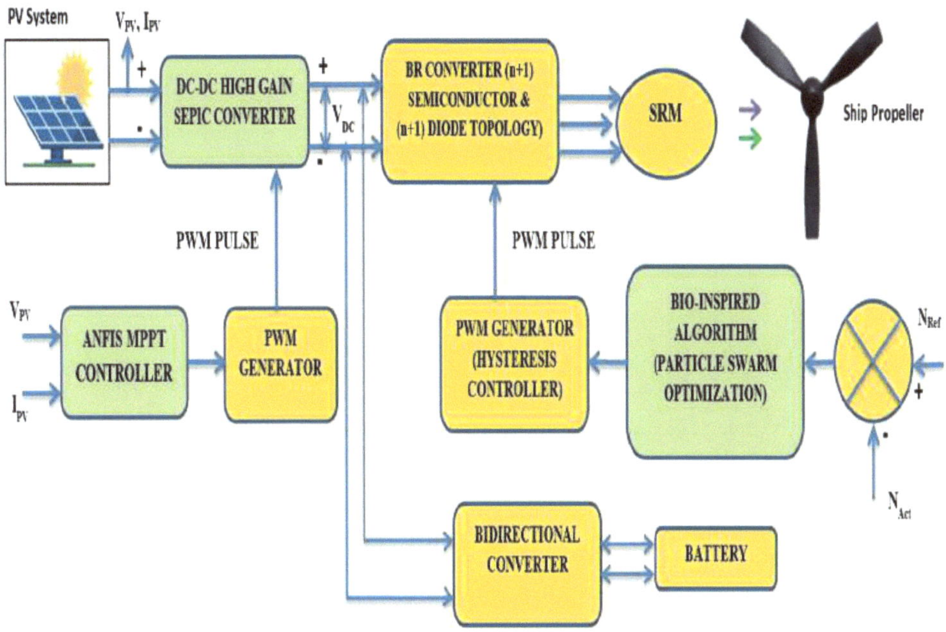

Fig. (1). Proposed system.

SIMULATION RESULTS AND DISCUSSION

The speed control of the 8/6 SR motor driven by a solar-fed high-gain converter is examined in this section. An MPPT algorithm based on ANFIS is used to control the converter, and evaluate its effectiveness. Temperature, irradiance, voltage, current, and other critical variables influencing PV systems are examined, and the associated waveforms are produced for evaluation. Figs. (**2a-d**) display the waveforms of a solar panel under different conditions. In Fig. (**2a**), the temperature is maintained at 25°C for the first 0.2 seconds before rapidly increasing to 35°C and levelling off.

The radiation increased sharply to 1000 w/sq.m. at 0.2s after remaining steady at 800 w/sq.m. This constant level is further maintained in Fig. (**2b**). Solar panel voltage is depicted in Fig. (**2c**). After 0.2 seconds of stability at 125 V, the voltage suddenly increases to 149 V, where it remains constant. It is noted that the current initially increases noticeably. But the current gradually decreases, plateaus at 60A, and then increases once again, reaching its highest point at 70A at 0.2s. In 0.2 seconds, the current stays the same. The current that was drawn from the solar panel is shown in Fig. (**2d**). The output current and voltage responses of the high-gain converter, produced by the ANFIS-based MPPT, are depicted in Figs. (**3a** and **3b**).

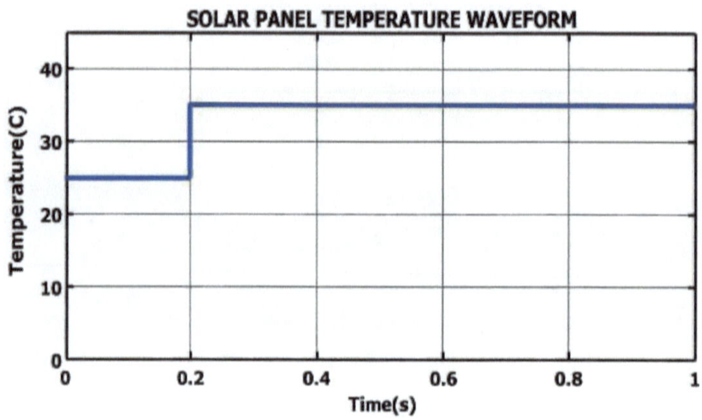

Fig. (2a). Solar: Temperature.

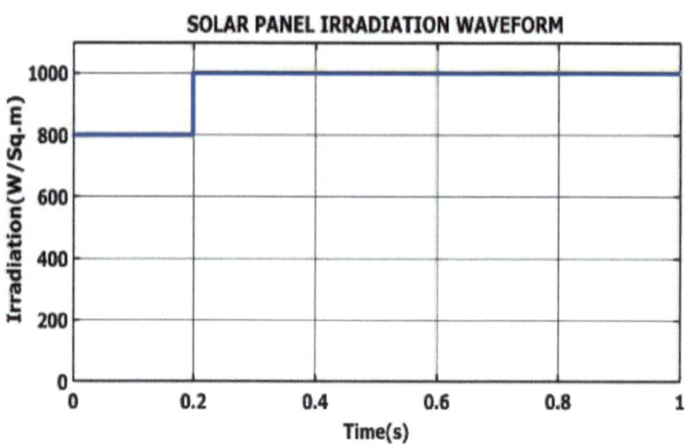

Fig. (2b). Solar: Irradiation.

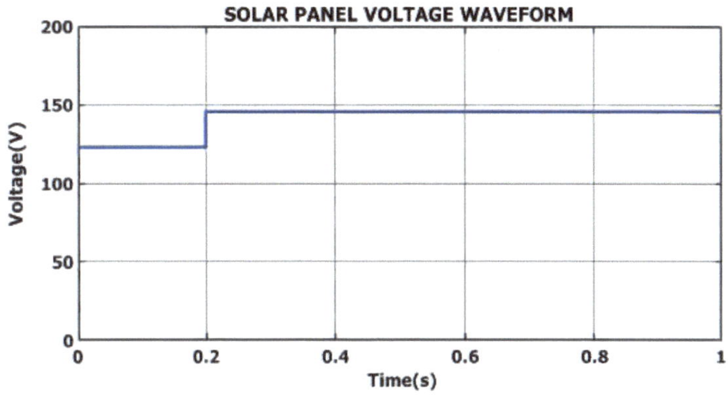

Fig. (2c). Solar: Voltage.

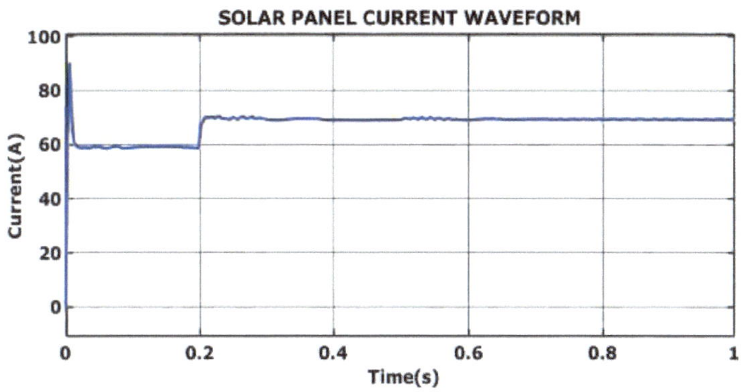

Fig. (2d). Solar: Current.

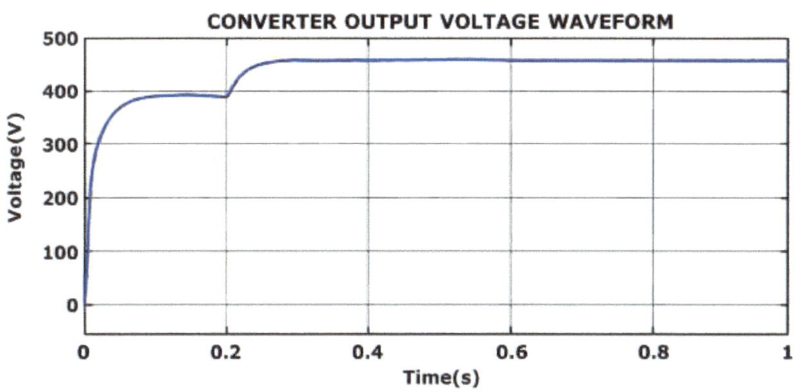

Fig. (3a). Sepic Converter: Voltage Waveform.

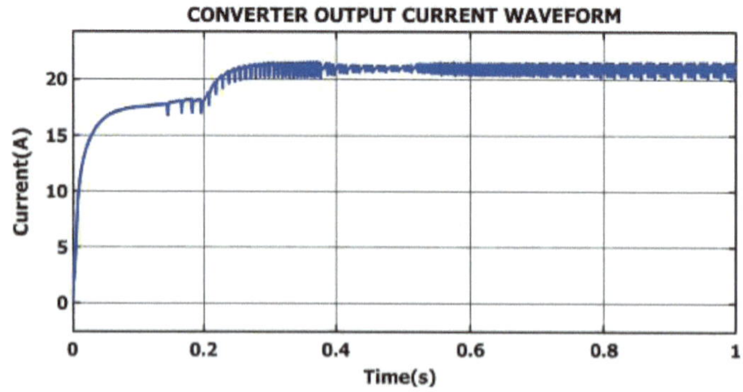

Fig. (3b). SEPIC converter: Current Waveform.

The SEPIC converter is effectively boosting the voltage from a 140V solar panel to an output of around 450V with a high efficiency of 97%. The solar panel voltage is increased by an SEPIC converter before being passed into a Bridge Resonance converter or (n+1) semiconductor and (n+1) diode converter. The motor's phase windings are driven by this converter. The SEPIC converter voltage output is illustrated in Fig. (**3a**). The high-gain converter achieves an output current of about 22A. The current obtained from the converter is displayed in Fig. (**3b**). The slight difference accounts for conversion losses. The decrease in the current from 70A to 22A compensates for the increase in voltage, maintaining the overall power balance. The observed phenomenon of voltage increasing from 140V to 450V and current decreasing from 70A to 22A using the step-up SEPIC converter can be explained through the principles of power conservation, converter efficiency, and design considerations. The SEPIC converter effectively steps up the voltage while proportionally decreasing the current to maintain power balance, enhance system efficiency, and ensure the safe operation of the energy storage system. The energy storage system typically operates at a much lower voltage compared to the PV array. The high-gain converter is employed to cut down the high voltage from the solar array (420V) to a level suitable for the battery (24V). This step-down process is essential to match the operating voltage of the battery, ensuring safe and efficient charging. The efficiency of the SEPIC converter plays a role in the observed voltage. Although modern converters are highly efficient, losses still occur due to components such as inductors, capacitors, and switching elements. These losses, albeit small, contribute to the slight reduction in voltage. The battery charging process often requires a specific current profile, which may necessitate lower current levels to ensure the longevity and safety of the battery. High currents can lead to overheating and degradation of battery cells; thus a lower current (1.2A) is applied. Figs. (**4a-c**) illustrate the response of output current, voltage, and State of Charge waveforms, respectively, for an energy storage system utilized by a bi-directional converter.

The battery's output voltage is roughly 24V, as illustrated in Fig. (**4a**). The battery's output current, approximately 1.2A, is illustrated in Fig. (**4b**). Finally, the battery's state of charge is approximately 80%, as shown in Fig. (**4c**). The initial SOC of the battery is set based on calibration and initial conditions. Before the battery begins to store excess energy from the PV array, the battery was likely pre-charged to a known SOC value, which in this case is 80%. This pre-charging ensures that the battery operates within a safe and efficient range, avoiding the extremes of overcharging or deep discharging. At the start of the operation, the battery is at rest or under a minimal load, leading to a constant SOC. This is because there is no significant current flow into or out of the battery, resulting in no substantial change in the SOC. The SOC value of 80% is determined through a combination of initial condition settings, accurate estimation methods, and thorough calibration. The constant SOC within the first seconds is due to a lack of significant current flow, system initialization phases, and potential lag in measurement systems.

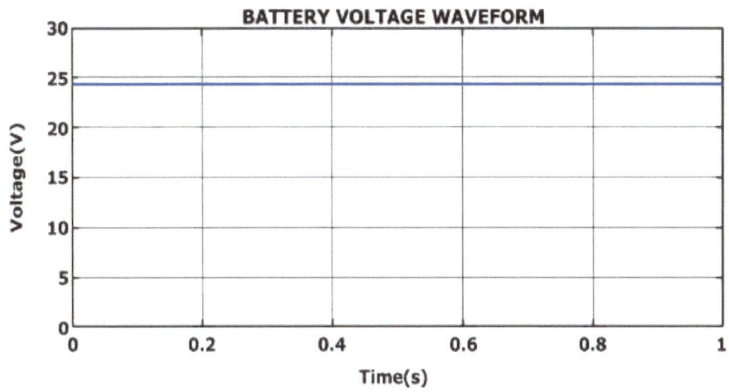

Fig. (4a). Battery: Voltage Waveform.

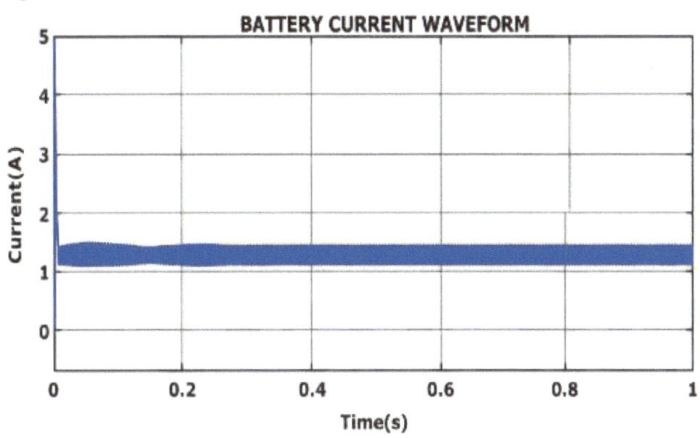

Fig. (4b). Battery: Current Waveform.

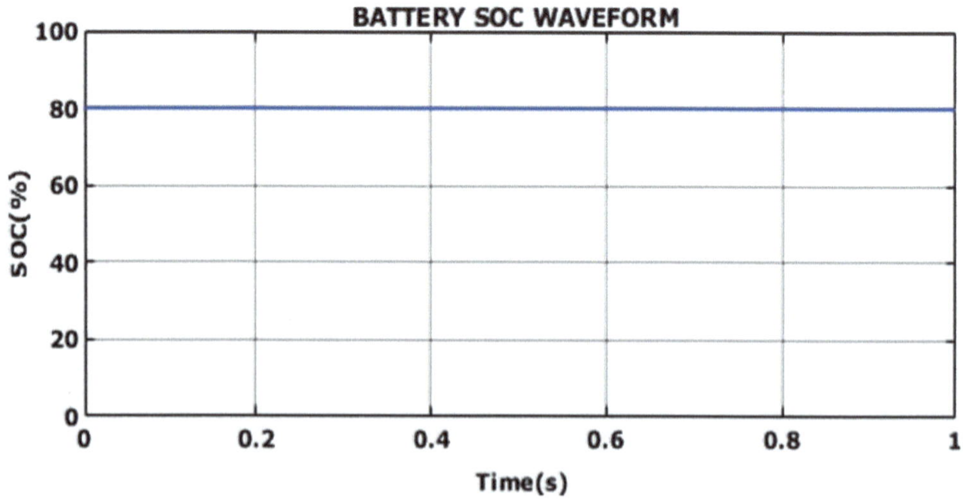

Fig. (4c). SOC_Battery.

SR MOTOR SPEED REGULATION USING PROPORTIONAL INTEGRAL CONTROLLER

Simulation studies are conducted to evaluate the effectiveness of SRM speed control using a PI controller. Figs. (**5a-d**) depict the proper torque, flux, and current responses for time intervals ranging from 0 to 1 second. The flux behavior of the Switched Reluctance Motor with a PI controller is shown in Fig. (**5a**). According to the response, the flux first rises, then progressively falls for 0.5 seconds until stabilizing at 0.084 Wb at 1 Nm.

The behavior of the motor with a PI is depicted in Fig. (**5b**). The current rises strongly before falling, as the response shows. It stabilizes at a steady 10 A at 1 Nm after a few small oscillations. Fig. (**5c**) depicts the torque behavior of the Switched Reluctance Motor with a PI controller. According to the response, the torque initially spikes and then decreases at 0.5 seconds. After a brief period, it stabilizes at a constant value of 2.5 Nm. In-depth simulation studies have been conducted to examine the speed behavior of the Switched Reluctance Motor. The speed is intended to reach 300 rpm at 1 Nm, according to the results. Fig. (**5d**) illustrates the response, which shows a longer response time, an extended oscillation period, and a greater maximum deviation. The speed behavior of the SRM while using a PI is depicted in this figure. The PI adjusted parameters coefficient, which produced the speed response in Fig. (**5d**), is displayed in Table **1**.

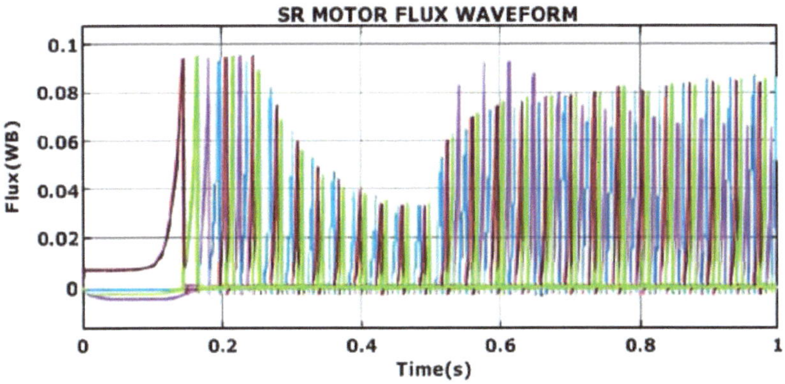

Fig. (5a). PI: Flux Waveform.

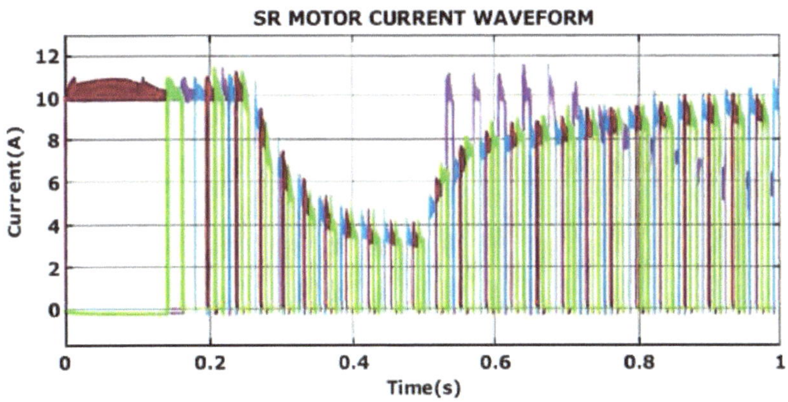

Fig. (5b). PI: Current Waveform.

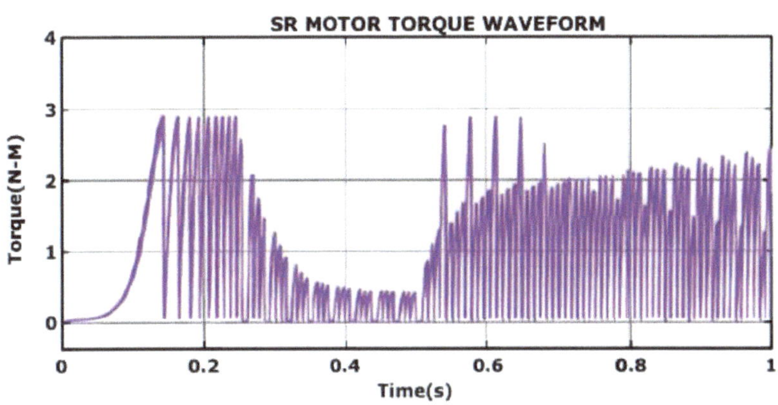

Fig. (5c). PI: Torque Waveform.

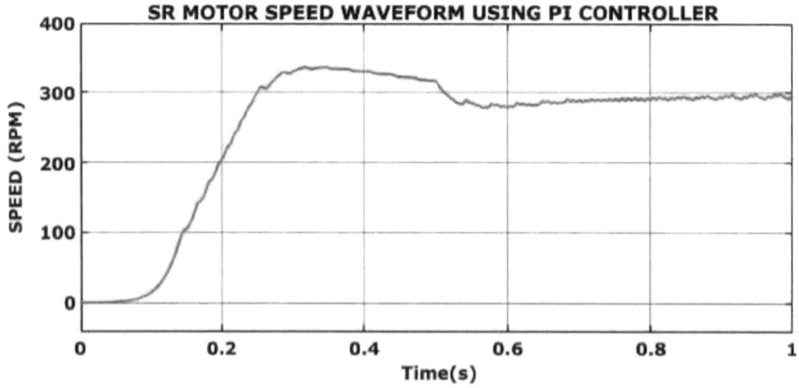

Fig. (5d). PI: Speed Waveform.

Table 1. Parameters of PI.

Parameter	Value
P	0. 0035478
I	0. 0064678

The efficacy and toughness of the PI concerning time domain specification are listed in Table **2**

Table 2. Efficacy and toughness.

Parameter	Tuned
Rise time	0.32
Peak Time	0.34
Overshoot	0.5
Settling Time	0.9
Steady State error	0.82
Maximum Peak Overshoot	0.56
Torque ripple in %	89.90
Integral Absolute error	16.81

The proportional-integral (PI) controller results in a relatively large torque ripple of 89.90% in the context of speed control of the Motor. In response to this issue, various optimization algorithms are employed. The forthcoming findings may provide a more in-depth understanding of how these optimization techniques contribute to torque ripple reduction and overall control effectiveness.

SR MOTOR SPEED REGULATION USING PSO - PI

The effectiveness of SRM-based speed control using the PSO-PI has been assessed through simulation trials. The matching speed, flux, torque, and current responses across a 0–1 second time range are shown in Figs. (**6a-d**). Fig. (**6a**) displays the flux response, which shows that the flux first rises, then gradually falls at 0.3 seconds before stabilizing at 0.052 Wb at 1 Nm. The SRM's current response with the PSO-PI controller is shown in Fig. (**6b**). The waveform indicates a sharp increase in current followed by a decline. It stabilizes at 6 A at 1 Nm after experiencing slight variations. The torque waveforms below demonstrate how the torque spikes and then falls. Following slight oscillations, the torque stabilizes at 0.8 NM. The torque response of SRM employing PSO-PI is shown in Fig. (**6c**).

Expansion of simulation studies to analyze the speed behavior of SRM reveals that the speed is precisely 300 rpm at 1 NM. The response clearly indicates oscillation, despite the relatively short rise and settling times. The speed behavior of SRM employing PSO-PI is shown in Fig. (**6d**). The PSO method's parameters are displayed in Table **3**. The PSO-PI controller's adjusted parameter coefficients, which produced the speed response graph in Fig. (**6d**), are displayed in Table **4**.

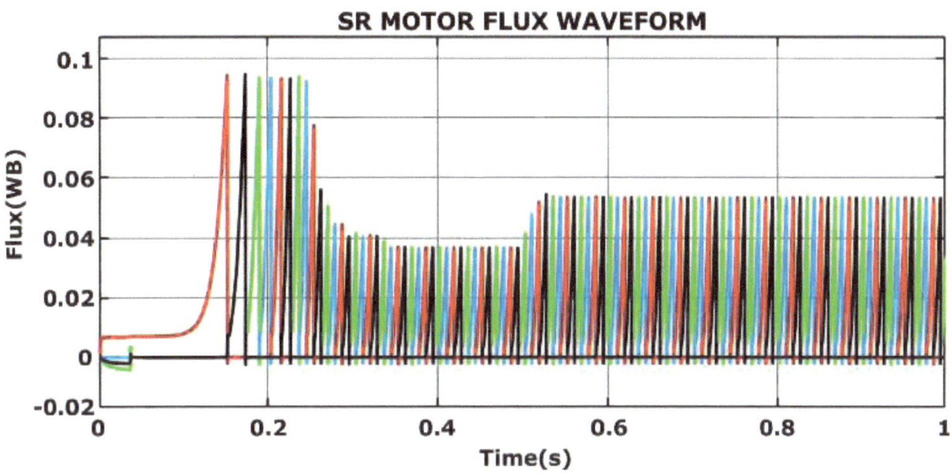

Fig. (6a). PSO-PI: Flux Waveform.

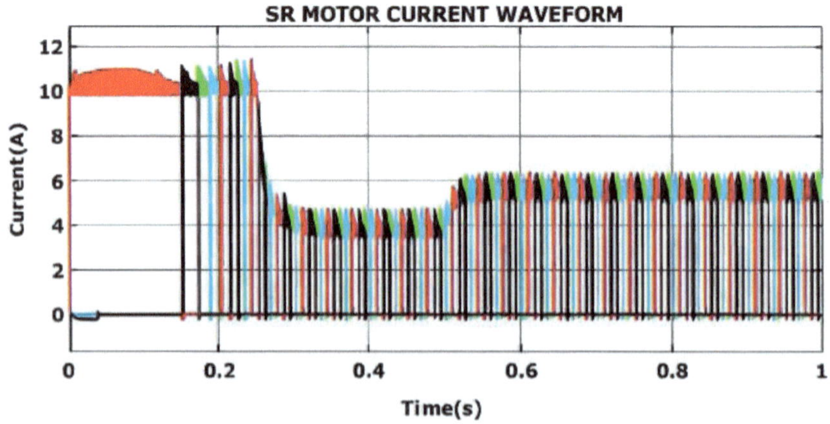

Fig. (6b). PSO-PI: Current Waveform.

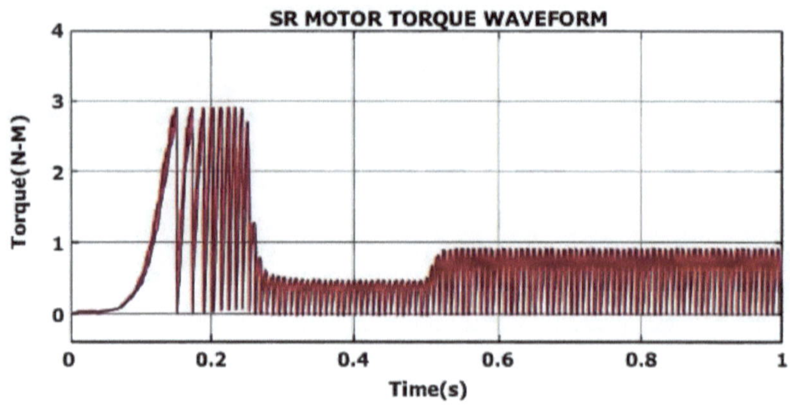

Fig. (6c). PSO-PI: Torque Waveform.

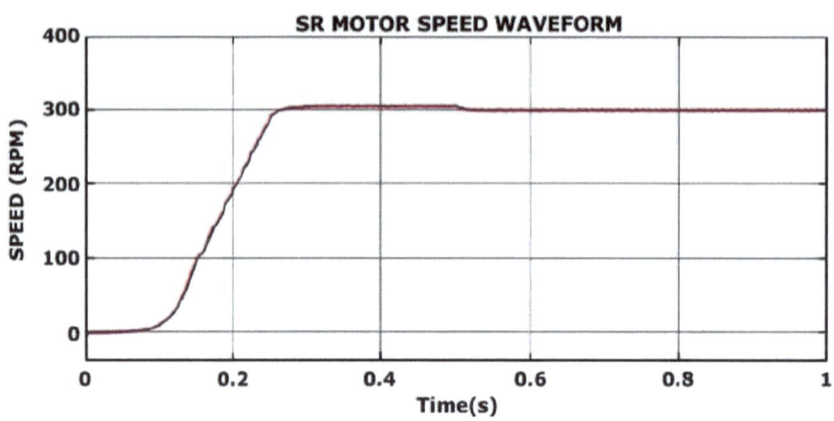

Fig. (6d). PSO-PI: Speed Waveform.

Table 3. Parameters of PSO.

Parameters	PSO
Population Size	25
Number of Iterations	100
Cognitive Constant c1	4
Social Constant c2	4

Table 4. Tuned PI values using PSO.

Parameters	Values
K_P	0.6601
K_I	0.0293

The efficacy and toughness of the PSO-PI concerning time domain specification are shown in Table **5**.

Table 5. Efficacy and toughness of PSO-PI.

Parameter	Tuned (300 RPM)
Rise time	0.19
Peak Time	0.25
Overshoot	0.0045
Settling Time	0.5
Maximum Peak Overshoot	0.41
Torque ripple in %	55.25
Steady State Error	0.43
IAE	8.5

The torque ripple in the PSO-PI controller is comparatively low at 55.25% in comparison to the PI shown in Fig. (**7**), regarding crucial time-domain parameters such as peak time, overshoot, steady-state error, rising time, and settling time. The superior performance of the PSO-PI over the PI is clearly shown in Table **5**. This illustrates how effectively the proposed PSO-PI control solution reduces torque ripple and improves settling time while maintaining a stable speed for the SRM.

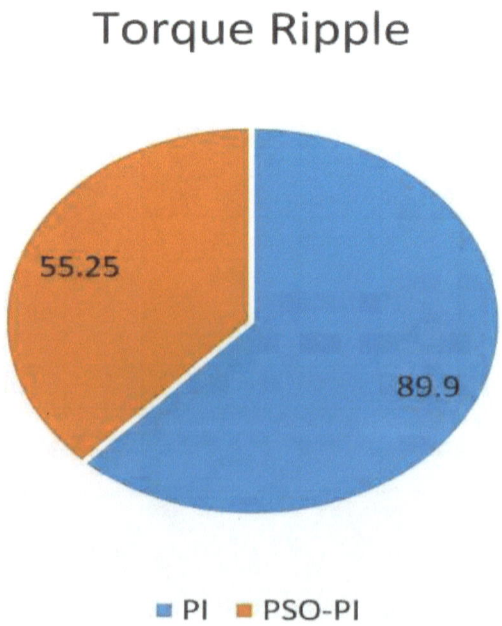

Fig, (7). Comparison of torque ripple.

CONCLUSION

To minimize torque ripples in switched reluctance motors, this chapter optimizes PI controller tuning using optimization methods like Particle Swarm Optimization (PSO). A comparison of the previously indicated method's Time Domain specification, SSE, IAE, and Torque Ripple has been carried out. The simulated findings show that the PSO-based PI controller increases efficacy in a dynamic environment, especially in the case of SRM, with a torque ripple of 55.25% smaller than the traditional PI. It is also highly efficient, accurate, and simple. The torque improvement percentage and torque ripple value are investigated in different circumstances of the proposed model. Efficiency gains and torque ripple reduction enhance SRM performance. The use of SRM for marine propulsion systems may propagate as a result of the proposed approach.

REFERENCES

[1] G. Jegadeeswari, D. Lakshmi, and B. Kirubadurai, "Renewable Energy Powered Switched Reluctance Motor for Marine Propulsion System Using Soft Computing Techniques", In: *Soft Computing in Renewable Energy Technologies*. CRC Press, 2024, pp. 189-205. [http://dx.doi.org/10.1201/9781003462460-9]

[2] G. Jegadeeswari, D. Lakshmi, B. Kirubadurai, and Z. Harith, "Performance Evaluation of Four Phase 8/6 Switched Reluctance Motor for Ship Propulsion System," Journal of Engineering Science and Technology, Special Issue on ICIT2022, vol. 19, no. 1, pp. 109–120, 2024.

[3] G. Jegadeeswari, D. Lakshmi, and B. Kirubadurai, "Grey Wolf Optimization Algorithm for Tuning PI Controller Based Speed Control of Switched Reluctance Motor for Ship Propulsion Systems", *International Conference on Future Technologies in Manufacturing, Automation, Design and Energy,* Trans Tech Publications Ltd., 2023. [http://dx.doi.org/10.4028/p-T96f23]

[4] G. Jegadeeswari, D. Lakshmi, and B. Kirubadurai, "ANN and Fuzzy Logic Based Direct Instantaneous Torque Control for 8/6 Switched Reluctance Motor", In: *Advances in Manufacturing, Automation, Design and Energy Technologies (ICoFT 2020), Lecture Notes in Mechanical Engineering.* Springer: Singapore, 2023. [http://dx.doi.org/10.1007/978-981-99-1288-9_31]

[5] G. Jegadeeswari, G. Ezhilarasi, V. Pramila, J. Vijayanand, and B. Kirubadurai, "Performance Comparison of Dynamic Responses & Speed Control of Switched Reluctance Motor Using PI & Fuzzy Logic Controller," in 2023 9th International Conference on Electrical Energy Systems (ICEES), Chennai, India, 2023, pp. 674–680. [http://dx.doi.org/10.1109/ICEES57979.2023.10110237]

[6] M. Das, and V. Agarwal, "Novel High-Performance Stand-Alone Solar PV System With High-Gain High-Efficiency DC–DC Converter Power Stages", *IEEE Trans. Ind. Appl.,* vol. 51, no. 6, pp. 4718-4728, 2015. [http://dx.doi.org/10.1109/TIA.2015.2454488]

[7] R. Errouissi, A. Al-Durra, and S.M. Muyeen, "Experimental Validation of a Novel PI Speed Controller for AC Motor Drives With Improved Transient Performances", *IEEE Trans. Control Syst. Technol.,* vol. 26, no. 4, pp. 1414-1421, 2018. [http://dx.doi.org/10.1109/TCST.2017.2707404]

[8] P. Prabhu, and V. Urundady, "One-cycle controlled bridgeless SEPIC with coupled inductors for PAM control-based BLDC drive", *Arab. J. Sci. Eng.,* vol. 44, no. 8, pp. 6987-7001, 2019. [http://dx.doi.org/10.1007/s13369-019-03740-x]

[9] H. Lan, J. Dai, S. Wen, Y-Y. Hong, D. Yu, and Y. Bai, "Optimal tilt angle of photovoltaic arrays and economic allocation of energy storage system on large oil tanker ship", *Energies,* vol. 8, no. 10, pp. 11515-11530, 2015. [http://dx.doi.org/10.3390/en81011515]

[10] J.F. Hansen, and F. Wendt, "History and State of the Art in Commercial Electric Ship Propulsion, Integrated Power Systems, and Future Trends", *Proc. IEEE,* vol. 103, no. 12, pp. 2229-2242, 2015. [http://dx.doi.org/10.1109/JPROC.2015.2458990]

[11] K. Kavitha, and J. Ebenezer, "Synchronous Cuk Converter Based Photovoltaic Energy System Design and Simulation", *International Journal of Scientific and Research Publications,* vol. 2, no. 10, pp. 1-8, 2012.

[12] G. Jegadeeswari, "Design and implementation of THD reduction for cascaded multilevel H-bridge inverter", *Journal of Advanced Research in Dynamical and Control Systems,* vol. 11, pp. 638-644, 2017. [JARDCS].

[13] V. R, K. A, and I. Selwynraj A, "A Comparison of Instantaneous and Extension p-q Methods for Current Controlled Voltage Source Inverter in Microgrid", *Int. J. Electron.,* vol. 109, no. 11, pp. 1896-1914, 2022. [http://dx.doi.org/10.1080/00207217.2021.2001859]

[14] R. Vinifa, G. Suriya and G. R. Charan, "Optimizing Power Conversion Technologies for Sustainable Electric Vehicle Mobility," 2024 10th International Conference on Communication and Signal Processing (ICCSP), Melmaruvathur, India, 2024, pp. 638-642. [http://dx.doi.org/10.1109/ICCSP60870.2024.10543571]

CHAPTER 10

Experimental Framework for Bio-inspired Algorithms in Wireless Communication: An Industry 5.0 Perspective.

Zaiba Khan[1,*]

[1] *Department of Computer Science, RNB Global University, Bikaner, Rajasthan, India*

Abstract: Advancements in wireless networks are crucial for the transformative potential of Industry 5.0, particularly in smart manufacturing and industrial automation. However, this new era demands solutions for persistent challenges, such as limited communication range, real-time data processing, and privacy concerns. Bio-inspired algorithms provide a novel approach to addressing these challenges, leveraging patterns observed in nature to enhance optimization and efficiency in wireless communication systems. This paper proposes an experimental framework using bio-inspired techniques to address specific industrial wireless communication needs, with a focus on edge intelligence, ultra-reliable low-latency communication, and energy efficiency. By emulating message protocols found in social animals, bio-inspired algorithms can optimize aspects like dynamic channel allocation and energy-saving topologies. The framework facilitates real-world testing in small to medium-sized industrial network settings, enabling an enhanced understanding of Industry 5.0 scenarios. Case studies demonstrate the effectiveness of bio-inspired solutions in optimizing network topology and energy consumption across smart factory networks, achieving notable results in scenarios requiring efficient data handling and reliable connectivity. This research highlights the importance of interdisciplinary approaches in supporting Industry 5.0 goals, demonstrating bio-inspired algorithms as promising tools for scalable, adaptive, and human-centered industrial wireless systems. The findings point towards sustainable advancements in wireless technology, fostering a deeper integration of nature-inspired solutions within next-generation industrial communication networks.

Keywords: Bio-inspired algorithms, Industrial automation, Industry 5.0, Optimization, Real-time data processing, Smart manufacturing, Wireless networks.

[*] **Corresponding author Zaiba Khan:** Department of Computer Science, RNB Global University, Bikaner, Rajasthan, India; E-mail: zaiba.khan@rnbglobal.edu.in

Pijush Dutta, Sudip Mondal, Korhan Cengiz and S. Balamurugan (Eds.)

INTRODUCTION

Advancements in wireless networks have led to industrial revolutions, such as the Industrial Internet and intelligent manufacturing. However, challenges remain in the communication range, real-time communication, and privacy protection [1]. The evolution of Industry 5.0 will bring more sophisticated requirements, improving the performance and capability of next-generation communication systems. Key technologies and concepts, such as edge intelligence, cell-free massive MIMO, ultra-reliable low-latency communication, spectral sharing, communication separation, and fusion, will be essential components. Bio-inspired algorithms can optimize specific components in future wireless communication systems, enhance performance, and refine algorithmic structures. An experimental framework for bio-inspired algorithms in wireless communication at the physical layer is presented, supporting various components throughout the system [2]. The proposed wireless experimental environment can construct local, small to medium-sized internal communication systems for factory scenes, providing a better understanding and verification in high-definition and high-precision industrial case instruments.

Background and Motivation

The recent revolution is changing the paradigms of various sectors of the modern economy, leading to integrated cooperation among heterogeneous entities, which enables a more efficient standard of living and accelerates the challenges that society is facing. Wireless communication has had a prominent role in both small and large projects. Wireless communication is everywhere, and shortly, it is expected that billions of devices will be able to transmit and receive at different scales of communication [3]. As the fourth industrial revolution paves the way for the digitalization of all processes, concepts, and services, it becomes essential to communicate even better and be recognized in advance. Thus, bio-inspired algorithms play an important role in processing the information necessary to bring life to prediction theories.

Although Industry 5.0 brings promising results by aligning security, comfort, and low processing latency, it also reveals certain flaws. One key issue is that the current peak in data processing demand—driven by the economy and intelligent services—has outpaced the system's ability to effectively manage and control. Data transmission based on an increasing number of connected devices does not give such precedence, if we think of large numbers of users who, at distinct intervals, decide to send large volumes of data simultaneously [4]. Hence, the teachings and strategies discussed can benefit such services, thereby minimizing traffic.

Scope and Objectives

To integrate the vast amount of unexploited principles on distributed computing provided by the biologically inspired algorithms community, whose focus is entirely on problem-solving and not on specific communication networks, this paper describes the main challenges and possible applications of specially tailored bio-inspired algorithms in industrial wireless communication networks, which constitute the basis for the monitoring, control, and automation of Industry 5.0 systems [5]. More specifically, after a review of the basics of bio-inspired algorithms, message protocols in social animals, and herd behavior phenomena, we identify the key features of wireless networks that might be overcome by properly mimicking mainly the message protocols employed by social animals, with the hope of contributing to renewing the stimulus underpinning original interdisciplinary research—characterizing symbiosis with nature typical of the engineering domains [6]. The considered categories of message protocols—specifically, the algorithmic strategies that allow nodes to adapt their messaging based on received signals, inspired by animal communication—can be leveraged to enhance the spatial reuse of network resources. This approach supports the analysis, design, and optimization of protocols that enable crowded networks to dynamically select small subsets of peer energy sources for time-shared use. Such mobile-to-mobile recharging services represent a promising energy provisioning solution for mobile networks, offering benefits in both performance and environmental sustainability.

BIO-INSPIRED ALGORITHMS IN WIRELESS COMMUNICATION

The Biologically Inspired Approach (BIA) has gained importance in solving complex optimization problems in communication systems due to its real-world analogy in biological systems [7]. BIA models randomized problems based on parameters, potential values, limitations, and convergence processes. Metaheuristic algorithms play a significant role in discrete and population optimization problems, focusing on limits and problem-specific knowledge. BIA design problem-solving focuses on the given solution and its costs. BIA can use direct or antibody-based metaheuristic algorithms for modulation classification and error functions for transmitted signal parameters. BIA achieves considerable performance, complexity, and convergence gain compared to current signal detection solutions. It monitors covariance matrices, confirming the accuracy of the data model and the deterministic process of optimization. Compared to additional algorithms, BIA significantly reduces redundant training time and achievable gains [8]. The signal's nearest neighbor is processed using Békédy's trigger mechanism for improved accuracy. BIA effectively meets the competitive needs of the wireless industry, driven by its growing data requirements.

Overview of Bio-inspired Algorithms

Bio-inspired algorithms are a combination of behaviors and solutions from various disciplines, aiming to model the natural world to solve complex problems in optimization, search, pattern recognition, and modeling domains [9]. Table **1** highlights the comparison of bio-inspired algorithms for optimizing wireless communication systems in Industry 5.0, highlighting their applications, strengths, limitations, and relevance. This table provides a concise comparison of algorithms like Particle Swarm Optimization (PSO), Ant Colony Optimization (ACO), and Bat Algorithm, highlighting their use in dynamic channel allocation, energy efficiency, and latency reduction. It helps readers quickly grasp the suitability of each algorithm for specific Industry 5.0 challenges. These algorithms have gained widespread use in networking and wireless communication applications, with a comprehensive experimental research framework provided in this chapter from the Industry 5.0 perspective. Over the past decade, bio-inspired algorithms, along with intelligent optimization techniques like particle swarm optimization, differential evolution, and the bat algorithm, have matured and gained rapid acceptance in various fields. Simulations and expert testing in a specialist environment showcase the strength of research and testing, and several algorithms are tested and applied to solve

Table 1. Comparison of bio-inspired algorithms for wireless communication optimization.

Algorithm	Key Application in Wireless Communication	Strengths	Limitations	Industry 5.0 Relevance
Particle Swarm Optimization (PSO)	Dynamic channel allocation, topology control	Fast convergence, simple implementation	Risk of local optima, parameter tuning	Edge intelligence, real-time data processing
Ant Colony Optimization (ACO)	Routing, energy-saving topologies	Robust for multi-hop networks	High computational complexity	Ultra-reliable low-latency communication
Bat Algorithm	Signal processing, spectral sharing	Adapts to dynamic environments	Limited scalability for large networks	Energy efficiency, smart factory automation
Differential Evolution	Modulation classification, error correction	High accuracy in optimization	Slow for real-time applications	Privacy protection, secure communication

complex practical problems [10]. These findings have led to the development of bio-inspired optimization and machine-learning techniques to solve complex problems quickly and accurately.

Applications for Wireless Communication

Bio-inspired algorithms are being used in various wireless communication systems, including learning, communication, and signal processing [11]. The challenges in Industry 5.0 can be divided into reviewed methods and new ones. Interest in innovative solutions based on bio-inspired algorithms is growing, particularly in sectors, such as transportation, urban life, social interactions, industrial environments, and agriculture. These sectors have raised demands for their integration into future communication systems. The versatility and numerous achievable applications of wireless communication networks make it an attractive option for users with high QoS requirements. The list of needs for wireless services is not conclusive, showcasing the versatility and numerous applications of wireless communication networks.

INDUSTRY 5.0 AND ITS RELEVANCE TO WIRELESS COMMUNICATION

Industry 5.0 is a concept rooted in wireless communication, aiming for the responsible redesigning of industries to enhance people's lives through a global vision based on a human-centered, sustainable, and inclusive approach [12]. The concept is guided by the 5 Hubs Principle, which emphasizes sustainable business, trusted technology, human augmentation, public inclusion, and cultural empathy. The pandemic has reinforced these strategies, influencing various economic sectors. The application of bio-inspired algorithms in technology development has shown success in communication networks. Core technologies like 6G, fog/edge computing, future internet, internet of energy, internet of production, and internet of things are influencing changes in wireless communication. Table **2** shows the mapping of Industry 5.0 technologies to bio-inspired algorithm applications in wireless communication, highlighting the key challenges and expected outcomes.

Table 2. Mapping of industry 5.0.

Industry 5.0 Technology	Wireless Communication Challenge	Bio-Inspired Algorithm	Application Example	Expected Outcome
6G	Ultra-low latency	PSO	Dynamic channel hopping	Reduced latency in smart factories
Edge/Fog Computing	Real-time data processing	ACO	Edge analytics optimization	Faster decision-making at the edge
Digital Twins	Bi-directional communication	Bat Algorithm	Network topology optimization	Enhanced reliability for IoT devices

(Table 2) cont.....

Industry 5.0 Technology	Wireless Communication Challenge	Bio-Inspired Algorithm	Application Example	Expected Outcome
Internet of Things (IoT)	Energy efficiency	Differential Evolution	Energy-harvesting node management	Prolonged device lifespan

Bio-inspired computing is advantageous for solving wireless communication problems due to its ability to execute specific target scenarios and provide rational yet efficient outcomes [13]. This has led to the development of research, experimentation, and teaching frameworks for pre-operational testing of bio-inspired algorithms to solve specific problems within the wireless communication spectrum.

Key Concepts and Technologies

Bio-inspired technologies are gaining attention due to their security and cognitive functions, inspired by the natural functionality of living beings. These technologies, such as teamwork, intelligence, and problem-solving, are incorporated into Industry 5.0 standards, aiming to fuse the synthetic and real worlds for better functionalities. Digital twin technology requires various heterogeneous services, including analytics, periodic updates, detailed modeling, and bi-directional communications. However, interactions between a dense number of nodes for edge analytics and cloud resources can lead to bottlenecks. Bio-inspired communications and computation concepts discovered in the natural world could be suitable solutions [11]. However, industries and engineers may require less standardization fuzziness to promote and evolve their ecosystem. Standardized solutions will improve the maturity, interoperability, and productivity of systems. The proposed framework selects and integrates available software technologies for research on signal processing problems.

DESIGN AND IMPLEMENTATION OF THE EXPERIMENTAL FRAMEWORK

Industry 5.0 aims to regain the human touch through wireless communication, which requires high reliability, low latency, and the ability to work in crowded environments. Bio-inspired techniques provide solutions to these problems, but experimental validation may face challenges in real industrial environments or theoretical approaches [8]. This research aims to provide an experimental framework for studying the feasibility of bio-inspired techniques for solving demanding wireless industry problems. The experimental platform's physical components, connectivity, and role are described, followed by a summary of the tools used for designing the framework. A hybrid framework is built, characterizing the relationship of different tools in a single model. Key features and challenges are highlighted for both the industry and the scientific community [12].

Architecture and Components

Biomorphic or bio-inspired algorithms are commonly applied to key components in Wireless Communication Networks (WCNs) for intelligent control operations, such as dynamic channel hopping systems, cyber-platform layers, and traffic management systems [9]. These algorithms also aim to achieve energy-efficient wireless networks, with a bio-innovation layer applied for wireless power transfer and a multispecies competition algorithmic for an intelligent optimization module. These algorithms often form secondary cognitive user-specific living resource elements in primary WCN systems, such as the Sun beside Earth architecture, which includes promotions, interactive communications solutions, ubiquitous terminals, high-speed shared bandwidth applications, signal access, information gathering, care, management, monitoring, message-oriented middleware applications, data mining, and user-suggested front-end resources [10].

Integration of Bio-inspired Algorithms and Industry 5.0 Technologies

The integration of CDoC can contribute to bio-inspired algorithm research in real wireless system optimization problems, fostering Industry 5.0. This symbiosis of bio-inspired algorithms, design science, co-robotics, and human-technology interface can create new value and collaboration between engineering models and applications in wireless communication [11, 13]. The design engineering model base can serve as a template for optimization problems, while real-world optimization problems can validate research results and generate new empirical data. This approach reflects the known knowledge and unknown issues of current bio-inspired algorithms in wireless communication, stimulating future research and innovation in this field.

CASE STUDIES AND RESULTS

This is a case study on two bio-inspired algorithms to evaluate their applicability and identify the challenges that need to be addressed when considering the use of such approaches in the context of wireless communication. The experimental campaign is framed within the development of Industry 5.0 systems and investigates the cooperation of multiple smart factories through wireless industrial communication networks. In this context, bio-inspired algorithms are increasingly applied to address the complex optimization problems that arise when power management, topology control, and routing need to be solved in multi-hop wireless networks. Such approaches mimic the behavior of natural systems, such as ants or fish, to find lightweight, energy-saving, connected topologies at design time or during network operation.

Two case studies are presented; both are addressed in a testbed implementation of industrial wireless communication systems. The results suggest that ACO is a good solution when dealing with topology control and that the communication between different smart factories through energy-harvesting wireless nodes is possible over short and medium distances with the protocols and technology. However, for larger distances, a higher degree of energy usage reduction is needed, which must be addressed with other techniques and strategies. It is important to note that bio-inspired algorithms have multiple parameters that need to be tuned, and the quality of the obtained solution varies with the selected parameters. The results must be considered carefully, and they may change significantly according to the specific topology design and MAC protocols.

Experimental Setup and Parameters

This section provides a detailed description of the experimental framework for the real testbed implemented to test the proposed biologically related algorithms in emerging radio environments at 28 GHz. The purpose is to detail the experimental parameters used in the case studies (*e.g.*, ACO for topology control), providing transparency and enabling replication. Description: This table lists key parameters for the testbed implementation at 28 GHz, such as the network size, frequency band, and algorithm settings. It supports the chapter's discussion of real-world testing in industrial settings.

Table **3** describes the experimental parameters for bio-inspired algorithms in different case studies, detailing network settings and performance metrics for topology control and energy harvesting [8]. Various layers and the realization platform will be described first, from the first layer, which deals with the physical interface between the concrete radio frequency (RF) and digital (BB) worlds of typical agile communication devices, to the topmost layer that must verify the obtained results.

Table 3. Experimental parameters for bio-inspired algorithms.

Parameter	Case Study 1: ACO for Topology Control	Case Study 2: Energy-Harvesting Nodes	Description
Network Size	20 nodes	15 nodes	Number of wireless nodes in the testbed.
Frequency Band	28 GHz	28 GHz	Operating frequency for mm Wave testing.

(Table 3) cont.....

Parameter	Case Study 1: ACO for Topology Control	Case Study 2: Energy-Harvesting Nodes	Description
Algorithm Iterations	100	80	Number of iterations for optimization.
Energy Constraint	50 mW max per node	30 mW max per node	Maximum power consumption per node.
Performance Metric	Topology stability (95%)	Energy savings (20%)	Key outcome measured in the experiment.
Simulation Tool	MATLAB	NS-3	Software used for emulation and analysis.

Each hardware setting is provided to control a specific state of the emulator, enabling it to properly handle the testing procedure for each algorithm. These parameter settings are not discussed here due to scope and space limitations. First of all, the hardware underpinnings, having recalibrated the involvement of swarm intelligence to provide ad-hoc solutions for this specific problem, have to be described in a very simple way, distracting attention from the technique mainly adopted to solve the problem with the actual imitation of the heterogeneity of the Industry 5.0 system at hand through deterministic points and attributes of metaheuristic algorithms. Only the most important variations on standard hardware for wireless communication must be highlighted, emphasizing the high alignment with the representation of mechatronic systems in the Industry 5.0 perspective and the abstract representation of the problems to be solved in this electromagnetic environment that asks for robustness, not only in performance but also in physical understanding and finding solutions.

Performance Evaluation and Comparison

The proposed approach extends the use of bio-inspired algorithms in wireless communication and provides an experimental framework for designing and implementing these algorithms. Bio-inspired algorithms have intrinsic features such as superior scalability, robustness, and generalization, making them widely used to solve wireless communication-related problems. They have been applied to optimize various wireless networks at different levels of abstraction. Some bio-inspired algorithms applied in current wireless networks at seven network abstraction levels are summarized. Future research directions include building integrated activities based on open-source testing platforms with bio-inspired algorithm-based wireless network optimization, implementing engineering design, functional testing, and performance evaluations. This is strategically important, as an open-source testing platform designed to support bio-inspired algorithm navigation in current wireless networks must be distinctive. It should capture enterprise-driven innovations while also preparing for future wireless communication systems that align with evolving industrial standards and practices.

CONCLUSION AND FUTURE DIRECTIONS

Summary of Findings

The study focuses on the technical merit and potential of Biological Inheritance (BIA) in wireless communication. It aims to compare BIA's performance in key wireless communication ingredients, revealing that BIA achieves the same performance as a parallel counterpart scheme for discrete signal data transmission, but also achieves point-to-point signal data communication. BIA's quick operability and the importance of the annealing process in ensuring correct behavior in complex future applications are highlighted. The quantum-inspired BIA used in the study also sustains the transmission propagation of coupled signals. The study also provides additional technical insights about data flow and hardware complexity reduction. Despite being limited to the number of naturally growing cells, the promising service provided by nature led to the realization of a bio-inborn alternative, maintaining the predictability gained in prior investigations through the BIA behavior of the dynamic process.

Potential Applications in Industry 5.0

The implementation of the Industry 5.0 paradigm is based on cyber-physical systems, cognitive data collection, processing, and feedback to the real world. Such systems are also characterized by efficient data transmission between the constituent elements nearby. Wireless solutions, when feasible, are advantageous in industrial environments. However, stringent requirements make wireless communications a challenging research area. Distributed solutions with low implementation complexity, the ability to auto-configure, and support diverse traffic loads and functional reliability, ultra-reliable low-latency communications, and intra-border scalability are essential. Protocols with the ability to adapt to bio-inspired ideas may constitute efficient solutions for the problems associated with industrial wireless systems.

REFERENCES

[1] M. Noor-A-Rahim, F. Firyaguna, and J. John, "Toward Industry 5.0: Intelligent Reflecting Surface in Smart Manufacturing", *Communications,* 2022. [http://dx.doi.org/10.1109/MCOM.001.2200016]

[2] S. Zeb, A. Mahmood, S.A. Khowaja, and K. Dev, "Industry 5.0 is coming: A survey on intelligent NextG wireless networks as technological enablers", *arXiv preprint arXiv,* 2022.

[3] A.T. Khan, S. Li, and X. Cao, "Control framework for cooperative robots in smart home using bio-

inspired neural network", *Measurement,* 2021.
[http://dx.doi.org/10.1016/j.measurement.2020.108253]

[4] P. Aghelpour, H. Bahrami-Pichaghchi, and O. Kisi, "Comparison of three different bio-inspired algorithms to improve ability of neuro-fuzzy approach in prediction of agricultural drought, based on three different indexes", *Computers and Electronics,* 2020.
[http://dx.doi.org/10.1016/j.compag.2020.105279]

[5] A. Verma, P. Bhattacharya, N. Madhani, and C. Trivedi, "Blockchain for Industry 5.0: Vision, opportunities, key enablers, and future directions", *IEEE,* 2022.
[http://dx.doi.org/10.1109/ACCESS.2022.3186892]

[6] B. Chander, S. Pal, D. De, and R. Buyya, "Artificial intelligence-based Internet of Things for Industry 5.0.", *Artificial Intelligence-Based Internet of Things.,* Springer, 2022.
[http://dx.doi.org/10.1007/978-3-030-87059-1_1]

[7] T. Sibalija, and J.P. Davim, "Soft computing in smart manufacturing: Solutions toward Industry 5.0", *Smart Manufacturing,* 2021.
[http://dx.doi.org/10.1515/9783110693225]

[8] R. Tallat, A. Hawbani, and X. Wang, "Navigating Industry 5.0: A survey of key enabling technologies, trends, challenges, and opportunities", *Communications,* 2023.

[9] A.A. Qidan, T. El-Gorashi, and J.M.H. Elmirghani, "Blind interference alignment in 6G optical wireless communications", *arXiv preprint,* 2021.

[10] A. Adnan-Qidan, and M. Morales-Céspedes, "Load balancing in hybrid VLC and RF networks based on blind interference alignment", *IEEE Access,* 2020.
[http://dx.doi.org/10.1109/ACCESS.2020.2987545]

[11] N. Petroulakis, M.O. Mattsson, and P. Chatziadam, "NextGEM: Next-generation integrated sensing and analytical system for monitoring and assessing radiofrequency electromagnetic field exposure and health", *Environmental Studies,* 2023.
[http://dx.doi.org/10.3390/ijerph20126085]

[12] Y. Azzoug, and A. Boukra, "Bio-inspired VANET routing optimization: An overview: A taxonomy of notable VANET routing problems, overview, advancement state, and future perspective", *Artificial Intelligence Review,* 2021.

[13] T.H. Pham, and B. Raahemi, "Bio-inspired feature selection algorithms with their applications: A systematic literature review", *IEEE Access,* 2023.
[http://dx.doi.org/10.1109/ACCESS.2023.3272556]

CHAPTER 11

Artificial Intelligence and Robotic Process Automation in the Indian Banking Industry: Implementation Strategies, Applications, Benefits, and Sustainability

Sourav Mazumder[1,*] and **Somnath Chakraborty**[2]

[1] *Department of Management, Eminent College of Management and Technology, Moshpukur, Barberia, Barasat, Kolkata 700126, West Bengal, India*

[2] *Department of Management Studies, Brainware University, Barasat 700125, West Bengal, India*

Abstract: Recent developments in technology within the Indian banking sector, specifically the implementation of Artificial Intelligence (AI) and Robotic Process Automation (RPA), have significantly transformed banking operations and customer experience. This study examines the implementation strategies, applications, and benefits of AI and RPA in Indian banking by reviewing secondary data from government and private reports, publications, books, and journals. The findings indicate that AI is used for building knowledge graphs, recommending services, and detecting financial fraud, whereas RPA delivers AI insights in real time. Applications include customer service, risk management, fraud detection, and personalized financial advice. The benefits of integrating AI and RPA include operational cost reductions of 30-70%, improved accuracy, 24x7 operations, and enhanced customer experience. The challenges include data security, regulatory compliance, potential job shifting, and the requirement for staff training. The study concludes that the successful integration of AI and RPA requires a strategic approach that focuses on organizational readiness, stakeholder engagement, and ethical considerations. Future research should find the long-term effects, ethical implications, strategies for sustainable integration, and potential for promoting financial inclusion in India.

Keywords: Artificial intelligence, Indian banking industry, Machine learning techniques, Robotic process automation.

INTRODUCTION

The banking system forms the foundation of the economic and social development of a country. It is the most important pillar of the financial sector,

* **Corresponding author Sourav Mazumder:** Department of Management, Eminent College of Management and Technology, Moshpukur, Barberia, Barasat, Kolkata 700126, West Bengal, India; E-mail: sourav@ecmt.in

Pijush Dutta, Sudip Mondal, Korhan Cengiz and S. Balamurugan (Eds.)

which plays a pivotal role in economic development of a country [1]. It is also very important that the financial requirement of various sectors of the economy is fulfilled with a higher degree of commitment and responsibility. They play a crucial role in the mobilization of deposits and supply of credit to the industry, and perform a similar role to the heart of the human body. The primary component of a nation's economic strength is the financial system's ability to operate efficiently, which is the outcome of a stable and solvent banking system. The Indian banking industry has undergone significant technological development in recent years, with the adoption of digital technologies that transform the way banks function and serve their customers [2]. One of the key areas of technological development is mobile banking, with banks launching mobile apps that allow customers access to a variety of banking services on their smartphones. This has improved banking's accessibility and convenience, especially for clients in rural areas, who may not have easy access to physical bank branches.

Another important development in the Indian banking industry is the adoption of artificial intelligence and machine-learning technologies. These technologies are being used to improve fraud detection and prevention, as well as to enhance the level of customer service by providing personalized services and recommendations [3].

Regular tasks in the banking sector, such as handling customer data, detecting fraud, and processing transactions, can be automated with AI. However, repetitive operations like data entry, report generation, and onboard customer analysis can be automated with RPA. Banks may lower operating expenses, increase productivity, and improve customer happiness by utilizing AI and RPA [4]. One of the major advantages of AI in the banking industry is its ability to analyze large amounts of data quickly and accurately. Banks can use AI to identify patterns and trends in customer behavior, which can help them offer personalized services and improve their marketing strategies. Additionally, AI can be used to identify criminal behavior like identity theft and money laundering, which can help banks prevent financial losses and protect their customers' interests. RPA can also help banks automate their back-office operations, such as account opening, processing loans, and claims management. By automating these operations, banks can reduce the turnaround time and improve the precision of their processes. RPA can also be used to automate customer interactions, such as chatbots and virtual assistants, which can assist banks in offering their clients round-the-clock assistance. However, there are several obstacles to overcome when implementing AI and RPA in the banking sector. Banks must ensure that the data used for AI and RPA is accurate, secure, and compliant with the regulatory requirements [5, 6]. Banks also need to invest in the appropriate infrastructure and talent to support AI and RPA initiatives.

In conclusion, AI and RPA have the potential to completely change the Indian banking industry by increasing productivity, reducing costs, and improving the overall customer experience. Banks that embrace these technologies can gain competitive advantages and provide better services to their customers.

Objectives

The goals of the research are:

- To identify the need for the implementation of AI and RPA in the Indian banking industry.
- To study the benefits of adopting AI and RPA in the Indian banking industry, and
- To learn about the implementation strategies of AI and RPA in various Indian Banks.

METHODOLOGY

The foundation of this study is a thorough analysis of secondary data, which was gathered from a variety of public and private reports, websites, books, newspapers, journals, and magazines.

Information Technology in the Banking Industry

Around the world, information technology (IT) has altered how organizations operate. Offering cutting-edge goods and services through technology advancements has benefited the Indian banking industry as well [7]. Through the introduction of innovative delivery channels to consumers, such as ATMs and shared payment platforms, online banking, the deployment of core banking solutions, mobile banking, *etc*., information technology has greatly benefited the banking industry.

The main advantages of technological adoptions in the banking industry are:

- Reduction of operational cost
- Encouraging customers to transact efficiently

The RBI has increased its emphasis on integrating modern technologies into banks' daily operations over time. As stated in the IT Vision Document, 2011–17, the Reserve Bank of India lays out a comprehensive plan for implementing important IT applications in banking, with a focus on ensuring that banking services are delivered flawlessly through the effective use of Business Continuity Management (BCM), Information Security Policy, and Business Process Re-engineering (BPR) [8]. The Indian banking industry has always been committed to improving the efficiency of its operations, and its progress has been observed as steady and incremental. Exploring advanced technologies across the banking and financial sectors has gained significant importance in recent times. The banking industry in India has entered into a transformative era with the introduction of cutting-edge technologies like applications of Artificial Intelligence (AI) and Robotic Process Automation (RPA). Improved customer services resulting from system upgrades by the implementation of AI and RPA are rapidly gaining the attention of the banking sector. Banks are now increasingly interconnecting their software system not just among branches within a city but also to different geographical locations with a high-speed network [9]. With the use of technology, banks can provide valuable data about the dispersion of innovative advances. With the efficient usage of technology, Indian banking has made some excellent progress and is seen as just an instrument of socio-economic changes.

Artificial Intelligence

The multifaceted field of computer technology known as artificial intelligence (AI) is concerned with creating intelligent machines that can do tasks that call for human intelligence. The simulation of human intelligence techniques using technology, especially computer systems, is known as artificial intelligence. On the other hand, AI includes professional systems, speech recognition, language processing, and system vision. Artificial intelligence uses an extensive array of technology, together with Data Science, Internet of Things (IoT) [10], and Natural Language Processing (NLP) [11]. All those technologies strengthen the operations of the economic institutions. Most banks leverage AI to beautify their customer procedures because the generation has already proven its capability in different industries. Taking those elements into account, banks want to put money into this banking generation's operations. Fig. (**1**) represents the integration of AI and RPA in the Indian Banking sector.

Robotic Process Automation (RPA)

A computer software called robotic process automation (RPA) makes it simple to build, deploy, and operate robots that mimic human actions while interacting with virtual structures and instructions [12]. The quantity of unstructured records that the banks must process is increasing exponentially with the rise of the virtual economy. These are not the most effective banking transaction records; however, additionally different behavioral records that might permit banks to enhance and innovate the consumer service. With the aggregate of numerous technologies that allow cognitive and robot method automation, bankers can now understand consumer movement and make a judgment at a rapid pace, scale, and quality. It additionally reduces mistakes and permits financial institution personnel to deal with greater complicated queries and offer higher customer service.

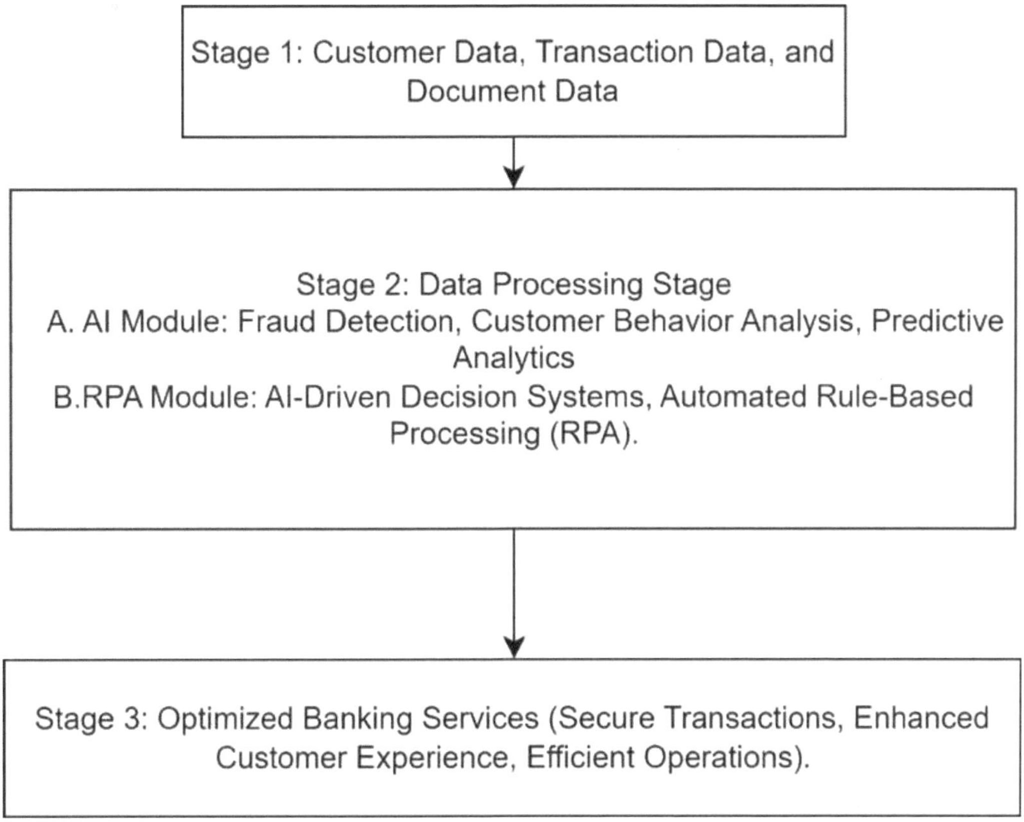

Fig. (1). AI and RPA integration in the indian banking industry.

Robotic tool automation is a software program that makes it simple to construct, control, and manipulate robots that mimic humans' movements, interacting with virtual structures and instructions. Robotic manner automation, additionally called software robotics, makes use of automation technology to perform back-office duties of human workers, which include extracting data, filling in forms, moving files, *etc*. Robotic Process Automation (RPA) can allow banks to lessen guide efforts, provide higher compliance, reduce risks, and improve the general customer experience [13]. Additionally, what makes automation maximally appropriate for banks and economic establishments is that there are no extra infrastructure necessities coupled with its low-cost approach. Not only does this assist in decreasing the operational costs, but it also saves the time taken to carry out the task. A comparative study between RPA and AI is shown in Table **1**. RPA inside the banking organization serves to deal with the issues faced by the banking sector and help them improve their overall performance with the resource in the following areas:

Table 1. Comparison of AI and RPA in the Indian Banking Industry

Aspect	Artificial Intelligence (AI)	Robotic Process Automation (RPA)
Definition	AI involves machine learning, NLP, and cognitive computing.	RPA automates repetitive, rule-based tasks without AI.
Application Scope	Advanced analytics, fraud detection, and customer support.	Data entry, report generation, transaction processing.
Complexity	High (requires advanced algorithms and data training).	Low to moderate (rule-based automation).
Human Intervention	Minimal, focuses on decision-making and predictive tasks.	Requires human setup for rule definition.
Scalability	High, with the ability to learn and adapt over time.	Moderate, limited to predefined tasks.
Cost of Implementation	High (requires skilled personnel and computational resources).	Moderate (relatively quick setup).
Sustainability	Adaptive, can be optimized for energy efficiency.	Fixed, may require frequent updates.
Risk of Errors	Can make mistakes without proper training.	Low (follows strict rules), but prone to failure if rules change.
Example Use Case	Fraud detection using ML algorithms.	Automating customer KYC verification.

Customer onboarding: The Customer onboarding process in banks is an extremely time-consuming procedure; in most cases, because of numerous files requiring verification. RPA could make the technique a great deal simpler by taking pictures of the facts from KYC (Know Your Customer) files by use of the Optical Character Recognition technique (OCR) [14]. The information provided in the form can be verified by these facts.

Know your customer (KYC) and Anti-Money Laundering (AML): In actuality, AML and KYC are both incredibly data-intensive procedures, which makes RPA the most suitable for them. When compared to traditional banking solutions, RPA adoption proved crucial in terms of saving time and money, whether it was through the identification of questionable transactions or the conversion of manual operations to automated processes that direct methods [15].

Account opening: Account opening procedures are made much faster, more error-free, and simpler with RPA. By automating the process, mistakes between new account opening requests and core banking rules and regulations can be eliminated, strengthening the process of removing risks from the entire banking system [16].

Customer service: The enormous volume of regular customer inquiries in banks makes it challenging for employees to reply to them quickly. Banks may greatly reduce response time by using RPA solutions to optimize such laborious and ineffective rule-based processes so they can effectively respond to inquiries in real-time.

Loan processing and mortgage lending: For any financial institution, lending is the area that generates the most income and profits. The advancement process is highly regulated and time-consuming, which makes it appropriate for RPA. RPA facilitates the automation of several crucial lending process operations, such as loan commencement, application processing, borrower financial statement analysis, and risk management.

Credit card processing: Credit card application forms usually require several man-hours to verify the data provided by the applicants in the application forms before approval. Moreover, RPA can assist the banks in making prompt choices for approval or disapproval of the application with a system-based approach upon verifying the credit scores of each applicant [17]. RPA offers the banking and financial services sector several advantages. Among the well-known ones are:

Scalability: The most important feature of RPA is that highly scalable robots allow financial institutions to handle large volumes even in prime business hours by adding more machines, and help in resolving any issue much more quickly. Additionally, the implementation of RPA enables banks to focus on creative ways to expand their business by relieving workers of monotonous and ineffective tasks.

Cost-effectiveness: With the automation drive in the banking industry, banks and financial institutions can save a substantial amount of man-hours and thereby can reduce around 25–50% by saving significant time and cost.

Increased operational efficiency: Banks and other financial organizations can increase the speed, productivity, and efficiency of their operations by implementing robotics.

Risk and compliance reporting: In banking, RPA can maintain a high level of compliance while lowering company risk by creating complete audit trails for every process.

Available 24x7: Since robots work around the clock to accomplish given tasks, banks employing RPA are also aiming to reduce human error while simultaneously achieving a higher degree of accuracy at a lower cost, reinforcing the constant availability.

Usage of software to curb fraudulent activities in banks and financial institutions: Recently, instances of banking fraud have been happening regularly in India. However, frauds in banking in India have been considered a cost of business. But post liberalization, the frequency and nature of banking frauds have increased manifold, resulting in a rising alarm for the regulators and management [18]. A survey report published in the Times of India dated 17 January 2022 reveals that 78% of bankers see fraudulent activities in the banking industry rising in the next 2 years. The scope of fraud has been triggered by the reduction of human intervention [19]. This is the result of remote working and an increase in customers using online banking channels for transactions. According to the report published by Deloitte on the Indian Banking Fraud Survey, the highest concern for bankers is loan fraud (24%) followed by internet fraud and mobile banking (14%). It was further revealed that limited monitoring of loans and advances (38%), economic slowdown (24%), and inadequate due diligence (21%) are the top three factors leading to higher instances of fraud. The survey showed that the number of frauds over the last two years appears to have increased [20]. However, bankers can detect fraud largely at the time of audit and data reconciliation, followed by measures through internal automated data analysis and high-end software. Regulation of AI in financial technology has been implemented in India so far in a sector-wise and phased manner, particularly in the areas of payments, lending, and insurance. The regulation of AI must be framed in such a manner to cover a broad-based area and should be cross-sectional and with transparency in line with the government policy [21, 22].

LITERATURE REVIEW

Artificial Intelligence (AI) and Robotic Process Automation (RPA) have revolutionized the Indian banking industry, offering significant improvements in efficiency, customer service, and risk management. AI technologies are changing various banking services, including customer service, fraud detection, and personalized financial advice [12]. RPA, a subfield of AI, is used to automate repetitive processes, minimizing workload and time for human agents while improving accuracy, quality, and speed [18]. These technologies address challenges in the Indian banking sector by enhancing operations and efficiency [11]. Interestingly, although AI and RPA offer numerous benefits, there are potential risks and challenges. The adoption of AI-based systems, such as RPA, can lead to operational risks, particularly if models are immature or not well-trained, potentially decreasing productivity and increasing errors from unsupported or wrong decisions [17]. Additionally, the implementation of these technologies requires strategic planning, stakeholder engagement, and organizational readiness [17]. To sum up, RPA and AI are essential to the digital transformation of the Indian banking industry. They are used in some fields, including back-office operations, risk management, fraud detection, and customer service [4, 16]. Although challenges exist, including potential job displacement and cybersecurity risks [1], the overall impact of these technologies is positive. They enable banks to convert challenges into opportunities, streamline operations, and provide personalized services [1, 8]. The importance of research on Artificial Intelligence and robotic process automation in the Indian banking industry cannot be overstated. Rapid advancements in AI and RPA technology have the potential to revolutionize the banking sector, enabling more efficient and streamlined processes, as well as improving customer experiences. Through this research, we can better understand the implementation strategies, applications, and benefits of these technologies in the Indian banking context. By identifying the best practices and potential challenges, research can help guide the successful integration of AI and RPA, ultimately leading to increased productivity, reduced operational costs, and enhanced competitiveness for banks in India.

The research conducted a primary survey among the 112 customers of various banks and concluded that Artificial Intelligence (AI) has brought revolutionary changes in the field of banking, as per the feedback received by the respondents, and is found to be valuable and user-friendly [6]. As online banking fraud is a major concern nowadays, fraudsters can easily hack into the banking system. 81.4% of respondents believe that the use of artificial intelligence can protect and strengthen the security system in banks. several challenges faced by Indian banks in implementing AI have been discussed. The study concludes that artificial intelligence offers many benefits to the banking sector [12]. It has a big role in transforming business processes and providing customer-friendly services in the Indian banking sector. It is also being largely used by banks to meet regulatory compliance, fraud detection, measure the creditworthiness of individuals, and implement mechanisms against cybercrimes. The study was carried out to confirm the advantages of integrating blockchain technology and artificial intelligence, particularly in the banking industry, to lessen the workload for human workers and to comprehend the impact of these technologies [10]. The study was conducted to analyze the negative impact of Artificial Intelligence used in the Indian banking industry and summarizes the key issues as follows [13]:

- **High cost:** The installation and maintenance of artificial intelligence uses high-end machines and sophisticate software, and hence requires high costs as they require regular updates.
- **Distribution of power:** Artificial intelligence can provide power to the few individuals who have the responsibility to control it. Hence, implementing AI does not provide a foolproof system and carries the risk in the way that takes control away from humans to machines.
- **Unemployment:** In the broader sense, a wide-reaching unemployment can be a result of **the** replacement of the human workforce with machines, which cannot be ignored in a country like India.
- **Irrational behavior in ecosystems:** Artificial intelligence's inability to make decisions on its own is a disadvantage. AI may never be able to make judgments like humans because humans are able to weigh the circumstances and use judgment.

Findings: Indian banks are adopting AI and Robotic Process Automation (RPA) in various ways:

HDFC Bank: - Leveraging AI and ML for deeper customer insights and personalization - Using AI for data enhancement.

State Bank of India: - Employing AI and ML for generating quality Current Account leads.

Kotak Bank: - Building ML operations frameworks for faster deployment and model governance, enhancing cloud data platforms and data consumption tools.

ICICI Bank: - Utilizing AI-powered chatbots for customer support - Implementing AI for fraud detection through Enterprise Fraud Risk Management (EFRM) solution - Exploring Generative AI for internal tools to assist employees in serving customers better.

Axis Bank: - Deploying an AI-based chatbot named 'Adi' for branch employees - Exploring Generative AI for real-time call center assistance - Implementing a personalization engine. It has created nearly 3,500 robotic automated processes to accelerate delivery across businesses. In Retail Banking operations, they have 3,500+ bots running approximately 1,500 automated processes.

IndusInd Bank: - Introducing AI-driven ChatBot for natural conversation banking operations.

PNB (Punjab National Bank): - Incorporating AI and ML in various processes, including risk reduction, model development and implementation, optimization of cash retention in ATMs, transaction-based nudges for retail products, lead generation for sales, and customer retention.

Implementation Strategies

Key implementation strategies include the use of AI for building knowledge graphs, recommending products and services, and detecting financial fraud and money laundering, whereas RPA is utilized to implement and deliver these AI-generated insights in real-time scenarios [8].

Applications

The major areas for AI/ML applications in Indian banking include crime in the financial sector and compliance, customer service, and relationship management, credit risk assessment, and customer service [19]. For instance, chatbots are employed for customer service, forecasting analysis for credit scoring, and algorithmic trading for investment [12]. Interestingly, although RPA is known for its efficiency in handling repetitive tasks and large volumes of data [18], it faces limitations in processing data that are unstructured and involve complex decision-making processes [22]. This highlights the complementary nature of AI and RPA in banking applications, where AI can provide intelligence and RPA can implement processes rapidly [8]. In conclusion, AI and RPA are transforming the Indian banking sector by enhancing operational efficiency, improving decision-making, and providing personalized customer experiences. Leading Indian banks, such as ICICI, HDFC, and SBI, have already adopted these technologies, demonstrating their potential to revolutionize the financial ecosystem [4]. However, it is crucial to consider the ethical implications, regulatory framework, and potential societal impacts of AI and RPA implementation in the Indian banking industry.

Benefits

AI and RPA implementation in Indian banks has led to substantial cost reductions, with operational expenses decreasing by 30-70% [21]. This cost-saving is achieved through the automation of repetitive tasks, freeing up human resource activities for complicated value-added activities [14]. Leading Indian banks, such as ICICI Bank, HDFC Bank, and Axis Bank, have already implemented RPA, demonstrating its growing importance in the sector [21]. The integration of AI and RPA in banking processes has resulted in improved accuracy, 24x7 operational capabilities, and enhanced customer experience [21]. These technologies enable banks to offer innovative services, personalize product recommendations, and streamline operations in areas such as customer service, risk management, compliance, and back-office functions [8, 16]. Additionally, AI and RPA have proven effective in detecting financial fraud and money laundering in real time [8]. However, implementing AI and RPA in banking is challenging. Banks should consider data security, regulatory compliance, and the need for employee upskilling [14]. There are also concerns about potential job displacement and its long-term effects on the workforce [1, 14]. To address these challenges, banks should adopt a strategic approach to implementation that focuses on organizational readiness, stakeholder engagement, and ethical considerations [14, 16]. The Indian banking sector stands to gain a great deal from the combination of AI and RPA in terms of increased customer satisfaction, cost savings, and operational efficiency. As these technologies continue to evolve, banks that successfully implement them are better positioned to drive innovation and maintain an advantageous position in the digital age.

CONCLUSION

The implementation of Artificial Intelligence (AI) and Robotic Process Automation (RPA) in the Indian banking sector has demonstrated significant potential for transforming operations, enhancing customer experience, and improving overall efficiency. This study highlights several key findings:

- Implementation strategies for AI and RPA in Indian banks focus on areas such as knowledge graph construction, product recommendations, fraud detection, and real-time service delivery.
- Applications of these technologies span various banking functions, including customer service, risk management, compliance, and personalized financial advice. Chatbots, predictive analytics, and algorithmic trading are some of the most notable applications.
- The benefits of AI and RPA implementation are substantial, with operational cost reductions ranging from 30 to 70%.

These technologies have also improved accuracy, enabled 24x7 operations, and enhanced the customer experience. However, the adoption of AI and RPA remains challenging. Banks must address concerns regarding data security, regulatory compliance, potential job displacement, and the need for employee upskilling. To maximize benefits while mitigating risks, a strategic approach to implementation is crucial, focusing on organizational readiness, stakeholder engagement, and ethical considerations. As the Indian banking industry continues to evolve, the roles of AI and RPA are likely to expand. Future research should focus on the long-term impacts, ethical implications, and strategies for the sustainable integration of these technologies. Additionally, exploring the potential of AI and RPA in promoting financial inclusion and addressing unique challenges in India could provide valuable insights for policymakers and industry leaders.

REFERENCES

[1] N. A. Adewumi, E. Ewim, J. Sam-Bulya, and B. Ajani, *Advancing business performance through data-driven process automation: A case study of digital transformation in the banking sector,* 2024. [http://dx.doi.org/10.53430/ijmru.2024.8.2.0049]

[2] R. Ahmed, "Artificial Intelligence (AI) in Financial Sectors: Blessings or Threats?" *", *J. Bus. Manag.,* vol. 23, no. 3, pp. 20-25, 2021. [http://dx.doi.org/10.9790/487X-2303012025]

[3] A. Alzaidi, "Impact of Artificial Intelligence on Performance of Banking Industry in Middle East," *IJCSNS Int. J. Comput. Sci. Netw. Secur.*, vol. 18, no. 10, p. 140, 2018. Available from: http://paper.ijcsns.org/07_book/201810/20181021.pdf

[4] R. Dabbeeru and D. N. Rao, "Fintech Applications in Banking and Financial Services Industry in India," *SSRN Electron. J.*, 2021. [http://dx.doi.org/10.2139/ssrn.3881967]

[5] 5. A. Geetha, "A Study On Artificial Intelligence (AI) In Banking and Financial Services," *Int. J. Creat. Res. Thoughts (IJCRT)*, vol. 9, no. 9, pp. 110–114, 2021. Available from: https://www.ijcrt.org/papers/IJCRTG020019.pdf

[6] N. Kaur, S.L. Sahdev, M. Sharma, and L. Siddiqui, "The Influence of Artificial Intelligence on the Banking Industry & How AI is Changing the Face of Modern Day Banks", *Int. J. Manag.,* vol. 11, no. 6, pp. 577-585, 2020. [http://dx.doi.org/10.34218/IJM.11.6.2020.049]

[7] F. Königstorfer, and S. Thalmann, "Applications of Artificial Intelligence in commercial banks – A research agenda for behavioral finance", *J. Behav. Exp. Finance,* vol. 27, p. 100352, 2020. [http://dx.doi.org/10.1016/j.jbef.2020.100352]

[8] S. Kumar, S. Khanna, N. Ghosh, and S.O.D. Kumar, "Importance of Artificial Intelligence (AI) and Robotic Process Automation (RPA) in the Banking Industry: A Study from an Indian Perspective", In: *Confluence of Artificial Intelligence and Robotic Process Automation*, 2023, pp. 231-266. [http://dx.doi.org/10.1007/978-981-19-8296-5_10]

[9] K. Lakshminarayanan and R. Thennarasan, "Technological advancement in Banking Sector - How it brings effects to the People," *IJRAR1944555 Int. J. Res. Anal. Rev.*, vol. 5, no. 4, 2018. Available from: https://www.ijrar.org/papers/IJRAR1944555.pdf

[10] K. Meghani, "Use of Artificial Intelligence and Block chain in Banking Sector: A Study Of Scheduled Commercial Banks In India", *J. Appl. Res.,* vol. 10, no. 8, pp. 26-29, 2020. [http://dx.doi.org/10.13140/RG.2.2.28112.12801]

[11] D.V. Mouneswari, "A Contemporary Artificial Intelligence (Ai)", *Developments And Challenges In Indian Banking Sector,* pp. 71-80, 2024. [http://dx.doi.org/10.58532/V3BHMA4P1CH7]

[12] M. Shakyawar, and K. Shakya, "Using Artificial Intelligence to Improve Banking Services in India: A Review and Prospects for the Future", *Int. J. Res. Appl. Sci. Eng. Technol.,* vol. 12, no. 4, pp. 728-738, 2024. [http://dx.doi.org/10.22214/ijraset.2024.59549]

[13] V. Padmanabhan, "An Impact of Artificial Intelligence in Indian Banking Industries," *Int. Res. J. Educ. Technol.*, vol. 1, no. 4, pp. 39–45, 2021. Available from: https://www.irjweb.com/VII6IRJEdT-5.pdf

[14] L. Patrício, L. Varela, and Z. Silveira, "Integration of Artificial Intelligence and Robotic Process Automation: Literature Review and Proposal for a Sustainable Model", *Appl. Sci. (Basel),* vol. 14, no. 21, p. 9648, 2024. [http://dx.doi.org/10.3390/app14219648]

[15] P.R. Thumar, and P.R. Vaghasiya, "The Impact of Artificial Intelligence on the Financial Sector", *Int. J. Res. Appl. Sci. Eng. Technol.,* vol. 12, no. 5, pp. 4931-4933, 2024. [http://dx.doi.org/10.22214/ijraset.2024.62751]

[16] K. G. Rajput, S. Harsha C, M. Lingam, D. Duraisamy, C. Bhargavi, M. Sravanthi, and E. M. S., "Role of Intelligent Process Automation in the Banking and Financial Services Industry," *Adv. Comput. Intell. Robot. Book Ser.*, pp. 513–532, 2024. [http://dx.doi.org/10.4018/979-8-3693-5380-6.ch020]

[17] M. Romao, J. Costa, and C.J. Costa, "Robotic Process Automation: A Case Study in the Banking Industry", *14th Iberian Conference on Information Systems and Technologies (CISTI),* pp. 1-6, 2019. [http://dx.doi.org/10.23919/CISTI.2019.8760733]

[18] S. Sharma, A. Kataria, and J.K. Sandhu, "Applications, Tools and Technologies of Robotic Process Automation in Various Industries", *IEEE Xplore,* no. Mar, pp. 1067-1072, 2022. [http://dx.doi.org/10.1109/DASA54658.2022.9765027]

[19] A.K. Tiwari, and D. Saxena, "Application of Artificial Intelligence in Indian Banks", *IEEE Xplore,* no. Dec, pp. 545-548, 2021. [http://dx.doi.org/10.1109/ComPE53109.2021.9751981]

[20] C. Vijai, "Artificial Intelligence In Indian Banking Sector: Challenges And Opportunities", *Int. J. Adv. Res. (Indore),* vol. 7, no. 4, pp. 1581-1587, 2019. [http://dx.doi.org/10.21474/IJAR01/8987]

[21] C. Vijai, S.M. Suriyalakshmi, and M. Elayaraja, "The Future of Robotic Process Automation (RPA) in the Banking Sector for Better Customer Experience", *Shanlax International Journal of Commerce,* vol. 8, no. 2, pp. 61-65, 2020. [http://dx.doi.org/10.34293/commerce.v8i2.1709]

[22] X. Zhan, Z. Ling, Z. Xu, L. Guo, and S. Zhuang, "Driving Efficiency and Risk Management in Finance through AI and RPA", *Preprints,* 2024.

CHAPTER 12

Artificial Neural Network-Based Modelling of Hexagonal Slotted Microstrip Patch Antenna Operating at 4.5 GHz for 5G Communication in Industry 5.0

Kaushik Saha[1], **Arijit Mitra**[1] and **Sudip Mandal**[1,*]

[1] *Department of Electronics and Communication Engineering, Jalpaiguri Government Engineering College, Jalpaiguri, India*

Abstract: In a very fast communication world, the technology is inclining towards the 5G & 6G communication techniques. Among the available frequency bands for 5G, the n79 band (4.5 GHz) is very popular. It can be applied for many purposes like mobile communication, radios, *etc*. Even this band is also tested and deployed for 4G communication. A microstrip patch antenna is very popular for high-speed communication due to compact size, light weight, and ease of application. In this research work, we used Rogers 92 mL substrate, a copper ground and a copper patch with a hexagonal slot utilizing the inset feeding technique with the help of Computer Simulation Technology (CST) Studio Suite 2024. After adjusting the radius of the hexagonal slot and after shifting its centre to the exact location, satisfactory results have been achieved. For the best result, S_{11} falls up to -61.33dB at the exact 4.5GHz frequency and the corresponding bandwidth is 1.2919 GHz, which is suitable for 5G communication in the n79 band. Additionally, a mathematical model for the proposed patch antenna is developed using Artificial Neural Network models to predict antenna parameters like S_{11}, bandwidth, and resonant frequency based on the radius of the hexagonal slot and the position of the centre of the slot. Predicted results show satisfactory accuracy in comparison with the CST Studio 2024 values.

Keywords: Artificial Neural Network (ANN), Industry 5.0, Microstrip patch antenna, Modelling, 5G communication.

INTRODUCTION

Following the development of 4G communication, the fifth generation, *i.e.*, 5G, becomes more efficient in IoT technology, mobile communication, remote surgery, autonomous driving, and other applications. Therefore, industries require

* **Corresponding author Sudip Mandal:** Department of Electronics and Communication Engineering, Jalpaiguri Government Engineering College, Jalpaiguri, India; E-mail: sudip.mandal007@gmail.com

Pijush Dutta, Sudip Mondal, Korhan Cengiz and S. Balamurugan (Eds.)

small, portable, cost-efficient, and moderately priced antennas with good speed and communication capabilities. There are so many types of antennas, like parabolic antennas, horn antennas, Yagi-Uda antennas, *etc.*, among those, Microstrip Patch Antenna (MPA) [1] is preferable for being portable, durable, reliable, cost-efficient, and light-weight. An MPA is made up of a dielectric substrate element between the patch and the ground. Generally, the patch and the ground are made up of Gold or Copper with different shapes and sizes for better efficiency [2]. The patch is connected to the transmission line by the inset feeding technique. In our research for achieving 4.5 GHz frequency in the CST Studio Suite 2024, we selected Rogers 92 mL dielectric substrate, with Copper as the patch and the ground. To enhance the bandwidth, resonant frequency, and gain, we designed the patch with a hexagonal slot. After varying several parameters of the antenna, we observed that changing the radius of the hexagonal slot and the position along the transmission line axis gave the desired results. After designing the patch antenna, Surface fitting technique is applied through MATLAB software to predict the result with CTS values. After adjusting the layers and the nodes in the Artificial Neural Network, we observed the best output result compared with our designed antenna result in CST. Many authors have attempted to design a process of MPA process at this frequency band. Geetharaman *et al.* [3] have proposed A-shaped antenna of 40×50×1.6 mm^3 dimensions that operates at 4.5 GHz with -37.92 dB return loss, 4.14 dB gain, 1.024 VSWR, and 340 MHz bandwidth. Singh *et al.* [4] designed a symmetrical maze-shaped slots antenna of 15×15×1.6 mm^3dimensions, resonating at 4.5 GHz with -43 dB return loss and 500 MHz bandwidth. Maheshwari *et al.* [5] designed an antenna that resonates at 4.6 GHz with -25.93 dB return loss, 7.944 dB gain, and 0.8781 VSWR. Werfelli *et al.* [6] designed an antenna operating at 4.3 GHz with -30 dB return loss, 3.488 dB gain, 1.6-1.7 VSWR. On the other hand, Maurya *et al.* [7] proposed a hexagonal ring microstrip patch antenna with asymmetrical feed and DGS. Ahmed *et al.* [8] proposed a rectangular microstrip antenna design with a multi-slotted patch and partial grounding for 5G communication. Moreover, Maity *et al.* [9] also designed a circular patch antenna with DGS working at 3GHz.

The use of the 4.5 GHz frequency band in our research on hexagonal slotted MPA design is strategically important for 5G communications [9, 10] due to several key factors. This frequency falls within FR1 (Frequency Range 1) and the mid-band spectrum (1-6 GHz) of 5G, offering an optimal balance between coverage and capacity while providing good signal penetration through buildings and reasonable coverage areas. It is part of the standardized n79 band (4.4-5.0 GHz) for 5G New Radio (NR) and has been allocated for 5G deployment [11, 12] in many countries, particularly in Asia and parts of Europe. From an antenna design perspective, 4.5 GHz provides practical advantages as it allows for reasonable physical dimensions in microstrip patch antennas while maintaining good performance characteristics, making it suitable for mobile devices and advanced array implementations. This frequency represents an ideal choice for research as it enables the study of crucial 5G features [13] like beam forming, and the findings can apply to nearby frequencies within the mid-band spectrum, contributing valuable insights to the field of 5G antenna design and optimization.

METHODOLOGY

Fig. (**1**) represents a four-step process for optimizing antenna design using artificial intelligence. It starts with designing an antenna using CST software, followed by creating a database through systematic parameter variations. The third step involves developing and training an Artificial Neural Network (ANN) using this database. Finally, the trained ANN is used to predict antenna performance for new designs, with validation to ensure accuracy. This approach combines traditional electromagnetic simulation with machine learning to make antenna design more efficient and less time-consuming.

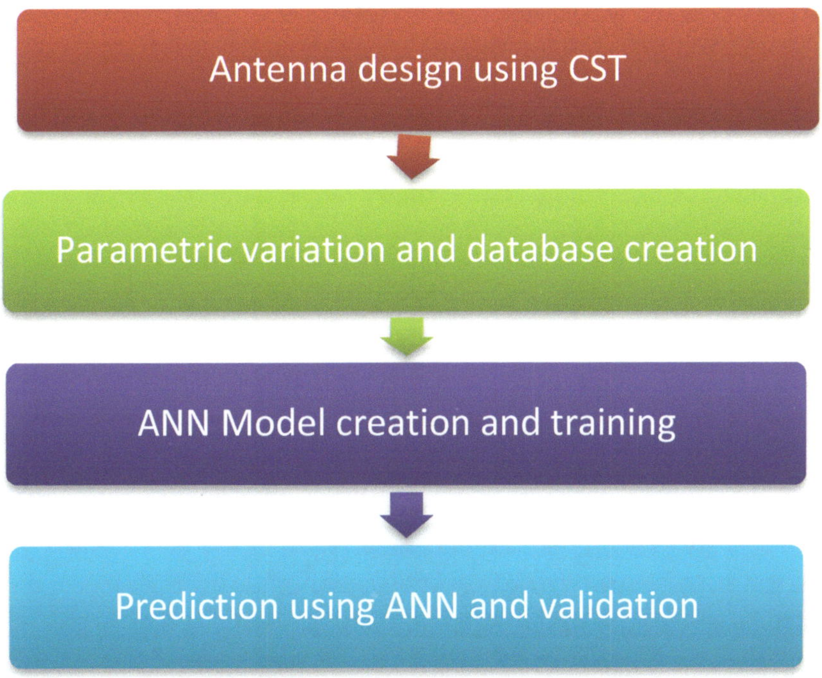

Fig. (1). Flowchart of our overall research.

Design of the Proposed Microstrip Patch

In the beginning, the width and the length of the antenna are calculated by the MPA calculator from the Pasternack [14] website. For making a Microstrip patch antenna, CST Studio Suite 2024 Simulation Software [15] is used. It can also be calculated by the given equations (1) and (2) below. Roger 92mL is used as a substrate whose dielectric constant is 5.13. Copper (annealed) is used for designing the patch and the ground shown in Fig. (2).

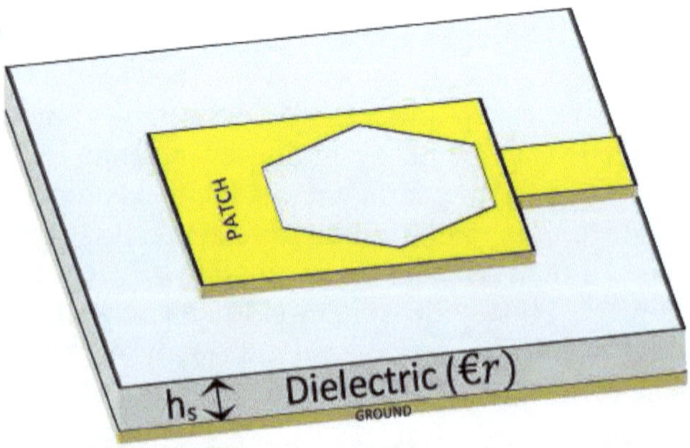

Fig. (2). Design of Proposed MPA.

$$Width(W) = \frac{c}{2f_0\sqrt{\frac{\varepsilon_R+1}{2}}} \tag{1}$$

$$Lenght = \frac{c}{2f_0\sqrt{\varepsilon_{eff}}} - 0.824h\left(\frac{(\varepsilon_{eff}+0.3)\left(\frac{W}{h}+0.264\right)}{(\varepsilon_{eff}-0.258)\left(\frac{W}{h}+0.8\right)}\right) \tag{2}$$

$$\varepsilon_{eff} = \frac{\varepsilon_R+1}{2} + \frac{\varepsilon_R-1}{2}\left[\frac{1}{\sqrt{1+12\left(\frac{h}{W}\right)}}\right] \tag{3}$$

Where,

$\mathcal{E}_R$ = the dielectric constant of the substrate, which is 5.13 in this design;

C = Speed of light, given as $(3 * 10^8)$ m/s;

f_0 = Operating frequency, which is 4.5GHz;

h = Height of the Substrate, which is 2.00055 mm in this design;

For designing the MPA, the ground and the substrate are constructed in the same width and length by the corresponding materials mentioned before shown in Fig. (**2**). Then the rectangular patch is built within the calculated dimensions. An inset feeding technique is applied. However, the result was not in our desired frequency range. So, the patch is cut into the hexagonal slot, and the dimensions of the ground are adjusted to get a 4.5 GHz frequency shown Figs. (**3** and **4**). All the dimensions and materials are described in the given Table **1**:

Table 1. Parametric value of the proposed mpa for the best result.

Parameters	Value
Radius of Hexagon patch (R)	6.9 mm
Position of the center of the Hexagon patch along X- axis	0.00
Position of the center of the Hexagon patch along Y- axis	-0.72mm
Width of Hexagon patch (Wp)	20.462 mm
Length of Hexagon patch (Lp)	14.5673 mm
Height of Hexagon patch	0.035 mm
Used material in the patch	Copper(annealed)
Width of Substrate (Ws)	26.2 mm
Length of Substrate (Ls)	25 mm
Height of Substrate (Hs)	2.00055 mm
Used material of substrate and its dielectric constant	Rogers 92 mL (Lossy), Epsilon= 5.13
Width of Ground (Wg)	19.0011 mm
Length of Ground (Lg)	15.0665 mm
Height of Ground	0.035 mm
Used material in the Ground	Copper(annealed)
Width of Transmission Line (Wt)	3.422 mm

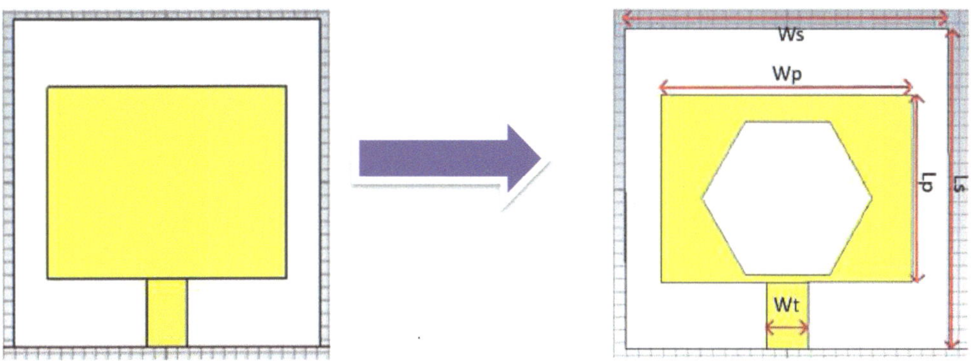

Fig. (3). Radiating plane of proposed MPA.

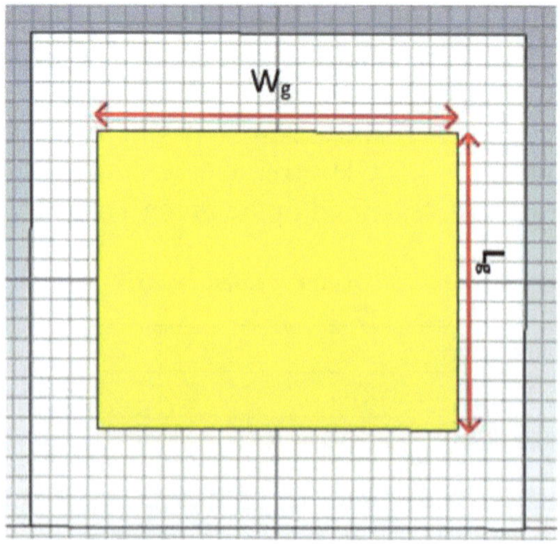

Fig. (4). Ground plane of proposed MPA.

Parametric Variation and Database Creation

In this part, after designing the MPA, two parameters (radius of the hexagonal slot and the position of the slot) are chosen to make a dataset where the inputs (chosen two parameters) will be varied to obtain variations of the outputs (Resonant Frequency, S_{11}, Bandwidth). Thus, a database is made in Table **2**.

Table 2. ANN model training data.

Outer Radius (mm)	Position along Y-shift (Center of Slot) (mm)	S_{11} (dB)	Resonant Frequency (GHz)	Bandwidth (GHz)
4	-0.72	-32.45	4.745	1.3001
4.5	-0.72	-29.9	4.7	1.3425
5	-0.72	-29.9	4.68	1.3656
5.5	-0.72	-29.1	4.65	1.389
6	-0.72	-30.6	4.61	1.3741
6.5	-0.72	-38.05	4.57	1.3385
6.6	-0.72	-40.68	4.56	1.3268
6.7	-0.72	-45.4	4.54	1.3126
6.8	-0.72	-48.65	4.52	1.3099
7	-0.72	-46.4	4.48	1.2715
7.1	-0.72	-41	4.45	1.2285
7.2	-0.72	-37.2	4.42	1.2041
7.3	-0.72	-36.8	4.41	1.1955

(Table 2) cont.....

Outer Radius (mm)	Position along Y-shift (Center of Slot) (mm)	S_{11} (dB)	Resonant Frequency (GHz)	Bandwidth (GHz)
7.4	-0.72	-38.6	4.42	1.2069
6.9	-0.9	-43	4.48	1.2207
6.9	-0.8	-48.3	4.49	1.26882
6.9	-0.72	-61.4	4.5	1.2904
6.9	-0.6	-46.8	4.51	1.3223
6.9	-0.5	-38.6	4.52	1.333
6.9	-0.4	-35.9	4.52	1.3506
6.9	-0.3	-33.9	4.52	1.3751
6.9	-0.2	-32.15	4.53	1.3906
6.9	-0.1	-31.24	4.53	1.4084
6.9	0	-30.5	4.53	1.4232
6.9	0.1	-30.5	4.54	1.433
6.9	0.2	-29.98	4.54	1.4444
6.9	0.3	-30	4.54	1.446
6.9	0.4	-29.4	4.55	1.4531
6.9	0.5	-29.1	4.55	1.4641
6.9	0.6	-28.2	4.55	1.4677
6.9	0.7	-28.9	4.55	1.4727
6.9	0.8	-28.6	4.55	1.4761
6.9	0.9	-28.5	4.56	1.4747
6.9	1.0	-28.24	4.56	1.4768
6.9	1.1	-28.4	4.55	1.4849
6.9	1.2	-28.1	4.54	1.4877

Artificial Neural Network (ANN) Model Creation and Training

In the next part, a mathematical model is designed to train the output results like S_{11} value, Bandwidth, and Resonant Frequency with the variation of the Radius of the hexagonal slot and the position of the center of the hexagonal slot (along the Y-axis) shown in Fig. (**5**). The model is built by a Neural Network and further trained with the input of different variations of the Radius of the hexagonal slot and the position of the hexagonal slot, and the output is the corresponding parameters, *i.e.*, Resonance Frequency, S_{11} value, and Bandwidth. After the training, we obtained our desired performance result.

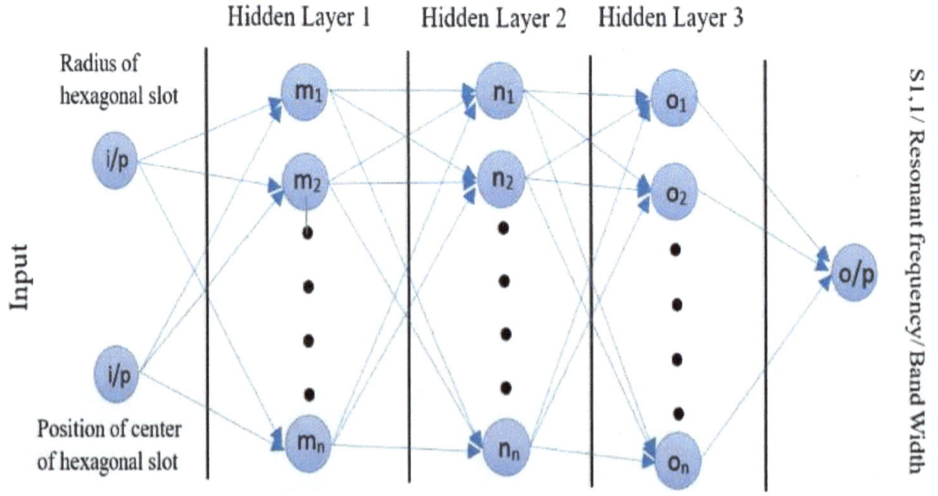

Fig. (5). Artificial Neural Network Building Structure

Prediction of Untrained Data using an ANN Model

After training the Artificial Neural Network (ANN), predictions were made using a new set of data that varied the radius and center position of the hexagonal slot (unseen during training). The differences between the ANN-predicted values and the CST simulation results were then calculated. This comparison helps evaluate the model's efficiency and determine the Root Mean Square Error (RMSE)

RESULT AND DISCUSSION

Results for the Best Case

Here, the best results given by the proposed MPA through CST Software have been discussed.

Tuning for Getting 4.5 GHz Resonant Frequency

Initially, to get the desired resonant frequency, *i.e.*, 4.5 GHz, we made a rectangular patch antenna with a hexagonal slot cut in the copper patch and adjusted the ground as well. After tuning, the best output at our desired frequency is observed.

S11 Curve

In Fig. (**6**), it can be seen that the S_{11} curve falls at 4.5 GHz and the S_{11} value is -61.46815 dB. Therefore, it can be clearly understood that the antenna resonates at 4.5 GHz, which is the desired frequency.

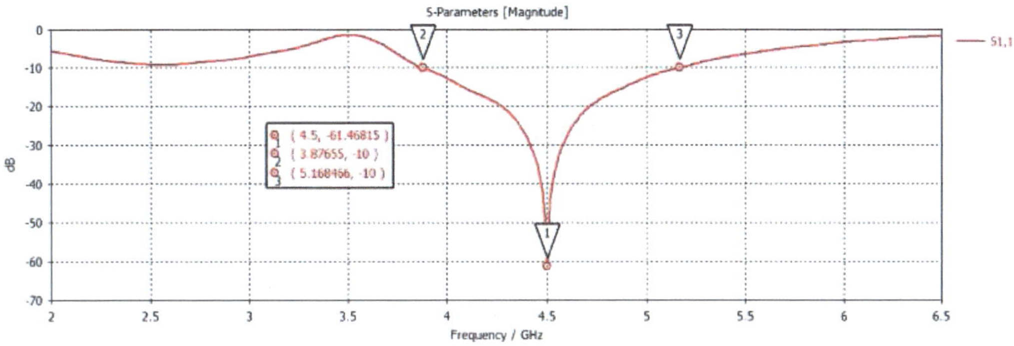

Fig. (6). Variation of S11 *vs.* frequency.

3.1.3. Bandwidth

In Fig. (**6**), it can be seen that the lower frequency is 3.87655 GHz and the upper frequency is 5.168466 GHz. When the upper frequency is subtracted from the lower frequencies, the bandwidth of 1.291916 GHz is obtained, which is considered a very satisfactory result for the proposed Antenna.

Gain

Fig. (**7**) shows the variation gain of our proposed antenna with respect to its frequency, and a gain of 0.89 dB has been observed up to the frequency of 4.5 GHz, which is our desired frequency.

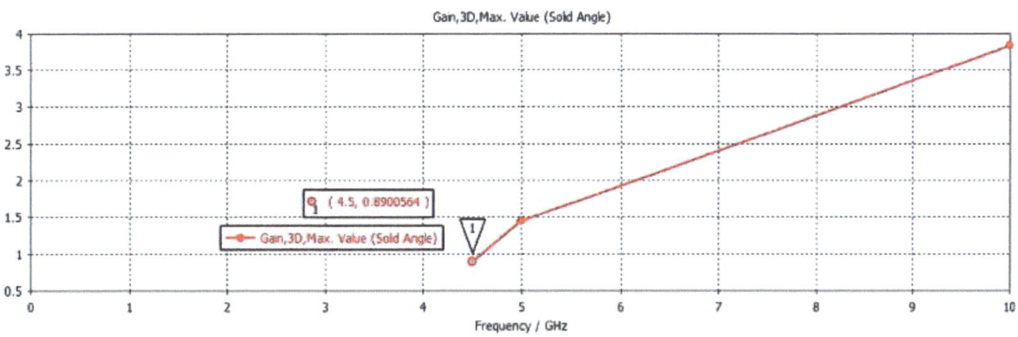

Fig. (7). Variation of gain *vs.* frequency.

VSWR

Fig. (**8**) shows the Voltage Standing Wave Ratio (VSWR) curve with Frequency. The VSWR value is near about 1.00169 observed on the frequency of 4.5 GHz, which is our desired frequency.

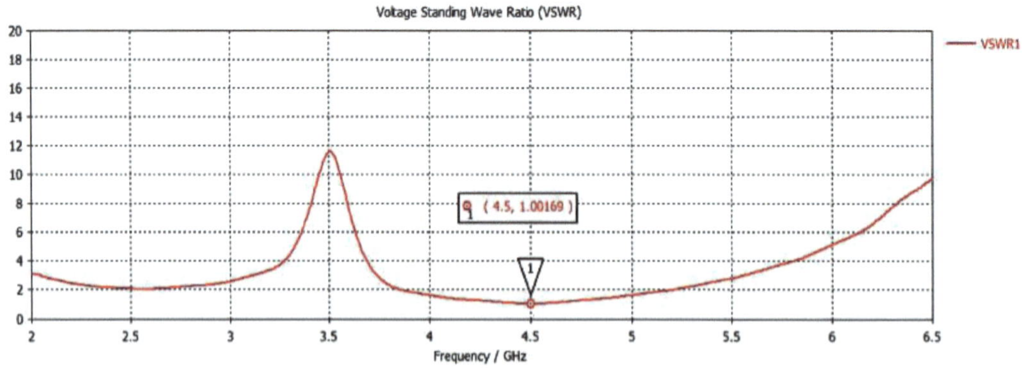

Fig. (8). Variation in VSWR *vs*. frequency.

Impedance

In Fig. (**9**), Z-Parameters or Impedance Parameters (in Ohms) concerning Frequency have been observed, which is around 48.18 Ohms at the frequency of 4.5 GHz. The antenna radiates maximum power when the impedance is 50 Ohms, and our result approximately matches this required value, which makes it efficient.

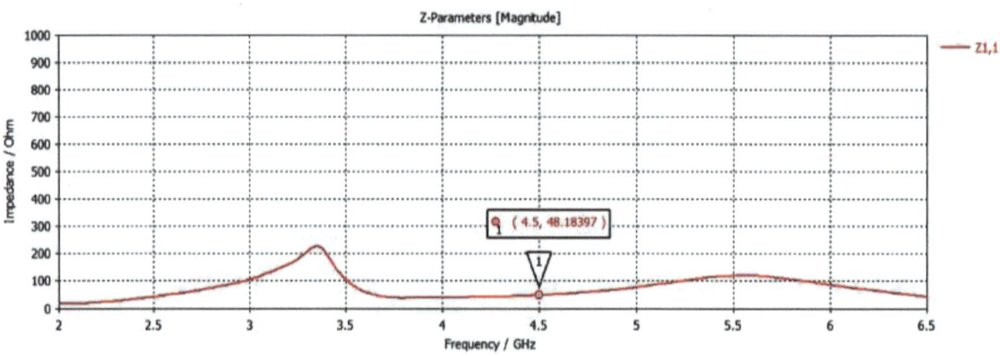

Fig. (9). Variation of impedance vs frequency.

Radiation Pattern

In Fig. (**10**), the far-field radiation pattern of the antenna has been observed. The HPBW of the proposed Rectangular Microstrip Patch Antenna is 81.4 degrees.

Creation of an Artificial Neural Network Model of the Proposed MPA

The objective is to create a mathematical model that can predict three antenna characteristics (S_{11} value, Bandwidth, and Resonant Frequency) based on changes in two physical parameters (the Radius of the hexagonal slot and the position of the centre of the hexagonal slot). This prediction model uses Neural Network

Fitting in MATLAB. It is trained by feeding it different combinations of the radius of the hexagonal slot and the position of the hexagonal slot and their corresponding outputs (*i.e.*, Resonant Frequency, S_{11} value, and Bandwidth) from CST Studio Suite 2024. The final part indicates that the model achieved the desired results and performance, which will be detailed below.

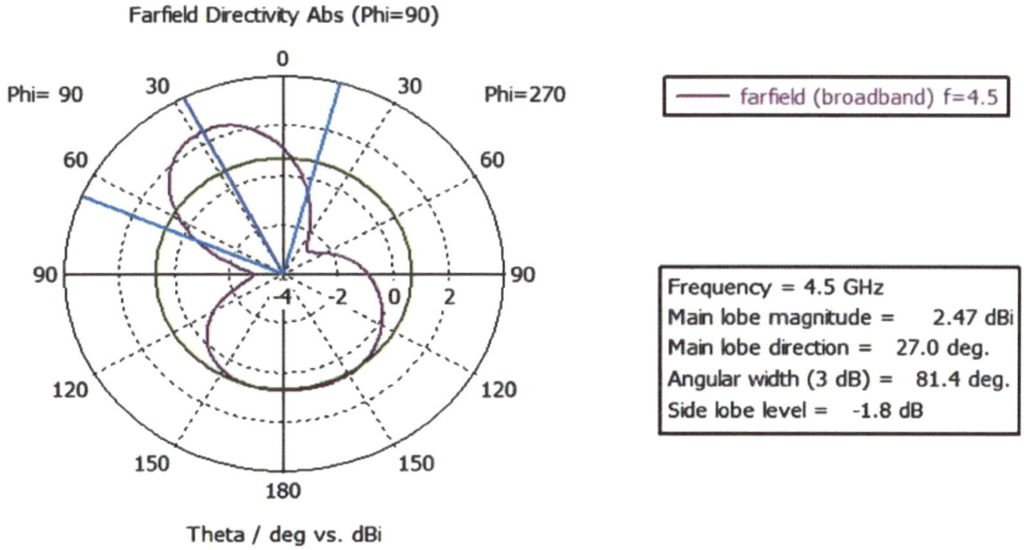

Fig. (10). Radiation pattern of the proposed antenna.

Input Data to Train the ANN Model

ANN Model Node Layer Structure and corresponding outputs.

For the S_{11} parameter prediction, the network was structured with 2 hidden layers containing 3 and 8 nodes, respectively shown in Table **3** and Fig. (**11**). This configuration achieved excellent results with a Root Mean Square Error (RMSE) of 0.0738. The training correlation (R) value was remarkably high at 0.99961, while both validation and test sets achieved perfect correlation values of 1. The overall correlation across all datasets was 0.9994, indicating highly accurate predictions. The Resonant Frequency prediction model used a more complex structure with 3 hidden layers, containing 10, 10, and 9 nodes, respectively, shown in Table **3** and Fig. (**12**). This model achieved a very low RMSE of 0.0013, demonstrating exceptional accuracy. The training correlation was 0.99769, with perfect correlations (R=1) for both validation and test sets. The overall correlation was 0.953, showing strong predictive capability across all data. For Bandwidth prediction, the network employed 2 hidden layers with 2 and 8 nodes, shown in

Table **3** and Fig. (**13**). This configuration produced a very low RMSE of 0.0011, indicating high precision. While the training correlation was slightly lower at 0.93371, both validation and test sets achieved perfect correlation values of 1. The overall correlation was 0.93452, demonstrating reliable prediction performance across all datasets. These results collectively indicate that the neural network models are performing exceptionally well in predicting all three antenna parameters, with particularly strong performance in the validation and testing phases.

Table 3. Inner Structure of the ANN Model with outputs.

Outputs	No. of Hidden Layers & Corresponding Nodes	Performance	Training (R)	Validation (R)	Test (R)	All (R)
S_{11}	2 & [3, 8]	0.0738	0.99961	1	1	0.9994
Resonant Frequency	3 & [10, 10, 9]	0.0013	0.99769	1	1	0.953
Band Width	2 & [2, 8]	0.0011	0.93371	1	1	0.93452

Validation of New Data from the ANN Model

After training, we predicted the output values with a combination of untrained data (variations of the Radius of the hexagonal slot and the position of the center of the hexagonal slot). We also measure the difference between the predicted data and the CST-given data and the error of the outputs given by the ANN model (discussed below).

$$\text{Error} = (\text{CST Value} - \text{Predicted Value}) \quad (4)$$

$$\text{RMSE} = \sqrt{\frac{\sum_{i=1}^{n}\left(\frac{\text{Actual}_i - \text{Predicted}_i}{\text{Actual}_i}\right)^2}{N}} \quad (5)$$

$$\text{Accuracy} = [1 - (\text{RMSE})] \times 100\% \quad (6)$$

Validation of Resonant Frequency with New Data (Untrained Data)

After the ANN Model was trained in MATLAB [16], the Resonating Frequency values were predicted with 20 different values [Table **4**] of the Radius of the hexagonal slot and the position of the center of the hexagonal slot, which were not trained in the model. Later, the error was compared, which is the difference between the given CST resonant frequency data and the ANN Model-predicted resonant frequency data.

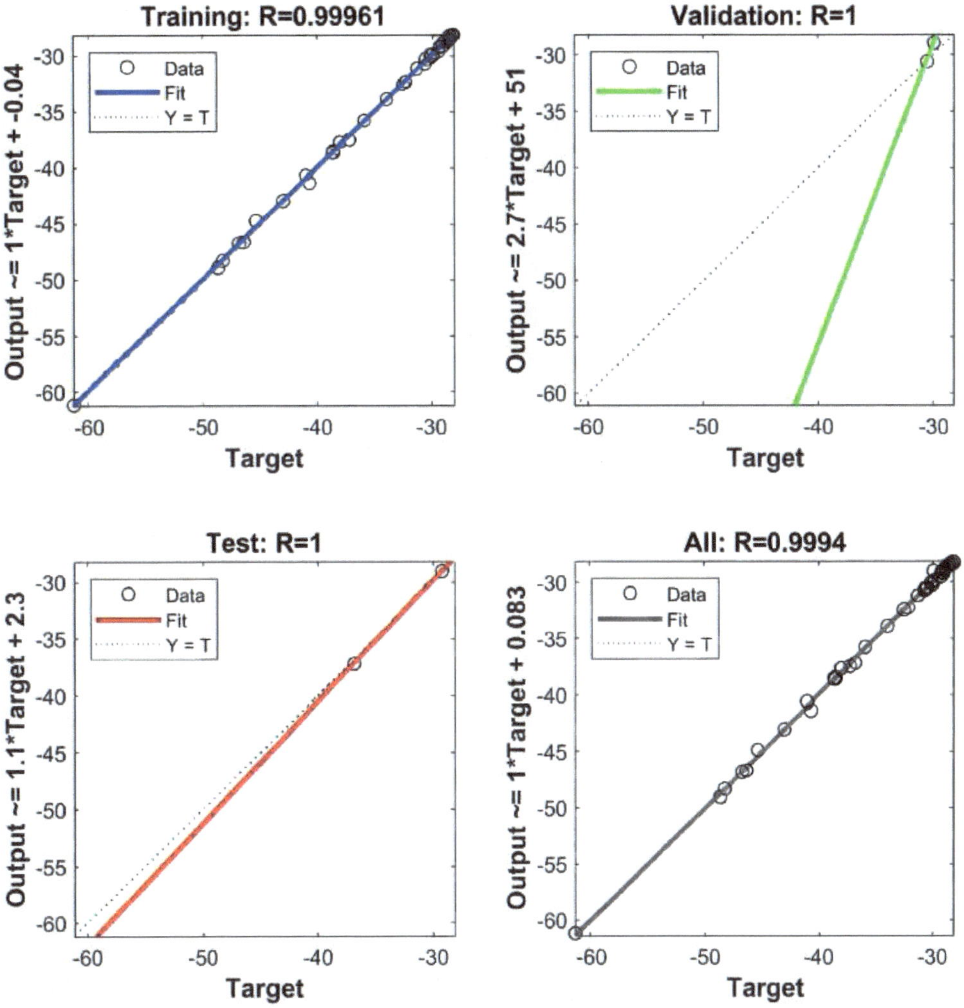

Fig. (11). ANN Model Regression Curve (S11).

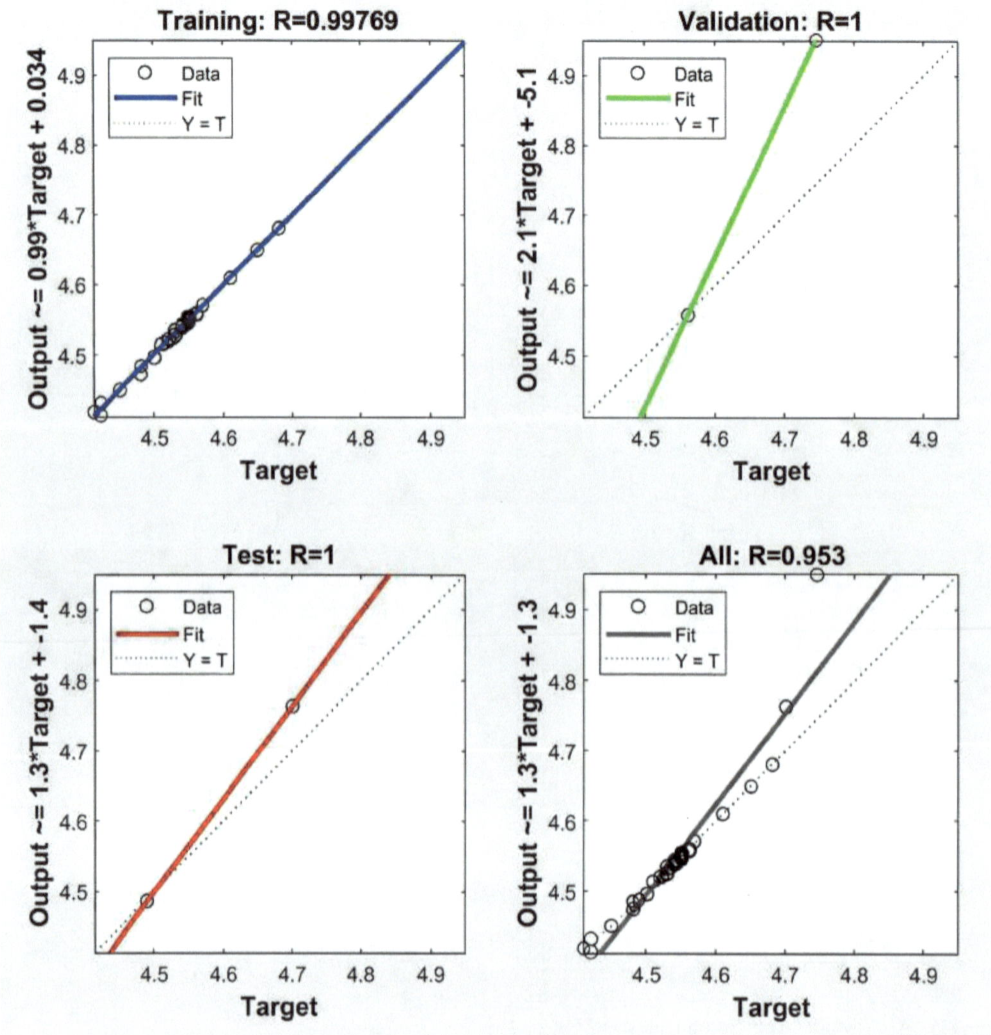

Fig. (12). ANN Model Regression Curve (Resonating Frequency).

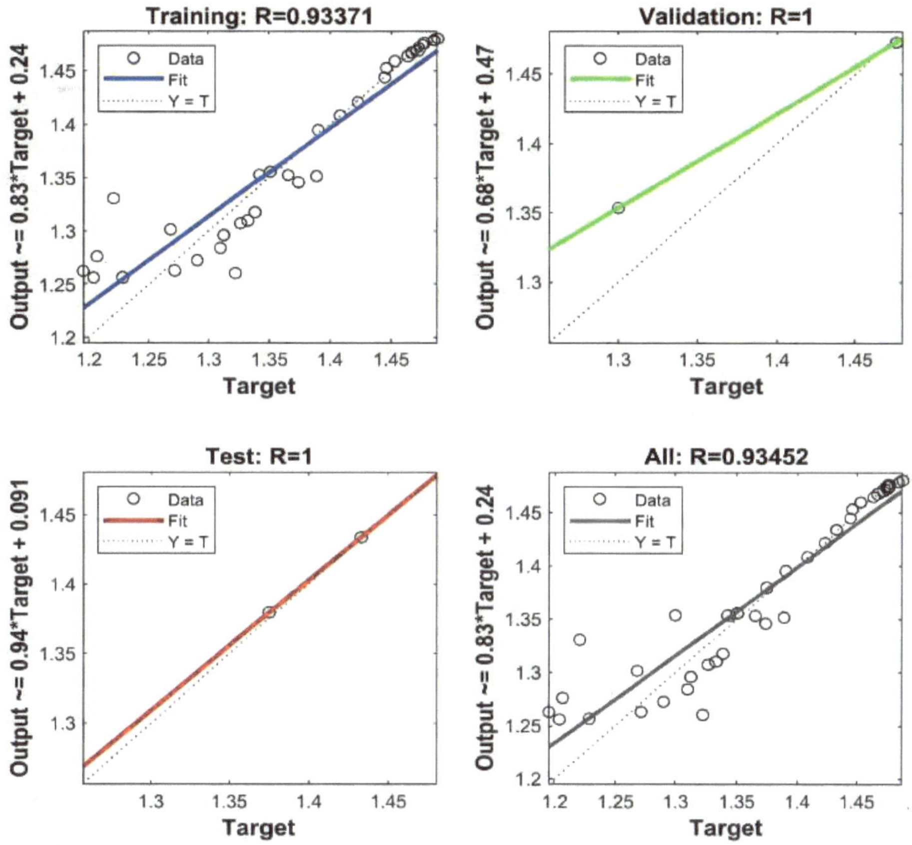

Fig. (13). ANN Model Regression Curve (Bandwidth).

Table 4. Predicted Data by ANN Model (Resonant Frequency)

Outer Radius (mm)	Position along Y-shift (centre of slot) (mm)	Resonant Frequency (GHz) CST	Resonant Frequency (GHz) MATLAB	Error
3.8	-0.72	4.75	4.7762	-0.0262
4.3	-0.72	4.72	4.7576	-0.0376
4.6	-0.72	4.7	4.7333	-0.0333
4.7	-0.72	4.69	4.7245	-0.0345
4.9	-0.72	4.69	4.7097	-0.0197
5.3	-0.72	4.67	4.6835	-0.0135
5.7	-0.72	4.64	4.6622	-0.0222
5.9	-0.72	4.62	4.6531	-0.0331

(Table 4) cont.....

Outer Radius (mm)	Position along Y-shift (centre of slot) (mm)	Resonant Frequency (GHz) CST	Resonant Frequency (GHz) MATLAB	Error
6.3	-0.72	4.59	4.6161	-0.0261
6.9	-0.72	4.5	4.503	-0.003
6.9	-0.7	4.5	4.5037	0.0037
6.9	-0.55	4.52	4.5088	0.0112
6.9	-0.35	4.52	4.5171	0.0029
6.9	-0.15	4.53	4.5286	0.0014
6.9	0.15	4.54	4.5629	0.0229
6.9	0.35	4.54	4.5146	0.0746
6.9	0.55	4.55	4.5312	0.0812
6.9	0.75	4.55	4.5649	0.0149
6.9	0.95	4.56	4.5563	0.0037
6.9	1.15	4.55	4.5409	0.0091
-	-	-	**RMSE**	**0.03111**
-	-	-	**Accuracy (in %)**	**96.89**

Validation of S11 with New Data (untrained Data)

After the ANN Model was trained in MATLAB, the S_{11} values were predicted with 20 different values (Table **5**) of the Radius of the hexagonal slot and the position of the center of the hexagonal slot, which were not trained to the model. Later, the error was compared, which is the difference between the given CST S_{11} data and the ANN Model predicted S_{11} data.

Table 5. Predicted Data by ANN Model (S_{11} Values)

Outer Radius (mm)	Position along Y-shift (center of slot) (mm)	S_{11}(dB) CST	S_{11}(dB) MATLAB	Error
3.8	-0.72	-32.6	-34.1391	1.5391
4.3	-0.72	-30.53	-30.6584	0.1284
4.6	-0.72	-29.6	-29.6134	0.0134
4.7	-0.72	-29.4	-29.3889	-0.0111
4.9	-0.72	-29.8	-29.0782	-0.7218
5.3	-0.72	-29	-28.9005	-0.0995
5.7	-0.72	-29.27	-29.4224	0.1524
5.9	-0.72	-30.15	-3.01588	0.0088
6.3	-0.72	-33.54	-33.5159	-0.0241

(Table 5) cont.....

Outer Radius (mm)	Position along Y-shift (center of slot) (mm)	S_{11}(dB) CST	S_{11}(dB) MATLAB	Error
6.9	-0.72	-61.4	-61.2435	-0.1565
6.9	-0.7	-57	-60.9574	3.9574
6.9	-0.55	-43.1	-41.6018	-1.4982
6.9	-0.35	-34.87	-34.8127	-0.0573
6.9	-0.15	-31.7	-31.6391	0.0609
6.9	0.15	-30.2	-30.2104	-0.0104
6.9	0.35	-29.85	-29.7225	-0.1275
6.9	0.55	-28.9	-29.1502	0.2502
6.9	0.75	-28.75	-28.6774	-0.0726
6.9	0.95	-28.3	-28.3615	0.0615
6.9	1.15	-28.2	-28.187	-0.013
-	-	-	**RMSE**	**0.09497**
-	-	-	**Accuracy (in %)**	**90.50**

Validation of Bandwidth with New Data (untrained Data)

After the ANN Model was trained in MATLAB, the Bandwidth values were predicted with 20 different values (Table **6**) of the Radius of the hexagonal slot and the position of the center of the hexagonal slot, which were not trained to the model. Later, the error was compared, which is the difference between the given CST bandwidth data and the ANN Model-predicted bandwidth data.

Table 6. Predicted Data by ANN Model (Bandwidth Values)

Outer Radius (mm)	Position along Y-shift (center of slot) (mm)	Bandwidth (GHz) CST	Bandwidth (GHz) MATLAB	Error
3.8	-0.72	1.2745	1.3851	0.1106
4.3	-0.72	1.3272	1.3742	0.047
4.6	-0.72	1.35	1.3664	0.0164
4.7	-0.72	1.3536	1.3637	0.0101
4.9	-0.72	1.355	1.3579	0.0029
5.3	-0.72	1.3788	1.3458	0.033
5.7	-0.72	1.3874	1.3329	0.0545
5.9	-0.72	1.3784	1.3263	0.0521
6.3	-0.72	1.3574	1.3127	0.0447

(Table 6) cont.....

Outer Radius (mm)	Position along Y-shift (center of slot) (mm)	Bandwidth (GHz) CST	Bandwidth (GHz) MATLAB	Error
6.9	-0.72	1.2904	1.2918	0.0001
6.9	-0.7	1.2947	1.2665	0.0282
6.9	-0.55	1.3336	1.2817	0.0519
6.9	-0.35	1.3666	1.3694	0.0028
6.9	-0.15	1.3994	1.4023	0.0029
6.9	0.15	1.4444	1.4396	0.0048
6.9	0.35	1.4507	1.4567	0.006
6.9	0.55	1.4675	1.4663	0.0012
6.9	0.75	1.4745	1.4718	0.0027
6.9	0.95	1.477	1.4757	0.0013
6.9	1.15	1.4828	1.4797	0.0031
-	-	-	**RMSE**	**0.125125**
-	-	-	**Accuracy (in %)**	**0.874875**

Comparative Study

The performance parameters (S_{11}, bandwidth, Gain, and HPBW) of the proposed 4.5 GHz rectangular patch antenna were evaluated against comparable microstrip patch antenna designs operating between 4.3 GHz to 4.6GHz. The comparison data presents five different antenna designs, including the proposed antenna, focusing on various performance parameters crucial for 5G and wireless applications, shown in Table 7. The first work by Geetharamani and Aathmanesan [3] presented a design with dimensions of 40×50×1.6, operating at 4.5 GHz with impressive performance characteristics including a return loss (S_{11}) of -37.92 dB, gain of 4.14 dB, very low VSWR of 1.024, and a bandwidth of 340 MHz. The second design by Singh, Kumar, and Gupta [4] featured a more compact structure of 15×15×1.6, also operating at 4.5 GHz, achieving an even better return loss of -43 dB and offering a wider bandwidth of 500 MHz. The third design by Maheswari *et al.* [5] operated at a slightly higher frequency of 4.6 GHz, achieving a return loss of -25.9338 dB and a notable gain of 7.944 dB with a VSWR of 0.8781. The fourth design by Werfelli *et al.* [6] operated at a lower frequency of 4.3 GHz, with S_{11} of -30 dB, gain of 3.488 dB, and a VSWR range of 1.6-1.7. The proposed antenna by Saha, Mitra, and Mondal with dimensions of 26.5×25×2.07035 operated at 4.5 GHz. It demonstrated superior S_{11} performance at -61.4 dB, though with a relatively lower gain of 0.89 dB. It achieved an excellent VSWR of 1.00169 and provided a bandwidth of 1.291916 GHz, which was significantly higher than the other designs where bandwidth information was available. This comparison suggests that while the proposed antenna may have lower gain, it excels in terms of S_{11}, VSWR, and bandwidth, making it potentially suitable for applications requiring wide bandwidth operation.

Table 7. Performance Analysis of Different MPA Designs Operating between 4.3 GHz to 4.6GHz

SL No	Work	Size of the MPA	Resonant Frequency (GHz)	S_{11} (dB)	Gain (dB)	VSWR	Bandwidth
1.	[3]	40*50*1.6	4.5	-37.92	4.14	1.024	340MHz
2.	[4]	15*15*1.6	4.5	-43	×	×	500 MHz
3.	[5]	×	4.6	-25.9338	7.944	0.8781	×
4.	[6]	×	4.3	-30	3.488	1.6-1.7	×
5.	Proposed Antenna	26.5*25*2.07	4.5	-61.4	0.89	1.0017	1.291916 GHz

CONCLUSION

The proposed hexagonal slotted microstrip patch antenna, designed on a Rogers 92 mL substrate and simulated using CST Studio, demonstrates exceptional performance characteristics for 5G wireless communications. With compact dimensions of 26.5×25×2.07035, the antenna achieves outstanding results at 4.5 GHz. The design exhibits a remarkable return loss (S_{11}) of -61.4 dB and a substantial bandwidth of 1.291916 GHz, significantly outperforming existing works in this frequency band. The antenna's near-ideal VSWR of 1.00169, combined with these superior parameters, makes it highly suitable for high-speed data transmission applications. Parametric analysis was conducted to optimize the antenna's performance by studying various design parameters and their effects on key metrics, including S_{11}, bandwidth, and center frequency. The implementation of an Artificial Neural Network (ANN) model represents a significant advancement in the design methodology, enabling accurate prediction of antenna parameters, including return loss, resonance frequency, and bandwidth. This machine-learning approach demonstrates promising prediction accuracy while substantially reducing the time and computational resources required for antenna design and optimization. The combination of exceptional antenna performance and sophisticated ANN modeling establishes a robust framework for future antenna designs. The results validate the effectiveness of the proposed design approach and suggest significant potential for applications in next-generation wireless communication systems, which is a typical example of Industry 5.0.

REFERENCES

[1] R. Garg, P. Bhartia, I. Bahl, and A. Ittipiboon, *Microstrip Antenna Design Handbook.* Artech House: Boston, MA, USA, 2001.

[2] E.C. Jordan, and K.G. Balmain, *Electromagnetic Waves and Radiating Systems.* 2nd ed. Pearson: Upper Saddle River, NJ, USA, 2015.

[3] G. Geetharamani, and T. Aathmanesan, "Design and development of novel patch antenna for 5G applications", *ICTACT J. Microelectron.,* vol. 4, no. 2, pp. 589-593, 2018.

[4] N. Singh, S. Kumar, and S. Gupta, "Compact and small planar monopole rectangular patch antenna with symmetrical maze-shaped slots for Bluetooth/WLAN/IMT applications", *Int. J. Latest Technol. Eng. Manag. Appl. Sci.,* vol. 5, no. 6, pp. 104-108, 2016.

[5] T. Maheswari, V.U. Sankar, S.S. Reddy, B.P. Kumar, and K. Rushendrababu, "Design of a microstrip patch antenna for 5G wireless applications", *Int. J. Res. Anal. Rev.,* vol. 6, no. 1, pp. 234-238, 2019.

[6] H. Werfelli, K. Tayari, M. Chaoui, M. Lahiani, and H. Ghariani, "Design of rectangular microstrip patch antenna", *Proc. 2nd Int. Conf. Adv. Technol. Signal Image Process. (ATSIP),* pp. 715-719, 2016.Monastir, Tunisia

[7] R.K. Maurya, B.K. Kanaujia, A.K. Gautam, S. Chatterji, and A.K. Singh, "Circularly polarized hexagonal ring microstrip patch antenna with asymmetrical feed and DGS", *Microw. Opt. Technol. Lett.,* vol. 61, no. 1, pp. 7-13, 2019.

[8] M.F. Ahmed, A.Z.M.T. Islam, and M.H. Kabir, "Rectangular microstrip antenna design with multi-slotted patch and partial grounding for performance enhancement", *Iran. J. Electr. Comput. Eng.,* vol. 12, no. 4, pp. 3859-3868, 2022. [IJECE].

[9] A. Maiti, and S. Mandal, "Surface fitting based modelling of a circular microstrip patch antenna operating at 3 GHz frequency", *International Journal of Wireless and Microwave Technologies,* vol. 14, no. 2, pp. 65-74, 2024.
[http://dx.doi.org/10.5815/ijwmt.2024.02.05]

[10] M.H. Mokhtar, M.K.A. Rahim, and H.A. Majid, "A compact slotted microstrip patch antenna for RFID applications", *Proc. 2013 IEEE Int. Conf. RFID Technol. Appl.,* pp. 1-5, 2013.Johor Bahru, Malaysia
[http://dx.doi.org/10.1109/RFID-TA.2013.6694536]

[11] S. Verma, L. Mahajan, R. Kumar, H.S. Saini, and N. Kumar, "A small microstrip patch antenna for future 5G applications", *Proc. 2016 5th Int. Conf. Rel., Infocom Technol. Optim. (ICRITO),* pp. 460-464, 2016.Noida, India
[http://dx.doi.org/10.1109/ICRITO.2016.7784999]

[12] U. Venkateshkumar, S. Kiruthiga, H. Mihitha, K. Maheswari, and M. Nithiyasri, "Multiband patch antenna design for 5G applications", *Proc. 4th Int. Conf. Comput. Methodol. Commun. (ICCMC 2020),* pp. 1-5, 2020.Erode, India
[http://dx.doi.org/10.1109/ICCMC48092.2020.ICCMC-00098]

[13] A. Nayak, S. Dutta, and S. Mandal, "Design of dual-band microstrip patch antenna for 5G communication operating at 28 GHz and 46 GHz", *International Journal of Wireless and Microwave Technologies,* vol. 13, no. 2, pp. 43-52, 2023.
[http://dx.doi.org/10.5815/ijwmt.2023.02.05]

[14] Pasternack, "Microstrip Patch Antenna Calculator," [Online]. Available from: https://www.pasternack.com/t-calculator-microstrip-ant.aspx

[15] Dassault Systèmes, "CST Studio Suite Learning Edition," 3DEXPERIENCE Edu. [Online]. Available from: https://www.3ds.com/edu/education/students/solutions/cst-le

[16] MathWorks, "MATLAB," [Online]. Available from: https://in.mathworks.com/products/matlab.html

CHAPTER 13

Comparative Study of Hybrid GAPSO for Parametric Optimization of the Liquid Flow Model

Sumanta Dey[1], **Anand Polamarasetti**[2], **Arindam Sadhu**[3] and **Gour Gopal Jana**[1,*]

[1] *Department of Electronics & Communication Engineering, Greater Kolkata College of Engineering and Management, Baruipur 743387, West Bengal, India*

[2] *Department of Computer Science, Andhra University, Visakhapatnam, AP, India*

[3] *Department of Electronics & Communication Engineering, Dr. Sudhir Chandra Sur Institute of Technology and Sports Complex, Kolkata, West Bengal, India*

Abstract: This study focuses on optimizing a nonlinear liquid flow control process model using advanced techniques. A total of 134 datasets were collected, with 117 used for training and 17 for validation. To check the performance of the best algorithm, a comparative study has been conducted between GA, PSO, and the proposed hybrid GAPSO techniques. The performance was evaluated using MAE, MAPE, RMSE, and computational time. The results showed that the hybrid algorithm outperformed others in terms of convergence speed, computation time, and accuracy.

Keywords: ANOVA, Genetic algorithm (GA), Liquid flow, Particle swarm optimization (PSO).

INTRODUCTION

In the process industry, optimization has been crucial during the past few decades, and Artificial Intelligence approaches have taken the lead in creating process models [1]. The optimization technique is typically applied to any nonlinear model to determine the best response. The liquid flow process model is a restriction of traditional optimization techniques because of the complex relationship between multiple inputs, response, and significant delay time. Because computational optimization reduces the computing time and accurately forecasts the possible input, researchers use it in the majority of complicated nonlinear process models [2]. Computational optimization performance is typically divided into two categories. In the first stage, the majority of the dataset,

* **Corresponding author Gour Gopal Jana:** Department of Electronics & Communication Engineering, Greater Kolkata College of Engineering and Management, Baruipur, West Bengal, 743387, India; E-mail: gour0202@gmail.com

Pijush Dutta, Sudip Mondal, Korhan Cengiz and S. Balamurugan (Eds.)

comprising input and output variables, is used to help develop the model. The model, which accounts for the input and output process variables, is verified and evaluated against the test data set in the second phase. Neural network control models are among the various AI techniques employed in numerous studies, namelyANFIS [3, 4], FLC [5, 6], GA [7], hybrid GA-ANN model [8, 9], *etc.* Nonlinear process plant train datasets are often modeled using empirical approaches such as ANOVA, RSM, and ANN [10 - 12]. For the liquid flow process industry, several studies have been conducted to optimize empirical models parametrically using various metaheuristic optimization techniques. These include improved FPA and enhanced versions of the ESWSA-integrated ANOVA and RSM model [13]. In addition, a hybrid HPSOGWO was suggested to execute this complex model, aiming to increase convergence speed [14]. In addition to providing better solutions and running faster than other metaheuristic algorithms, PSO is a highly effective algorithm [15], however, its main drawback is that it cannot find the global optimum [16]. The global optimum solution is provided by the genetic algorithm, which takes a considerable amount of computing time because it improves outcomes by increasing the number of iterations and computational steps [17]. Therefore, in this study, we used both PSO and GA to develop a hybrid optimization technique called HGAPSO, which enables faster performance [18]. HGAPSO is used as an optimization tool used in several fields, including medical diagnosis and potential attribute selections [19, 20], as an estimation tool for wear in a milling process [21], in cluster-based routing in WSN [22], hierarchical problem-solving in GP algorithm [23], transformer fault diagnosis [24], *etc.* The HGAPSO assessment indicates that the suggested optimization methods are practical and efficient in fulfilling the real-time control needs of the liquid flow control process.

Overall, the article is organized into the following sections: introduction, followed by a mathematical explanation, suggested technique, findings and discussion, and finally, conclusions.

EXPERIMENTAL PROCEDURE

The Liquid Flow experimental setup [2], as shown in Fig. (**1**), is used for the experimental work. Four independent variables have been included in 134-sample data collected for this work.

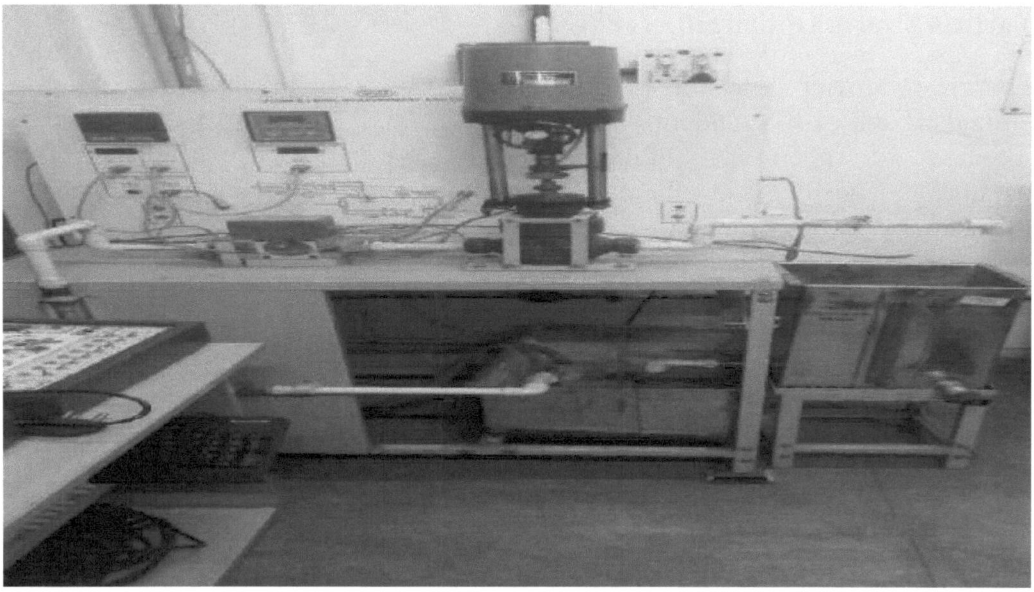

Fig. (1). Experimental setup [3].

A well-known nonlinear power equation, Analysis of Variance (ANOVA) [25 - 27], is formulated to represent the input and output variables as shown in Eq. (1)

$$F=\mu_1.E^{\mu_2}.D^{\mu_3}.k^{\mu_4}.n^{\mu_5} \quad \textbf{(1)}$$

The values of this coefficient can be obtained using computational intelligence techniques. Here, three distinct metaheuristic optimization strategies are used to fit the process with the experimental one and provide the optimal value of the process variable. We employed RMSE as an objective function in this study to minimize the metaheuristic. The error function for ANOVA-based modeling can be written as:

$$(Ei,Di,X)= \mu_1.E^{\mu_2}.D^{\mu_3}.k^{\mu_4}.n^{\mu_5}—F \quad \textbf{(2)}$$

$$X=\{\mu_1,\mu_2,\mu_3,\mu_4,\mu_5\} \quad \textbf{(3)}$$

PROPOSED METHODOLOGY

GA, PSO, and hybrid HGAPSO are explained first before the suggested methodology is further developed.

Particle Swarm Optimization (PSO)

Particle swarm optimization [28] is inspired by the interaction of a group of animals. Each of the random variables used at the beginning of the procedure indicates a potential solution to the optimization problem. Two parameters—position and velocity—represent each of the variables [29]. Whereas the velocity shows how a variable moves over the search space, the location shows how far the variable deviates from the optimal answer. G_{best} determines the swarm's overall best position, whereas P_{best} determines each particle's optimal position individually. PSO has been successfully used in a variety of research areas, including nuclear energy [30], nanoparticles [31], mathematical modeling [32, 33], renewable energy [34, 35], *etc.*

Genetic Algorithm (GA)

GA is a computational model inspired by Darwin's theory of evolution and natural selection [36]. It employs genetic operators like crossover and mutation to provide a population of candidate solutions. Crossover combines genetic information and introduces diversity by altering genetic structures. The GA process begins with initializing a population of potential solutions. New solutions are generated through crossover and mutations, and their fitness is evaluated. After this, a selection process determines which solutions advance to the next generation. This iterative process continues until the algorithm converges on an optimal solution. GA has been widely applied in optimization tasks across various fields, including operational research [37, 38], multidisciplinary optimization, fault diagnosis [39, 40], and aviation applications [41, 42].

Hybrid GAPSO

The GA-PSO algorithm sets a certain number of iterations and begins by creating a random population. We set the initial values for the GA and PSO parameters, iterations, and population counts. The GA algorithm is then run n/2 times since the GA algorithm's performance is primarily dependent on the technique used to encode solutions and to reduce the complexity of the suggested algorithm [43, 44]. The Global & Positional Best Position (G_{best} & P_{best}) can be determined by adjusting these parameter values after assessing the algorithm's performance on a few trial runs. This concept is also known as divide and conquer, where a single problem is divided into two sub-problems to produce a complexity equal to T(n)= $T(n) = 2 * T\left(\frac{n}{2}\right) + F(n)$, where F(n) is the conquering time [45].

Parameter Setting

List of parameters for the proposed algorithms:

- For GA, the crossover percentage (p_c), crossover factor (y), mutation percentage (p_m), and mutation rate (m_u) are 0.7, 0.4, 0.3, and 0.1, respectively.
- For PSO, the damping factor (W_{damp}), the personal learning coefficient (c_1), and global learning coefficient (c_2) are 0.99, 0.5, and 2, respectively.
- For HGAPSO, the mutation rate is 0.05, while single-point crossover, local (C_1) and global acceleration coefficient (C_1) are 1.5 and 2, r1 (0,1) and r2 (0,1), and the degree of importance is $\alpha 1$, $\alpha 2$, and $\alpha 3$ (0.4,04.,0.4) respectively.

PERFORMANCE ANALYSIS

We used the MATLAB 2013b version to model solar cells, and the PC specifications were 16 GB RAM, Intel(R) Core (TM) i5 processor, and Windows 7 OS. Overall performance was measured using computational time (CT), reliability test (RT), Fitness test (FT), and convergence test, as described in this section.

Computational Efficiency Test

Computational time is measured by how much time is taken by an optimization algorithm to achieve the optimum value of a model [46, 47]. Table **1** shows that the proposed hybrid HGAPSO algorithm has achieved an optimum computation time compared to GA and PSO.

Table 1. Result based on computational time.

Method	Avg. computational time
GA	165.7174Sec
PSO	119.0112Sec
HGAPSO	18.619Sec

Convergence speed is another important metric that indicates how fast an optimization algorithm reaches its minimum objective function value for several runs. For this purpose, we set the iteration number from 100 to 5000. The convergence speed of each algorithm is depicted in Fig. (**2**). In this case, the proposed HGAPSO shows a better convergence speed.

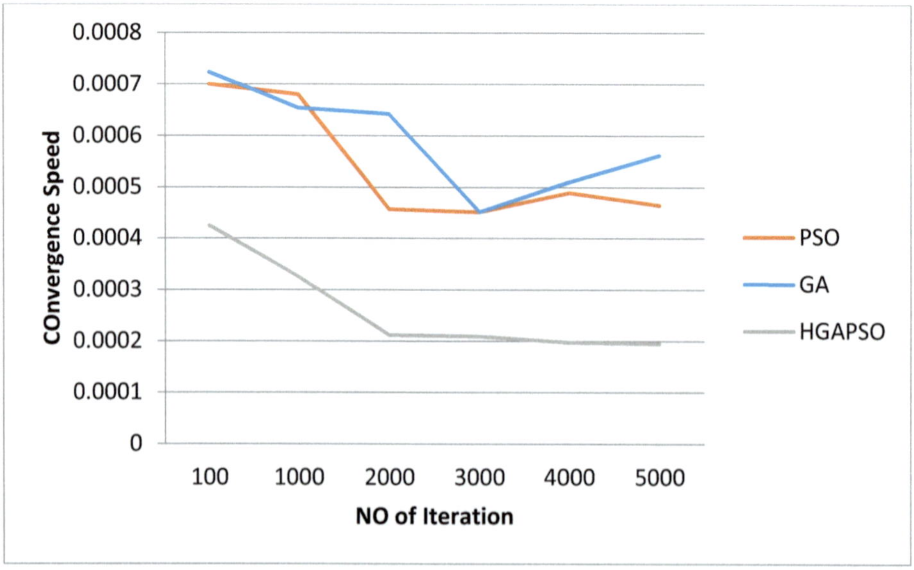

Fig. (2). Comparative study based on convergence speed.

Accuracy can be measured by comparing the actual value and measured value [2, 48]. Mean absolute error (*MAE*) and mean absolute percentage error (MAPE) are defined as Eqns. (5) and (6) are the two error indicator indices to quantify the accuracy of the model [49].

$$IAE=|F_{measured}-F_{calculated} \quad \textbf{(4)}$$

$$\text{MAPE} = \frac{1}{n}\sum_{i=1}^{n}\frac{IAE}{F_{measured}} \quad \textbf{(5)}$$

$$\text{MAE} = \frac{1}{n}\sum_{i=1}^{n} IAE_i \quad \textbf{(6)}$$

The optimal parameters of the nonlinear model obtained by the optimization techniques are shown in Table **2**.

Table 2. Estimated optimal parameters.

Algorithm	μ_1	μ_2	μ_3	μ_4	μ_5
PSO	15.00	10.045	-1.055	-3.629	-0.624
GA	15.00	8.407	-0.727	-1.384	-0.730
HGAPSO	09.42	8.366	-1.225	1.728	-1.131

Root Mean Square Error (RMSE), which is defined as follows, can be used to compute the prediction error.

$$\text{Accuracy} = (100\text{-RMSE})\ \% \quad \textbf{(7)}$$

Tables **3** and **4** explain how HGAPSO offers the optimum value in terms of MAPE, MAE, and RMSE. Fig. (**3**) compares the performance metrics between GA, PSO and HGAPSO.

Table 3. Result based on Mean absolute error (MAE).

Method	MAPE	MAE
PSO	16.001	0.036
GA	20.412	0.039
HGAPSO	2.153	0.012

Table 4. Results based on RMSE & Accuracy.

Method	RMSE	Accuracy
PSO	0.044	99.955
GA	0.049	99.950
HGAPSO	0.021	99.978

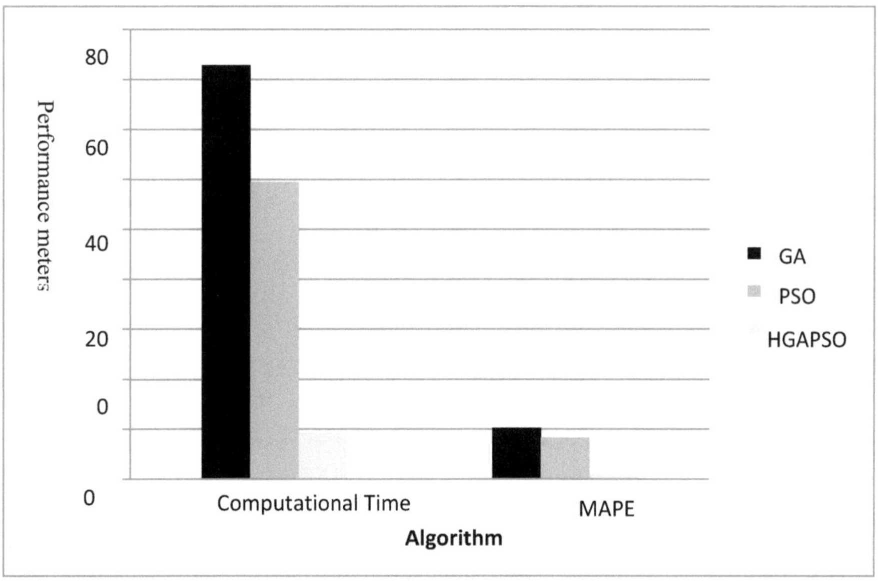

Fig. (3). Performance metric.

FINDING OPTIMAL CONDITIONS FOR LIQUID FLOW

In this phase, we determine the optimal value of input parameters to minimize the following rate. Here, an objective function (OF) is defined in which the flow rate is solely dependent on the numerical values of the potential attribute, regardless of its unit.

$$OF = \mathrm{F} = \mu_1 E^{\mu_2} . D^{\mu_3} 3 . K^{\mu_4} . n^{\mu_5}$$

$$\mathrm{OF} = 9.4281 . E^{8.366} . D^{-1.2252} . K^{1.7282} . n^{-1.1319} \tag{8}$$

To optimize this objective function, we chose the proposed HGAPSO algorithm, as it proved to be the best-fitted model with a higher degree of accuracy. The optimal condition, as determined by the completion of the iteration, is 0.218, 0.605, 0.898, and 0.025 for sensor output voltage, liquid conductivity, viscosity, and pipe diameter, respectively.

CONCLUSION

- **Nonlinear Complexity:** Modeling and optimizing parameters in nonlinear industrial processes is inherently complex and challenging.
- **Focus of Study:** The research aimed to optimize a nonlinear liquid flow process model using advanced optimization techniques.
- **Data Collection:** A total of 134 datasets were gathered—117 for training and 17 for validation.
- **Limitations of Traditional Methods:** Conventional computing approaches failed to effectively determine optimal parameters due to the nonlinear nature of the process.
- **Three-Phase Methodology:** In Phase 1, the implementation of the power algorithm ANOVA was realized to analyze the system. In Phase 2, the application of traditional algorithms (Genetic Algorithm and Particle Swarm Optimization) along with a hybrid HGAPSO algorithm was evaluated using MAE, MAPE, RMSE, and computational time, and in Phase 3, the HGAPSO algorithm was used to fine-tune parameters for minimizing the liquid flow rate.
- **Key Finding:** The hybrid HGAPSO algorithm proved effective in optimizing the nonlinear process parameters.
- **Significance:** The study underscores the value of improving optimization strategies for complex nonlinear systems.
- **Future Scope:** Further research could explore the integration of IoT-based AI models for smarter and more efficient process optimization.

REFERENCES

[1] B. Roy, "A Practically Validated Intelligent Calibration Technique using Optimized ANN for Ultrasonic Flow meter", *International Journal on Electrical Engineering andInformatics,* vol. 7, pp. 379-393, 2015.
[http://dx.doi.org/10.15676/ijeei.2015.7.3.2]

[2] P. Dutta, and A. Kumar, "Flow sensor analogue: realtime prediction analysis using SVM & KNN", *1st International conference on Emerging trends in Engineering & science (ETES) on 23rd-24th March,* 2018.

[3] P. Dutta, and A. Kumar, "Design an intelligent flow measurement technique by optimized fuzzy logic controller", *J. Eur. Syst. Autom.,* vol. 51, no. 1-3, pp. 89-107, 2018.
[http://dx.doi.org/10.3166/jesa.51.89-107]

[4] P. Dutta, and A. Kumar, "Intelligent calibration technique using optimized fuzzy logic controller for ultrasonic flow sensor", *Mathematical Modelling of Engineering Problems,* vol. 4, no. 2, pp. 91-94, 2017.
[http://dx.doi.org/10.18280/mmep.040205]

[5] P. Dutta, and A. Kumar, "Modelling of Liquid Flow control system Using OptimizedGenetic Algorithm. Statistics, Optimization &", *Inf. Comput.,* vol. 8, pp. 565-582, 2020.
[http://dx.doi.org/10.19139/soic-2310-5070-618]

[6] D.F. Cook, C.T. Ragsdale, and R.L. Major, "Combining a neural network with a genetic algorithm for process parameter optimization", *Eng. Appl. Artif. Intell.,* vol. 13, no. 4, pp. 391-396, 2000.
[http://dx.doi.org/10.1016/S0952-1976(00)00021-X]

[7] P. Dutta, and A. Kumar, "Design an intelligent calibration technique using optimized GA-ANN for liquid flow control system", *J. Eur. Syst. Autom.,* vol. 50, no. 4-6, pp. 449-470, 2017.
[http://dx.doi.org/10.3166/jesa.50.449-470]

[8] Liu H-G, Sun J-H, Zhang B, Zhang Y-S. ANFIS and its application in control system 2001; 15: 27–31.

[9] D. Pijush, and K. Asok, "Application of an anfis model to optimize the liquid flow rate of a process control system", *Chem. Eng. Trans.,* vol. 71, pp. 991-996, 2018.
[http://dx.doi.org/10.3303/CET1871166]

[10] P. Dutta, and A. Kumar, "Modeling and Optimization of a Liquid Flow Process using an Artificial Neural Network-Based Flower Pollination Algorithm", *Journal of Intelligent Systems,* vol. 29, no. 1, pp. 787-798, 2019.
[http://dx.doi.org/10.1515/jisys-2018-0206]

[11] P. Dutta, S. Mandal, and A. Kumar, "Application of FPA and ANOVA in the optimization of liquid flow control process", *Review of Computer Engineering Studies,* vol. 5, no. 1, pp. 7-11, 2019.
[http://dx.doi.org/10.18280/rces.050102]

[12] Dutta P, Mandal S, Kumar A. Comparative study: FPA based response surface methodology & ANOVA for the parameter optimization in process control. AMA_C 2018; 73: 23–7.
[http://dx.doi.org/10.18280/ama_c.730104]

[13] S. Mandal, P. Dutta, and A. Kumar, "Modeling of liquid flow control process using improved versions of elephant swarm water search algorithm", *SN Appl. Sci.,* vol. 1, no. 8, p. 886, 2019.
[http://dx.doi.org/10.1007/s42452-019-0914-5]

[14] P. Dutta, M. Majumder, and A. Kumar, "An Improved Grey Wolf Optimization Algorithm for Liquid flow", *Control Syst. (Tonbridge),* p. 12, 2021.

[15] F. Ebadifard, and S.M. Babamir, "A PSO-based task scheduling algorithm improved using a load-balancing technique for the cloud computing environment", *Concurr. Comput.,* vol. 30, no. 12, p. e4368, 2018.
[http://dx.doi.org/10.1002/cpe.4368]

[16] Y. Zhang, X. Liu, F. Bao, J. Chi, C. Zhang, and P. Liu, "Particle swarm optimization with adaptive learning strategy", *Knowl. Base. Syst.,* vol. 196, p. 105789, 2020. [http://dx.doi.org/10.1016/j.knosys.2020.105789]

[17] Y. Ren, C. Zhang, F. Zhao, H. Xiao, and G. Tian, "An asynchronous parallel disassembly planning based on genetic algorithm", *Eur. J. Oper. Res.,* vol. 269, no. 2, pp. 647-660, 2018. [http://dx.doi.org/10.1016/j.ejor.2018.01.055]

[18] Manasrah AM, Ba Ali H. Workflow scheduling using hybrid GA-PSO algorithm in cloud computing. Wireless Communications and Mobile Computing, 2018; 2018. [http://dx.doi.org/10.1155/2018/1934784]

[19] D. Sharma, P. Gaur, and A.P. Mittal, "Comparative analysis of hybrid GAPSO optimization technique with GA and PSO methods for cost optimization of an off- gridhybridenergy system", *Energy Technology & Policy,* vol. 1, no. 1, pp. 106-114, 2014. [http://dx.doi.org/10.1080/23317000.2014.969450]

[20] B.M. Sahoo, H.M. Pandey, and T. Amgoth, "GAPSO-H: A hybrid approach towards optimizing the cluster based routing in wireless sensor network", *Swarm Evol. Comput.,* vol. 60, p. 100772, 2021. [http://dx.doi.org/10.1016/j.swevo.2020.100772]

[21] X. Wu, Y. Wang, and T. Zhang, "An improved GAPSO hybridprogramming algorithm", *2009 International Conference on Information Engineering and Computer Science,* IEEE, pp. 1-4, 2009.

[22] S.S. Shrawane, M. Diagavane, and N. Bawane, "Optimal reactive power dispatch by furnishing UPFC using multi-objectivehybrid GAPSO approach for transmission loss minimisation and voltage stability", *2015 International Conference on Nascent Technologies in the Engineering Field (ICNTE),* IEEE, pp. 1-6, 2015.

[23] F. Ye, "Evolving the SVM model based on a hybrid method using swarm optimization techniques in combination with a genetic algorithm for medical diagnosis", *Multimedia Tools Appl.,* vol. 77, no. 3, pp. 3889-3918, 2018. [http://dx.doi.org/10.1007/s11042-016-4233-1]

[24] K.G. Parthiban, and S. Vijayachitra, "Spike detection from electroencephalogramsignals with aid of hybridgenetic algorithm-particle swarm optimization", *J. Med. Imaging Health Inform.,* vol. 5, no. 5, pp. 936-944, 2015. [http://dx.doi.org/10.1166/jmihi.2015.1480]

[25] Lei Z, Zhu Q, Zhou Y, Sun B, Sun W, Pan X. A GAPSO-EnhancedExtreme Learning Machine Method for Tool Wear Estimation in Milling Processes Based on Vibration Signals. International Journal of Precision Engineering and Manufacturing- Green Technology 2021; 8:745–59.

[26] H-X. Lei, N. Liu, D-J. Cui, T-J. Ma, and H-B. Xu, "Transformer faultdiagnosis based on optimized FCM clustering by hybrid GA and PSO", *Power System Protection and Control,* vol. 39, pp. 52-56, 2011.

[27] F. Fausto, E. Cuevas, A. Valdivia, and A. González, "A global optimization algorithm inspired in the behavior of selfish herds", *Biosystems,* vol. 160, pp. 39-55, 2017. [http://dx.doi.org/10.1016/j.biosystems.2017.07.010] [PMID: 28847742]

[28] B. Tran, B. Xue, and M. Zhang, "Variable-lengthparticle swarm optimization for feature selection on high-dimensional classification", *IEEE Trans. Evol. Comput.,* vol. 23, no. 3, pp. 473-487, 2019. [http://dx.doi.org/10.1109/TEVC.2018.2869405]

[29] O.H. Mohammed, Y. Amirat, and M. Benbouzid, "Particle swarm optimization of a hybridwind/tidal/PV/batteryenergy system. Application to a remote area in Bretagne, France", *Energy Procedia,* vol. 162, pp. 87-96, 2019. [http://dx.doi.org/10.1016/j.egypro.2019.04.010]

[30] A.H. Elsheikh, and M. Abd Elaziz, "Review on applications of particle swarm optimization in solar energy systems", *Int. J. Environ. Sci. Technol.,* vol. 16, no. 2, pp. 1159-1170, 2019.

[http://dx.doi.org/10.1007/s13762-018-1970-x]

[31] M. Hemmat Esfe, M.H. Hajmohammad, and S.H. Rostamian, "Multi-objective particle swarm optimization of thermal conductivity and dynamic viscosity of magnetic nanodiamond-cobalt oxide dispersed in ethylene glycolusing RSM", *Int. Commun. Heat Mass Transf.,* vol. 117, p. 104760, 2020. [http://dx.doi.org/10.1016/j.icheatmasstransfer.2020.104760]

[32] A. shafaei, and G.R. Khayati, "A predictive model on size of silver nanoparticles prepared by green synthesis method using hybrid artificial neural network-particle swarm optimization algorithm", *Measurement,* vol. 151, p. 107199, 2020. [http://dx.doi.org/10.1016/j.measurement.2019.107199]

[33] K. Kalita, I. Shivakoti, and R.K. Ghadai, "Optimizing process parameters for laser beam micro-marking using genetic algorithm and particle swarm optimization", *Mater. Manuf. Process.,* vol. 32, no. 10, pp. 1101-1108, 2017. [http://dx.doi.org/10.1080/10426914.2017.1303156]

[34] H. Wang, M. Peng, J. Wesley Hines, G. Zheng, Y. Liu, and B.R. Upadhyaya, "A hybrid fault diagnosis methodology with support vector machine and improved particle swarm optimization for nuclear power plants", *ISA Trans.,* vol. 95, pp. 358-371, 2019. [http://dx.doi.org/10.1016/j.isatra.2019.05.016] [PMID: 31171304]

[35] H.M. Pandey, and N. Jain, *Performance Evaluation of Reproduction Operators in Genetic Algorithm. Computer Communication, Networking and Internet Security.* Springer, 2017, pp. 451-460. [http://dx.doi.org/10.1007/978-981-10-3226-4_46]

[36] G. Celli, F. Pilo, G. Pisano, and G.G. Soma, "Distribution energy storage investment prioritization with a real coded multi-objective Genetic Algorithm", *Electr. Power Syst. Res.,* vol. 163, pp. 154-163, 2018. [http://dx.doi.org/10.1016/j.epsr.2018.06.008]

[37] Paliwal A, Gimeno F, Nair V, Li Y, Lubin M, Kohli P, et al. Reinforcedgenetic algorithm learning for optimizing computation graphs. ArXivPreprintArXiv:190502494 2019.

[38] O. Kor, and S. Acarer, *Aerodynamic Optimization of a Compressor Rotor Using Genetic Algorithm. DesigningEnginessering Structures Using Stochastic Optimization Methods.* CRC Press, 2020, pp. 187-202. [http://dx.doi.org/10.1201/9780429289576-14]

[39] R. Sharma, B.K. Jha, and V. Pahuja, "Optimization Techniques for Response Predication in Metal Cutting Operation: A Review", *Proceedings of the International Conference on Industrial and Manufacturing Systems (CIMS-2020),* Springer, pp. 77-92, 2022. [http://dx.doi.org/10.1007/978-3-030-73495-4_6]

[40] D. Zhang, W. Li, X. Wu, and X. Lv, "Application of simulated annealing genetic algorithm-optimized back propagation (BP) neural network in fault diagnosis", *International Journal of Modeling, Simulation, and Scientific Computing,* vol. 10, no. 4, p. 1950024, 2019. [http://dx.doi.org/10.1142/S1793962319500247]

[41] T. Ueda, J. Katagiri, T. Oki, and S. Koyanaka, "Genetic algorithm optimization in discreteelement simulation of electric parts separation from printed circuit board", *Struct. Multidiscipl. Optim.,* pp. 1-9, 2021.

[42] G. Xu, L. Zhuang, B. Dong, Q. Liu, and J. Wen, "Optimization design with an advanced genetic algorithm for a compact air-air heat exchanger applied in aero engine", *Int. J. Heat Mass Transf.,* vol. 158, p. 119952, 2020. [http://dx.doi.org/10.1016/j.ijheatmasstransfer.2020.119952]

[43] Y. Sun, N. Geng, S. Gong, and Y. Yang, "Research on improved genetic algorithm in path optimization of aviation logistics distribution center", *J. Intell. Fuzzy Syst.,* vol. 38, no. 1, pp. 29-37, 2020. [http://dx.doi.org/10.3233/JIFS-179377]

[44] F. Moslehi, A. Haeri, and F. Martínez-Álvarez, "A novel hybrid GA–PSO framework for mining quantitative association rules", *Soft Comput.,* vol. 24, no. 6, pp. 4645-4666, 2020. [http://dx.doi.org/10.1007/s00500-019-04226-6]

[45] V. Anand, and S. Pandey, "New approach of GA–PSO-based clustering and routing in wireless sensor networks", *Int. J. Commun. Syst.,* vol. 33, no. 16, p. e4571, 2020. [http://dx.doi.org/10.1002/dac.4571]

[46] A. Anand, and L. Suganthi, "Hybrid GA-PSO optimization of artificial neural network for forecastingelectricity demand", *Energies,* vol. 11, no. 4, p. 728, 2018. [http://dx.doi.org/10.3390/en11040728]

[47] J.H. Tam, Z.C. Ong, Z. Ismail, B.C. Ang, and S.Y. Khoo, "A new hybrid GA−ACO−PSO algorithm for solving various engineering design problems", *Int. J. Comput. Math.,* vol. 96, no. 5, pp. 883-919, 2019. [http://dx.doi.org/10.1080/00207160.2018.1463438]

[48] P. Dutta, S. Paul, and A. Kumar, Comparative analysis of varioussupervised machine learning techniques for diagnosis of COVID-19. [http://dx.doi.org/10.1016/B978-0-323-85172-5.00020-4]

[49] P. Dutta, S. Paul, A.J. Obaid, S. Pal, and K. Mukhopadhyay, "Feature Selection based Artificial Intelligence Techniques for the Prediction of COVID like Diseases", *J. Phys. Conf. Ser.,* vol. 1963, no. 1, p. 012167, 2021. [http://dx.doi.org/10.1088/1742-6596/1963/1/012167]

CHAPTER 14

Photovoltaic Cell Performance Assessment Using the Hybrid CSPSO Algorithm

Gour Gopal Jana[1], **Rudrajit Datta**[2] and **Arindam Sadhu**[3,*]

[1] *Department of Electronics & Communication Engineering, Greater Kolkata College of Engineering and Management, Baruipur, West Bengal, 743387, India*

[2] *Department of Electrical Engineering, Greater Kolkata College of Engineering and Management, Baruipur, West Bengal, 743387, India*

[3] *Department of Electronics & Communication Engineering, Dr. Sudhir Chandra Sur Institute of Technology and Sports Complex, Kolkata, West Bengal, India*

Abstract: The conventional model is limited to obtaining the optimal solution from a nonlinear system objective function. An effective method for determining the optimal solution for nonlinear objective functions is the use of evolutionary algorithms (EA). In this study, we suggested three optimization techniques: Cuckoo Search Optimization (CSO), Particle Swarm Optimization (PSO), and a hybrid algorithm of CSO & PSO (HCSPSO) to determine the single and double-diode solar cells' optimal parameters. The proposed algorithm was compared with the CSO and PSO in terms of statistical metrics for a single-diode (SDM) and double-diode model (DDM). According to a comparison analysis, a more precise model for estimating a solar cell's optimal parameter with fewer iterations is offered by the upgraded CSO optimization. As a result, we suggested HCSPSO as the top optimization tool for delivering the most promising results.

Keywords: Improved cuckoo search optimization, Metaheuristics, Parametric optimization, Solar cell.

INTRODUCTION

In the current period, renewable energy sources such as solar energy are becoming increasingly appealing due to the energy crisis and the negative environmental impacts of pollution [1 - 3]. A solar cell must be modeled to forecast how it will behave under varrying temperatures and sun intensity situations. Although there have been several research studies on solar cells, the most popular literature

* **Corresponding author Arindam Sadhu:** Department of Electronics & Communication Engineering, Dr. Sudhir Chandra Sur Institute of Technology and Sports Complex, Kolkata, West Bengal, India; E-mail: arindam.hit11@gmail.com

Pijush Dutta, Sudip Mondal, Korhan Cengiz and S. Balamurugan (Eds.)

review compares the SDM with the DDM [4 - 7]. An effective optimization approach is necessary in a photovoltaic system to determine the best parameter and anticipate the performance of a solar cell [8, 9].

There are diverse characteristics of bio inspired optimization experimented on SDM & DDM of PV modules such as Genetic Algorithm [10, 11], Differential Evolution [12, 13], ABC calculation [14, 15], Chaotic JAYA Algorithm [16], TLBO [17], SFLA [18], Moth-Flame Optimization (MFO) [19], Sine–Cosine Algorithm [21], Ant lion optimization (ALO) [20], FPA [22, 23], elephant swarm water search (ESWS) [24], PSO [25] and so on. To study the performance of an SDM, three optimization techniques, Bat algorithm (BA), CSO & Firefly algorithm (FA) [26], were used. Moreover, wind-driven optimization was also used for the optimization of DDM [27]. Apart from this metaheuristic optimization, some researchers also applied a fuzzy logic controller [28] and genetic algorithms [29]. In the theory of the "No Free Lunch hypothesis," [30] it is mentioned that no single metaheuristic is reasonable for taking care of a wide range of issues. Parametric optimization of a single diode, double diode and PV model was done by a hybrid teaching-learning and artificial bee colony (TLABC) [31, 32], improved version of whale optimization algorithm (IWOA) [33], ensemble differential evolution (EDE) [34], improved differential evolution (DE), and WOA [35], improved chaotic whale optimization algorithm (ICWOA) [36], improved ABC, and FPA [37], Hybrid PSO and SA (HPSOSA) [38], Hybrid FA and PSA (HFPSA) [39], Hybrid PSO & GWO algorithm [40]. There are still open challenges in achieving better computational time and convergence speed for optimizing mathematical models. PSO deals with only local search abilities in certain constraints [41 - 43]. Cuckoo Search Optimizer (CSO) is a powerful evolutionary algorithm [44, 45] that exhibits superior convergence ability. To improve the convergence speed and capability of searching the global optimum, we introduced a new hybrid algorithm, HCSPSO, constructed by incorporating PSO with CSO algorithms. The effectiveness of this technique lies in the single and double solar cell model problem with non-smooth cost functions like diode current in both cases. So far Hybrid HCSPSO has been applied to many problems such as for improving the convergence performance of electrical load forecasting [46], energy extraction from fuel cells [47], reconfiguration of electrical distribution network [48], multiobjective parametric optimization in hydropower station [49], self-adaptive knowledge learning in the education sector [50], identification of fault location in a distributed network [51], *etc.* The remaining part of this paper is presented as follows. SDM and DDM mathematical models are presented followed by a discussion on the objective function, the hybrid algorithm, and the analysis of results and conclusions.

MATHEMATICS MODEL OF SOLAR CELL

Single Diode Model (SDM)

Fig. (**1**) represents the equivalent circuit with a mathematical model for SDM [52].

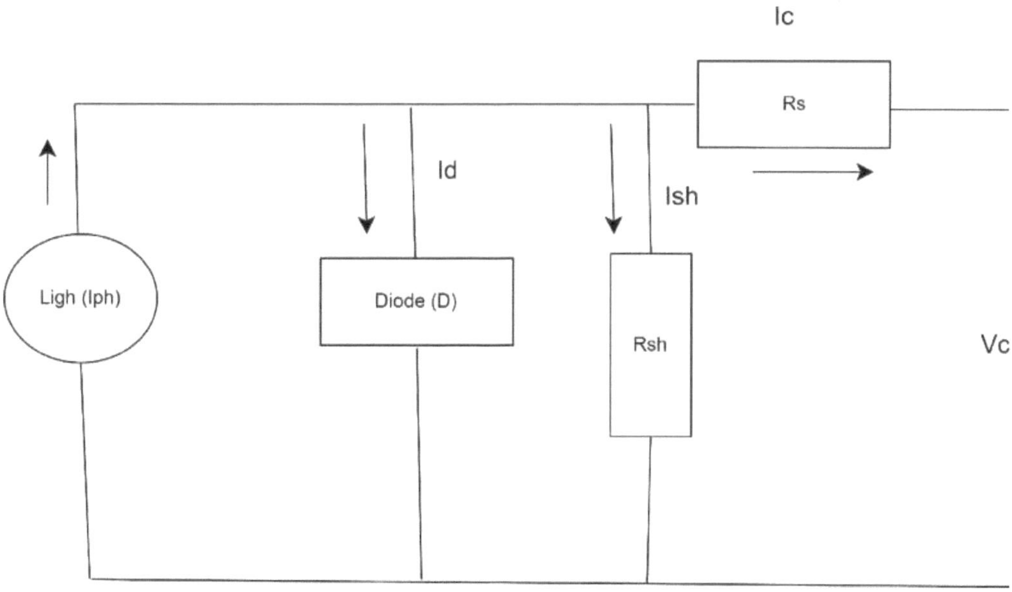

Fig. (1). Simplified model of SDM.

$$I_C = I_{ph} - I_{sh} - I_d \tag{1}$$

$$\text{Where, } I_d = I_{sd}\left[\exp\left(\frac{V_C + I_C R_s}{\eta V_t}\right) - 1\right] \tag{2}$$

$$I_{sh} = \frac{V_C + I_C R_s}{R} \tag{3}$$

After combining the equations, the resulting current equation is presented in Eq. (4)

$$I_C = I_{ph} - I_{sd}\left[\exp\left(\frac{V_C + I_C R_s}{\eta V_t}\right) - 1\right] - \frac{V_C + I_C R_s}{R_{sh}} \tag{4}$$

So, the equation contains five parameters (I_{ph}, I_{sd}, R_s, R_{sh}, η) that needs to be optimized.

Double Diode Model (DDM)

Fig. (**2**) represents the equivalent circuit with a mathematical model for SDM [53].

$$I_C = I_{ph} - I_{d1} - I_{d2} - I_{sh} \tag{4}$$

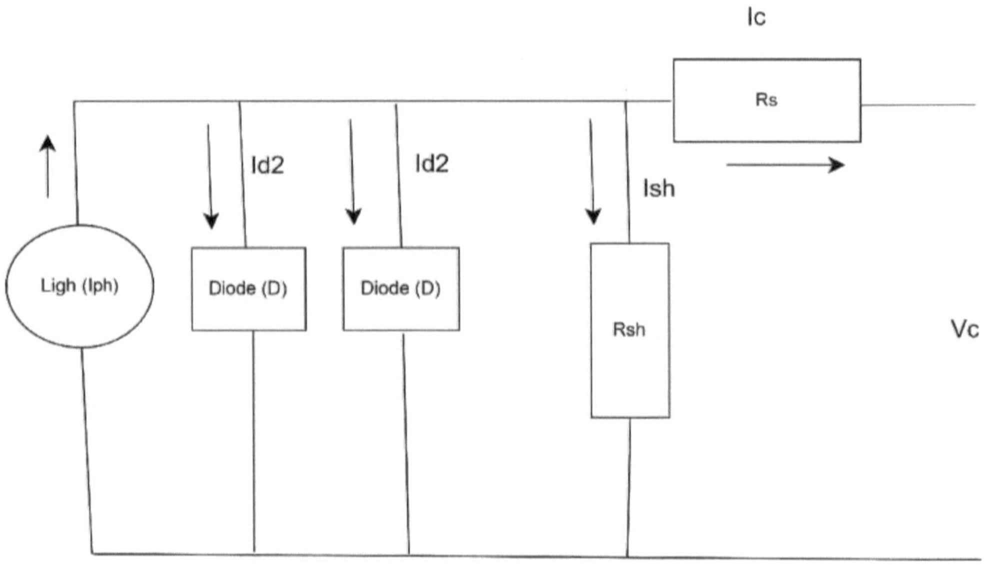

Fig. (2). Simplified model of DDM.

In DDM, the resulting current can be formulated as:

$$I_C = I_{ph} - I_{sd1}\left[\exp\left(\frac{V_C + I_C R_s}{\eta_1 V_t}\right) - 1\right] - I_{sd2}\left[\exp\left(\frac{V_C + I_C R_s}{\eta_2 V_t}\right) - 1\right] - \frac{V_C + I_C R_s}{R_{sh}} \tag{5}$$

The model contains seven optimization parameters (I_{ph}, I_{sd1}, I_{sd2}, R_s, R_{sh}, η_1, η_2)

PV Module Model

In the PV module, connected cells follow the same mathematical formulation.

OBJECTIVE FUNCTION

In the present model, the Root Mean Square Error (RMSE) [54] is considered as an objective function formulated in Eq. (6).

$$\mathrm{RMSE(X)} = \sqrt{\frac{1}{N}\sum_{i=1}^{N} f(V_{Ci}, I_{Ci}, X)^2} \quad \textbf{(6)}$$

For SDM, the objective function formulated in Eq. (7)

$$\mathrm{RMSE_{min}} = \sqrt{\frac{1}{N}\sum_{i=1}^{N}(I_{measured} - I_{calculated}\ (I_{ph},\ I_{sd},\ R_s,\ R_{sh},\ \eta))^2} \quad \textbf{(7)}$$

For DDM, the objective function is formulated in Eq. (8)

$$\mathrm{RMSE_{min}} = \sqrt{\frac{1}{N}\sum_{i=1}^{N}(I_{measured} - I_{calculated}\ (I_{ph}, I_{sd1}, I_{sd2}, R_s, R_{sh}, \eta_1, \eta_2))^2} \quad \textbf{(8)}$$

PROPOSED METHODOLOGY

In this section, a hybrid algorithm of CSO and PSO algorithms is presented. Every optimization technique has some advantages and disadvantages. The hybrid algorithm is designed by focusing on the positive aspects of both the traditional algorithms [55]. PSO is the most used traditional algorithm that offers a premature convergence speed in complex problems [56]. However, CSO has a more explorative search, but the convergence rate is comparatively slower than PSO [57]. No algorithm can efficiently optimize all optimization problems. The proposed methodology for the present research is shown in Fig. (**3**). The parameters of each algorithm are shown in Table **1**.

Table 1. Parameters setting.

-	PSO	CSO	HCSPSO
No. population (N)	25	25	25
Inertia weight	0.9 to 0.4	-	0.9 to 0.4
Other constant	$C_1 = C_2=2$	Abandoned probability P_a=0.25	Abandoned probability P_a=0.25, $C_1 = C_2$=2

RESULTS ANALYSIS AND DISCUSSION

In this research, we have considered 26 datasets of SDM and DDM solar cells [58, 59]. Here, we perform a comparison between HCSPSO and the other two traditional optimization techniques.

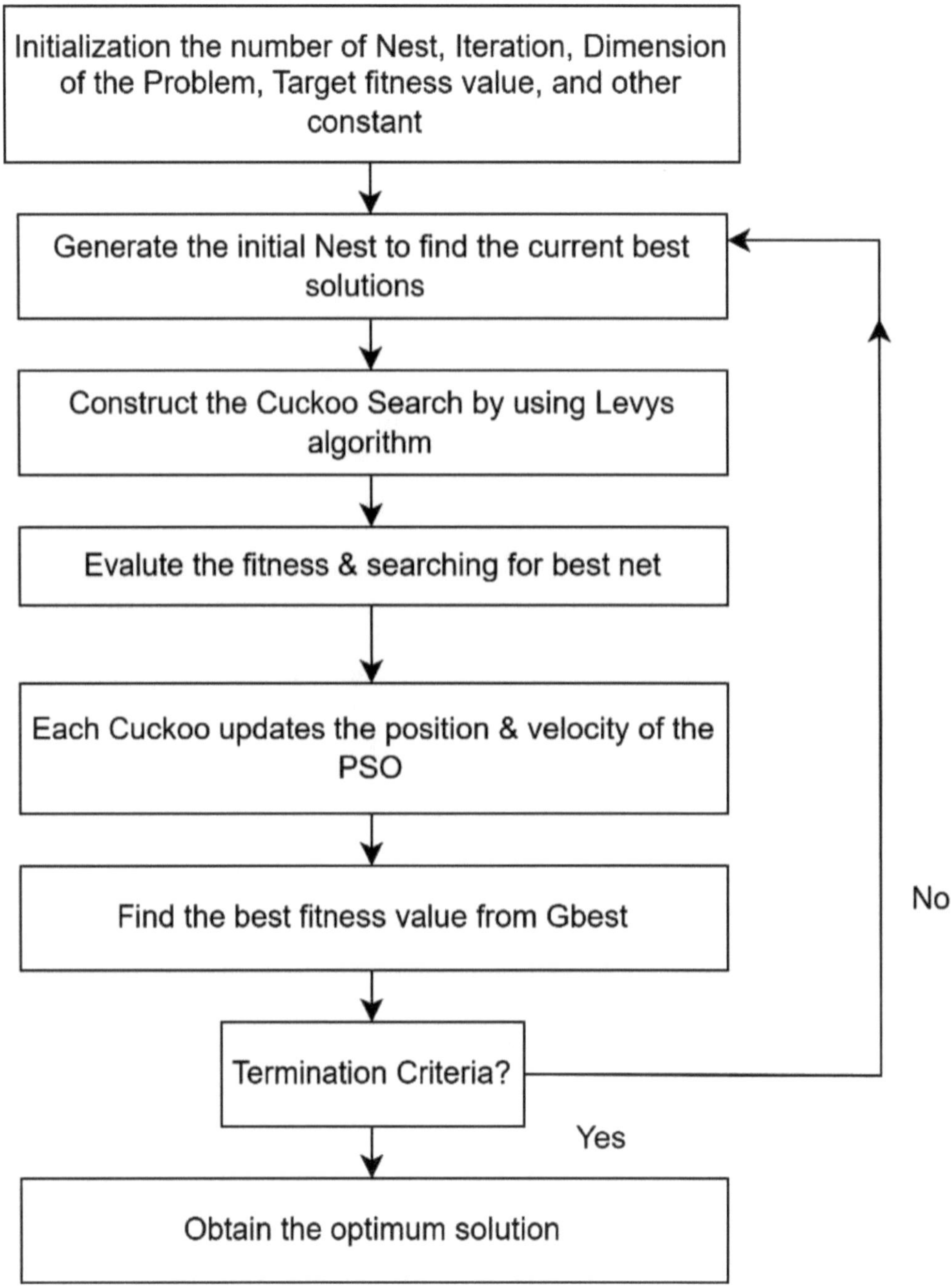

Fig. (3). Flowchart for the Proposed HCSPSO.

Table **2** shows the parameter search ranges for SDM and DDM.

Table 2. Parameters search ranges.

PV System	Ranges
Iph in Amp	(0,1)
Isd in μA	(0,1)
R_s in Ω	(0,0.5)
Rsh in Ω	(0,100)
n	(1,2)

Due to its stochastic nature, every optimization algorithm produces a distinctive output. To overcome this situation, we run each algorithm 20 times to complete the execution process. In our research, we used Matlab 2013b version and hardware specifications: 16 GB RAM, Intel(R) Core (TM) i5 processor, with a Windows 10 working System. The overall result analysis is described in the following section.

During the reliability test, we observed how an optimization technique reaches its global minimum with a small variation [60 - 62]. For this purpose, we calculated the standard deviation of each algorithm, as shown in Table **3**, for both SDM and DDM.

Table 3. Result based on standard deviation.

Case	Method	Standard Deviation
RTC-SDM	CSO	0.0088
	PSO	0.0289
	HCSPSO	0.0032
RTC-DDM	CSO	0.0065
	PSO	0.0264
	HCSPSO	0.0032

Computational time is measured by the amount of time an optimization algorithm takes to achieve the optimal value of a model [63 - 64]. Table **4** shows that the proposed hybrid HCSPSO algorithm has achieved an optimum computation time compared to CSO and PSO.

Table 4. Result based on average computational time.

Case	Method	Avg. Computational Time
RTC-SDM	CSO	78.89 Sec
	PSO	169.46 Sec
	HCSPSO	74.41 Sec
RTC-DDM	CSO	84.28 Sec
	PSO	294.37 Sec
	HCSPSO	68.64 Sec

Convergence speed is another important metric, which indicates how fast an optimization algorithm reaches its minimum objective function value for several runs [65 - 67]. For this purpose, we set the iteration number from 100 to 5000. The convergence speed of each algorithm is depicted in Figs. (**4** and **5**). In both cases (SDM and DDM), the proposed HCSPSO shows a better convergence speed.

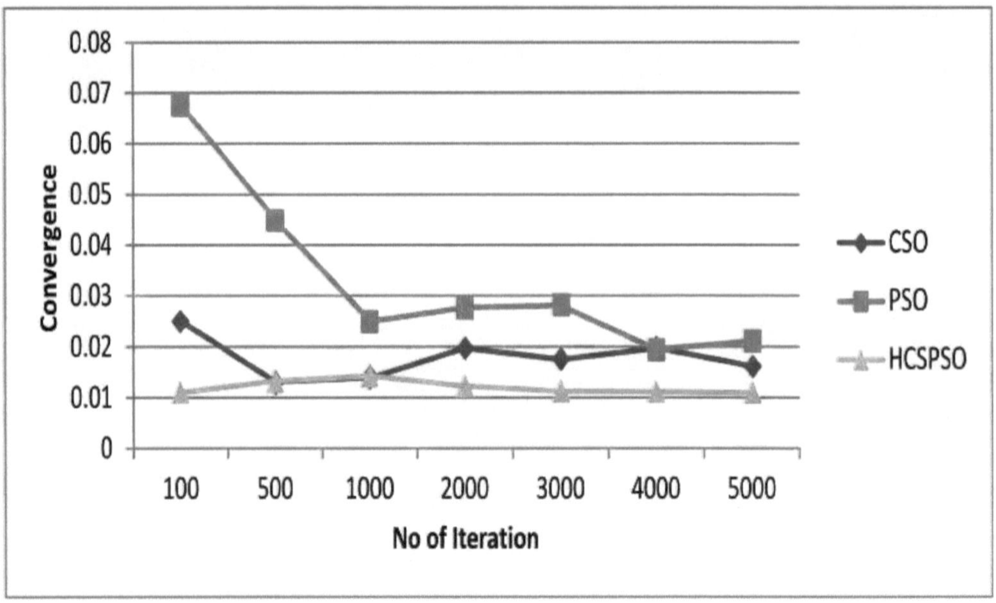

Fig. (4). Convergence speed for SDM.

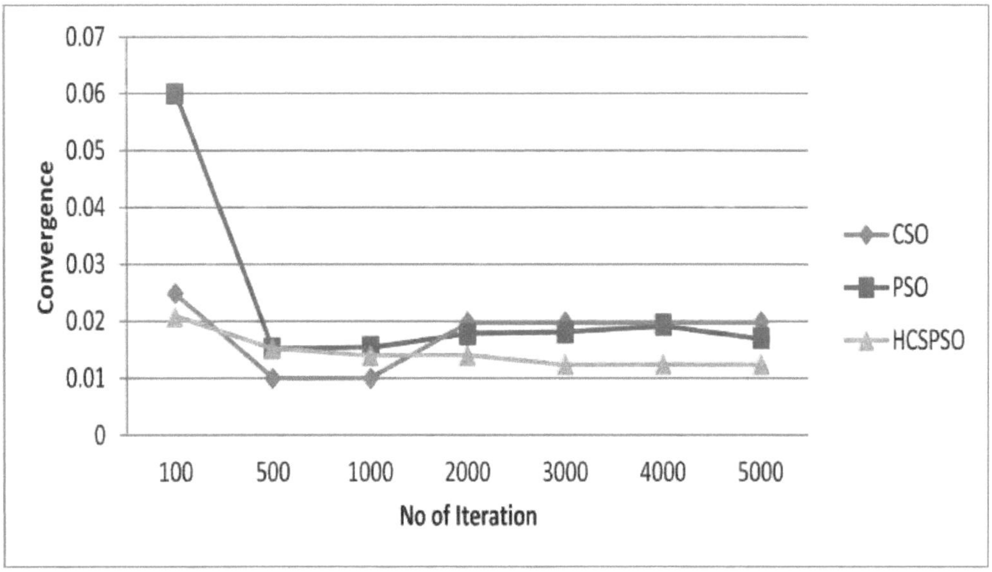

Fig. (5). Convergence speed for DDM.

Accuracy can be measured by how close the measured value is to the true value [67]. Here, we used Relative error (RE) and individual absolute error (*IAE*) as the error index represented in Eqs. (9) & (10).

$$IAE = |I_{measured} - I_{calculated}| \quad \textbf{(9)}$$

$$RE = \frac{I_{measured} - I_{Calculated}}{I_{Calculated}} \quad \textbf{(10)}$$

Where $I_{measured}$ and $I_{calculated}$ are the calculated and true value of current. Tables **5** and **6** represent the optimum parameters for both SDM and DDM.

Table 5. Optimal parameters of SDM.

Parameters	PSO	CSO	HCSPSO
I_{ph}	0.921	0.752	0.723
I_{sd}	0.452	0.458	0.711
R_s	0.0451	0.0398	0.0002
R_{sh}	20.14	60.23	10.33
n	1.8481	1.7874	1.6222

Table 6. Optimal parameters for DDM.

Parameters	PSO	CSO	HCSPSO
I_{ph}	0.734	0.701	0.759
I_{sd1}	0.928	0.591	0535
R_s	0.004	0.029	0.034
R_{sh}	85.32	70.938	100
n_1	1.712	1.582	1.534
I_{sd2}	0.00012	0.2351	0.1252
n_2	1.8	1.67	2

Tables **6** and **7** show that hybrid HCSPSO achieved the lowest RMSE & TAE for both SDM and DDM. Relative error characteristics concerning testing datasets for SDM and DDM are shown in Figs. (**6** and **7**).

Table 7. Result based on TAE.

Case	Method	Total Absolute Error (TAE)
RTC-SDM	CSO	0.02780
	PSO	0.02142
	HCSPSO	0.01584
RTC-DDM	CSO	0.02213
	PSO	0.02431
	HCSPSO	0.01648

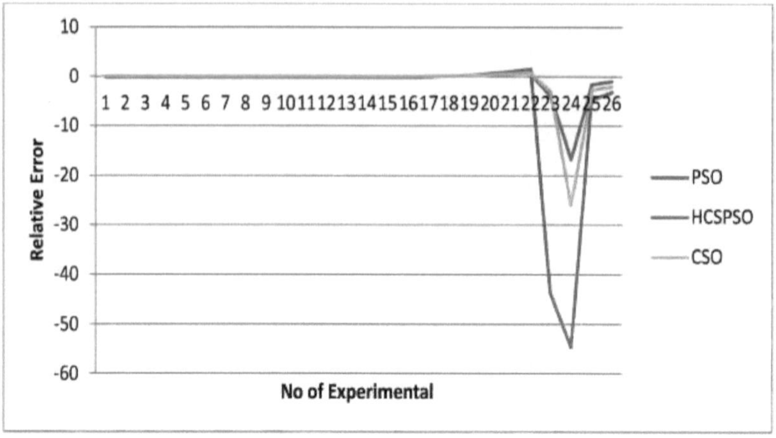

Fig. (6). Graphical characteristics of RE for SDM.

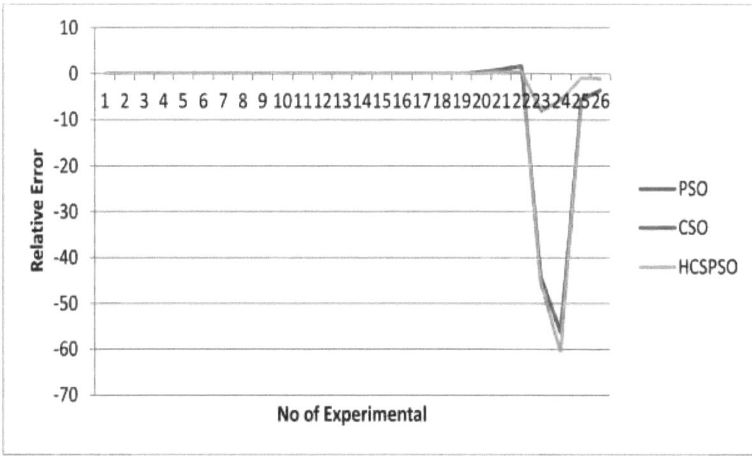

Fig. (7). Graphical characteristics of RE for DDM.

Table 8. Results based on RMSE & accuracy.

Case	Method	RSME	Accuracy
RTC-SDM	CSO	1.786	98.214
	PSO	2.896	97.103
	HCSPSO	0.885	99.115
RTC- DDM	GWO	1.768	98.231
	PSO	2.646	97.354
	HCSPSO	0.926	99.074

Overall Efficiency

For the overall performance of the applied algorithm, we allocated an exhibition score to every paradigm. Table **9** shows the close examination dependent on these scores to assess the general productivity of the proposed HCSPSO calculation, which outperformed other algorithms.

Table 9. Performance for all the proposed algorithms.

Method	Standard Deviation	Time	Convergence	TAE	RE	RMSE	Accuracy	Max.	Min.	Mean	Total Score
CSO	0.33	0.33	0.5	0	0.5	0.33	0.33	0.33	0.33	0.33	3.31
PSO	0	0	0	0.33	0	0	0.33	0.33	0.33	0.33	1.65
HCSPSO	0.66	0.66	0.5	0.66	0.5	0.66	0.33	0.33	0.33	0.33	4.96

CONCLUSION

The ideal solar cell characteristics for PV system control and design are presented in this research based on the experimental datasets of SDM and DDM RTC cells. A novel multi-objective hybrid optimization technique that incorporates both PSO and CSO is used because of the intricacy of the optimization issue. Additionally, the SDM and DDM objective functions are compared between HCSPSO, PSO, and CSO. The convergence speed suggested that the HCSPSO algorithm is a successful algorithm that can be used as an alternate technique for determining the modelling parameters of PV modules because of its capacity to seek the global optimum. However, the relative accuracy and standard deviation of HCSPSO are among its major drawbacks, which can be further improved by considering the proper selection of parameters and other hybrid algorithms.

REFERENCES

[1] P.G.V. Sampaio, and M.O.A. González, "Photovoltaic solar energy: Conceptual framework", *Renew. Sustain. Energy Rev.,* vol. 74, pp. 590-601, 2017.
[http://dx.doi.org/10.1016/j.rser.2017.02.081]

[2] T. Jia, Y. Dai, and R. Wang, "Refining energy sources in winemaking industry by using solar energy as alternatives for fossil fuels: A review and perspective", *Renew. Sustain. Energy Rev.,* vol. 88, pp. 278-296, 2018.
[http://dx.doi.org/10.1016/j.rser.2018.02.008]

[3] T.S. Ge, R.Z. Wang, Z.Y. Xu, Q.W. Pan, S. Du, X.M. Chen, T. Ma, X.N. Wu, X.L. Sun, and J.F. Chen, "Solar heating and cooling: Present and future development", *Renew. Energy,* vol. 126, pp. 1126-1140, 2018.
[http://dx.doi.org/10.1016/j.renene.2017.06.081]

[4] S. Bana, and R.P. Saini, "A mathematical modeling framework to evaluate the performance of single diode and double diode based SPV systems", *Energy Rep.,* vol. 2, pp. 171-187, 2016.
[http://dx.doi.org/10.1016/j.egyr.2016.06.004]

[5] M.B.H. Rhouma, A. Gastli, L. Ben Brahim, F. Touati, and M. Benammar, "A simple method for extracting the parameters of the PV cell single-diode model", *Renew. Energy,* vol. 113, pp. 885-894, 2017.
[http://dx.doi.org/10.1016/j.renene.2017.06.064]

[6] D.S.H. Chan, and J.C.H. Phang, "Analytical methods for the extraction of solar-cell single- and double-diode model parameters from I-V characteristics", *IEEE Trans. Electron Dev.,* vol. 34, no. 2, pp. 286-293, 1987.
[http://dx.doi.org/10.1109/T-ED.1987.22920]

[7] T. Ahmad, S. Sobhan, and M.F. Nayan, "Comparative analysis between single diode and double diode model of PV cell: concentrate different parameters effect on its efficiency", *Journal of Power and Energy Engineering,* vol. 4, no. 3, pp. 31-46, 2016.
[http://dx.doi.org/10.4236/jpee.2016.43004]

[8] A.M. Humada, M. Hojabri, S. Mekhilef, and H.M. Hamada, "Solar cell parameters extraction based on single and double-diode models: A review", *Renew. Sustain. Energy Rev.,* vol. 56, pp. 494-509, 2016.
[http://dx.doi.org/10.1016/j.rser.2015.11.051]

[9] M. Derick, C. Rani, M. Rajesh, M.E. Farrag, Y. Wang, and K. Busawon, "An improved optimization technique for estimation of solar photovoltaic parameters", *Sol. Energy,* vol. 157, pp. 116-124, 2017.
[http://dx.doi.org/10.1016/j.solener.2017.08.006]

[10] A. Fathy, and H. Rezk, "Parameter estimation of photovoltaic system using imperialist competitive algorithm", *Renew. Energy,* vol. 111, pp. 307-320, 2017. [http://dx.doi.org/10.1016/j.renene.2017.04.014]

[11] P.A. Kumari, and P. Geethanjali, "Adaptive genetic algorithm based multi-objective optimization for photovoltaic cell design parameter extraction", *Energy Procedia,* vol. 117, pp. 432-441, 2017. [http://dx.doi.org/10.1016/j.egypro.2017.05.165]

[12] T.O. Olowu, M. Jafari, and A.I. Sarwat, "A multi-objective optimization technique for volt-var control with high PV penetration using genetic algorithm", *2018 North American Power Symposium (NAPS),* pp. 1-6, 2018. [http://dx.doi.org/10.1109/NAPS.2018.8600557]

[13] S. Li, W. Gong, X. Yan, C. Hu, D. Bai, and L. Wang, "Parameter estimation of photovoltaic models with memetic adaptive differential evolution", *Sol. Energy,* vol. 190, pp. 465-474, 2019. [http://dx.doi.org/10.1016/j.solener.2019.08.022]

[14] S. Li, Q. Gu, W. Gong, and B. Ning, "An enhanced adaptive differential evolution algorithm for parameter extraction of photovoltaic models", *Energy Convers. Manage.,* vol. 205, p. 112443, 2020. [http://dx.doi.org/10.1016/j.enconman.2019.112443]

[15] D.C. Huynh, L.D. Ho, and M.W. Dunnigan, "Parameter estimation of solar photovoltaic cells using an improved artificial bee colony algorithm", *International Conference on Green Technology and Sustainable Development,* Springer, pp. 281-292, 2020.

[16] M. Premkumar, T.S. Babu, S. Umashankar, and R. Sowmya, "A new metaphor-less algorithms for the photovoltaic cell parameter estimation", *Optik (Stuttg.),* vol. 208, p. 164559, 2020. [http://dx.doi.org/10.1016/j.ijleo.2020.164559]

[17] M. Premkumar, P. Jangir, R. Sowmya, R.M. Elavarasan, and B.S. Kumar, "Enhanced chaotic JAYA algorithm for parameter estimation of photovoltaic cell/modules", *ISA Trans.,* vol. 116, pp. 139-166, 2021. [http://dx.doi.org/10.1016/j.isatra.2021.01.045] [PMID: 33551129]

[18] G. Xiong, J. Zhang, D. Shi, L. Zhu, and X. Yuan, "Parameter extraction of solar photovoltaic models with an either-or teaching learning based algorithm", *Energy Convers. Manage.,* vol. 224, p. 113395, 2020. [http://dx.doi.org/10.1016/j.enconman.2020.113395]

[19] A. Ramadan, S. Kamel, A. Korashy, and J. Yu, "Photovoltaic cells parameter estimation using an enhanced teaching–learning-based optimization algorithm", *Iran. J. Sci. Technol. Trans. Electr. Eng.,* vol. 44, no. 2, pp. 767-779, 2020. [http://dx.doi.org/10.1007/s40998-019-00257-9]

[20] M. Wang, Q. Zhang, H. Chen, A.A. Heidari, M. Mafarja, and H. Turabieh, "Evaluation of constraint in photovoltaic cells using ensemble multi-strategy shuffled frog leading algorithms", *Energy Convers. Manage.,* vol. 244, p. 114484, 2021. [http://dx.doi.org/10.1016/j.enconman.2021.114484]

[21] H. Sheng, C. Li, H. Wang, Z. Yan, Y. Xiong, Z. Cao, and Q. Kuang, "Parameters extraction of photovoltaic models using an improved moth-flame optimization", *Energies,* vol. 12, no. 18, p. 3527, 2019. [http://dx.doi.org/10.3390/en12183527]

[22] K. G, and Harish Kumar, "Modeling of solar cell under different conditions by Ant Lion Optimizer with LambertW function", *Appl. Soft Comput.,* vol. 71, pp. 141-151, 2018. [http://dx.doi.org/10.1016/j.asoc.2018.06.025]

[23] O. Aydin, H. Gozde, M. Dursun, and M.C. Taplamacioglu, "Comparative parameter estimation of single diode PV-cell model by using sine-cosine algorithm and whale optimization algorithm", [http://dx.doi.org/10.1109/ICEEE2019.2019.00020]

[24] M. Mohamed, M. Abdullah, and M. Yahia, *Parameters estimation of photovoltaic module using Grey Wolf Optimization method.* unpublished [http://dx.doi.org/10.15199/48.2021.02.26]

[25] M-U-N. Khursheed, M.A. Alghamdi, M.F. Nadeem Khan, A.K. Khan, I. Khan, A. Ahmed, A.T. Kiani, and M.A. Khan, "PV model parameter estimation using modified FPA with dynamic switch probability and step size function", *IEEE Access,* vol. 9, pp. 42027-42044, 2021. [http://dx.doi.org/10.1109/ACCESS.2021.3064757]

[26] A.K. Ryad, A.M. Atallah, and A. Zekry, "Photovoltaic parameters estimation using hybrid flower pollination with clonal selection algorithm", *Turkish Journal of Electromechanics and Energy,* vol. 3, pp. 15-21, 2018.

[27] P. Dutta, S. K. Biswas, S. Biswas, and M. Majumder, *Parametric optimization of Solar Parabolic Collector using metaheuristic optimization.* unpublished [http://dx.doi.org/10.36647/CIML/02.01.A004]

[28] S. Mandal, "Modeling of photovoltaic systems using modified elephant swarm water search algorithm", *International Journal of Modelling and Simulation,* vol. 40, no. 6, pp. 436-455, 2020. [http://dx.doi.org/10.1080/02286203.2019.1650488]

[29] J. Gupta, P. Nijhawan, and S. Ganguli, *Parameter estimation of different solar cells using a swarm intelligence technique, .* [http://dx.doi.org/10.21203/rs.3.rs-371558/v1]

[30] P. Dutta, R. Agarwala, M. Majumder, and A. Kumar, "Parameters extraction of a single diode solar cell model using bat algorithm, firefly algorithm & cuckoo search optimization", *Annals of the Faculty of Engineering Hunedoara,* vol. 18, pp. 147-156, 2020.

[31] D. Mathew, C. Rani, M. Rajesh Kumar, Y. Wang, R. Binns, and K. Busawon, "Wind-driven optimization technique for estimation of solar photovoltaic parameters", *IEEE J. Photovolt.,* vol. 8, no. 1, pp. 248-256, 2018. [http://dx.doi.org/10.1109/JPHOTOV.2017.2769000]

[32] P. Dutta, and A. Kumar, "Intelligent calibration technique using optimized fuzzy logic controller for ultrasonic flow sensor", *MATHEMATICAL MODELLING OF ENGINEERING PROBLEMS,* vol. 4, no. 2, pp. 91-94, 2017. [http://dx.doi.org/10.18280/mmep.040205]

[33] P. Dutta, and A. Kumar, "Design an intelligent flow measurement technique by optimized fuzzy logic controller", *J. Eur. Syst. Autom.,* vol. 51, no. 1-3, pp. 89-107, 2018. [http://dx.doi.org/10.3166/jesa.51.89-107]

[34] P. Dutta and A. Kumar, "Study of optimized NN model for liquid flow sensor based on different parameters," 2018.

[35] P. Dutta, and A. Kumar, "Modelling of liquid flow control system using optimized genetic algorithm", *Stat. Optim. Inf. Comput.,* vol. 8, no. 2, pp. 565-582, 2020. [http://dx.doi.org/10.19139/soic-2310-5070-618]

[36] K. Sharma, M. Cerezo, Z. Holmes, L. Cincio, A. Sornborger, and P.J. Coles, "Reformulation of the no-free-lunch theorem for entangled data sets", *arXiv preprint arXiv:2007.04900,* 2020.

[37] S. Li, W. Gong, L. Wang, X. Yan, and C. Hu, "A hybrid adaptive teaching–learning-based optimization and differential evolution for parameter identification of photovoltaic models", *Energy Convers. Manage.,* vol. 225, p. 113474, 2020. [http://dx.doi.org/10.1016/j.enconman.2020.113474]

[38] S. Li, W. Gong, X. Yan, C. Hu, D. Bai, L. Wang, and L. Gao, "Parameter extraction of photovoltaic models using an improved teaching-learning-based optimization", *Energy Convers. Manage.,* vol. 186, pp. 293-305, 2019. [http://dx.doi.org/10.1016/j.enconman.2019.02.048]

[39] G. Xiong, J. Zhang, D. Shi, and Y. He, "Parameter extraction of solar photovoltaic models using an improved whale optimization algorithm", *Energy Convers. Manage.,* vol. 174, pp. 388-405, 2018. [http://dx.doi.org/10.1016/j.enconman.2018.08.053]

[40] "https://doi.org/10.1016/j.enconman.2018.08.053.

[41] X. Chen, and K. Yu, "Hybridizing cuckoo search algorithm with biogeography-based optimization for estimating photovoltaic model parameters", *Sol. Energy,* vol. 180, pp. 192-206, 2019. [http://dx.doi.org/10.1016/j.solener.2019.01.025]

[42] J. Liang, K. Qiao, K. Yu, S. Ge, B. Qu, R. Xu, and K. Li, "Parameters estimation of solar photovoltaic models via a self-adaptive ensemble-based differential evolution", *Sol. Energy,* vol. 207, pp. 336-346, 2020. [http://dx.doi.org/10.1016/j.solener.2020.06.100]

[43] G. Xiong, J. Zhang, X. Yuan, D. Shi, Y. He, and G. Yao, "Parameter extraction of solar photovoltaic models by means of a hybrid differential evolution with whale optimization algorithm", *Sol. Energy,* vol. 176, pp. 742-761, 2018. [http://dx.doi.org/10.1016/j.solener.2018.10.050]

[44] D. Oliva, M. Abd El Aziz, and A. Ella Hassanien, "Parameter estimation of photovoltaic cells using an improved chaotic whale optimization algorithm", *Appl. Energy,* vol. 200, pp. 141-154, 2017. [http://dx.doi.org/10.1016/j.apenergy.2017.05.029]

[45] J.P. Ram, T.S. Babu, T. Dragicevic, and N. Rajasekar, "A new hybrid bee pollinator flower pollination algorithm for solar PV parameter estimation", *Energy Convers. Manage.,* vol. 135, pp. 463-476, 2017. [http://dx.doi.org/10.1016/j.enconman.2016.12.082]

[46] M.A. Mughal, Q. Ma, and C. Xiao, "Photovoltaic cell parameter estimation using hybrid particle swarm optimization and simulated annealing", *Energies,* vol. 10, no. 8, p. 1213, 2017. [http://dx.doi.org/10.3390/en10081213]

[47] A.M. Beigi, and A. Maroosi, "Parameter identification for solar cells and module using a Hybrid Firefly and Pattern Search Algorithms", *Sol. Energy,* vol. 171, pp. 435-446, 2018. [http://dx.doi.org/10.1016/j.solener.2018.06.092]

[48] S.F. Li, and C.Y. Cheng, "Particle swarm optimization with fitness adjustment parameters", *Comput. Ind. Eng.,* vol. 113, pp. 831-841, 2017. [http://dx.doi.org/10.1016/j.cie.2017.06.006]

[49] M. Ghasemi, E. Akbari, A. Rahimnejad, S.E. Razavi, S. Ghavidel, and L. Li, "Phasor particle swarm optimization: a simple and efficient variant of PSO", *Soft Comput.,* vol. 23, no. 19, pp. 9701-9718, 2019. [http://dx.doi.org/10.1007/s00500-018-3536-8]

[50] S. Mohanty, A. Mishra, B.K. Nanda, and B.C. Routara, "Multi-objective parametric optimization of nano powder mixed electrical discharge machining of AlSiCp using response surface methodology and particle swarm optimization", *Alex. Eng. J.,* vol. 57, no. 2, pp. 609-619, 2018. [http://dx.doi.org/10.1016/j.aej.2017.02.006]

[51] M. Saravanan, C. Thiyagarajan, and S. Somasundaram, "Parametric optimization of wirecut-electrical discharge machining through cuckoo search algorithm", *Mater. Today Proc.,* vol. 22, pp. 681-687, 2020. [http://dx.doi.org/10.1016/j.matpr.2019.09.127]

[52] P. Civicioglu, E. Besdok, M.A. Gunen, and U.H. Atasever, "Weighted differential evolution algorithm for numerical function optimization: a comparative study with cuckoo search, artificial bee colony, adaptive differential evolution, and backtracking search optimization algorithms", *Neural Comput. Appl.,* vol. 32, no. 8, pp. 3923-3937, 2020. [http://dx.doi.org/10.1007/s00521-018-3822-5]

[53] Z. Zhang, W.C. Hong, and J. Li, "Electric load forecasting by hybrid self-recurrent support vector

regression model with variational mode decomposition and improved cuckoo search algorithm", *IEEE Access,* vol. 8, pp. 14642-14658, 2020. [http://dx.doi.org/10.1109/ACCESS.2020.2966712]

[54] M. İnci, and A. Caliskan, "Performance enhancement of energy extraction capability for fuel cell implementations with improved Cuckoo search algorithm", *Int. J. Hydrogen Energy,* vol. 45, no. 19, pp. 11309-11320, 2020. [http://dx.doi.org/10.1016/j.ijhydene.2020.02.069]

[55] J. Li, Y. Li, S. Tian, and J. Xia, "An improved cuckoo search algorithm with self-adaptive knowledge learning", *Neural Comput. Appl.,* vol. 32, no. 16, pp. 11967-11997, 2020. [http://dx.doi.org/10.1007/s00521-019-04178-w]

[56] T.T. Nguyen, and T.T. Nguyen, "An improved cuckoo search algorithm for the problem of electric distribution network reconfiguration", *Appl. Soft Comput.,* vol. 84, p. 105720, 2019. [http://dx.doi.org/10.1016/j.asoc.2019.105720]

[57] X. Meng, J. Chang, X. Wang, and Y. Wang, "Multi-objective hydropower station operation using an improved cuckoo search algorithm", *Energy,* vol. 168, pp. 425-439, 2019. [http://dx.doi.org/10.1016/j.energy.2018.11.096]

[58] X. Huang, Z. Xie, and X. Huang, "Fault location of distribution network base on improved cuckoo search algorithm", *IEEE Access,* vol. 8, pp. 2272-2283, 2020. [http://dx.doi.org/10.1109/ACCESS.2019.2962276]

[59] P. Dutta, and M. Majumder, *An improved grey wolf optimization technique for estimation of solar photovoltaic parameters.* vol. Vol. 4. Int. J. Power Energy Syst, 2021.

[60] M.R. Chen, X. Li, X. Zhang, and Y.Z. Lu, "A novel particle swarm optimizer hybridized with extremal optimization", *Appl. Soft Comput.,* vol. 10, no. 2, pp. 367-373, 2010. [http://dx.doi.org/10.1016/j.asoc.2009.08.014]

[61] M. Zhang, H. Wang, Z. Cui, and J. Chen, "Hybrid multi-objective cuckoo search with dynamical local search", *Memet. Comput.,* vol. 10, no. 2, pp. 199-208, 2018. [http://dx.doi.org/10.1007/s12293-017-0237-2]

[62] A.M. Ibrahim, and M.A. Tawhid, "A hybridization of cuckoo search and particle swarm optimization for solving nonlinear systems", *Evol. Intell.,* vol. 12, no. 4, pp. 541-561, 2019. [http://dx.doi.org/10.1007/s12065-019-00255-0]

[63] S. Mandal, P. Dutta, and A. Kumar, "Modeling of liquid flow control process using improved versions of elephant swarm water search algorithm", *SN Appl. Sci.,* vol. 1, no. 8, p. 886, 2019. [http://dx.doi.org/10.1007/s42452-019-0914-5]

[64] P. Dutta, S. Mandal, and A. Kumar, "Application of FPA and ANOVA in the optimization of liquid flow control process", *Review of Computer Engineering Studies,* vol. 5, no. 1, pp. 7-11, 2019. [http://dx.doi.org/10.18280/rces.050102]

[65] P. Dutta, and A. Kumar, "Design an intelligent calibration technique using optimized GA-ANN for liquid flow control system", *J. Eur. Syst. Autom.,* vol. 50, no. 4-6, pp. 449-470, 2017. [http://dx.doi.org/10.3166/jesa.50.449-470]

[66] P. Dutta, S. Paul, and A. Kumar, "Comparative analysis of various supervised machine learning techniques for diagnosis of COVID-19", In: *Electronic Devices, Circuits, and Systems for Biomedical Applications.,* S.L. Tripathi, V.E. Balas, S.K. Mohapatra, K.B. Prakash, J. Nayak, Eds., Academic Press, 2021, pp. 521-540. [http://dx.doi.org/10.1016/B978-0-323-85172-5.00020-4]

[67] P. Dutta, S. Paul, A.J. Obaid, S. Pal, and K. Mukhopadhyay, "Feature selection based artificial intelligence techniques for the prediction of COVID-like diseases", *J. Phys. Conf. Ser.,* vol. 1963, no. 1, p. 012167, 2021. [http://dx.doi.org/10.1088/1742-6596/1963/1/012167]

CHAPTER 15

Design of Rectangular Microstrip Patch Antenna Using ANOVA at 26 GHz for Industry 5.0

Dipankar Saha[1], **Sudip Mandal**[2,*] and **Kabita Purkait**[3]

[1] *Department of Electronics & Communication Engineering, Global Institute of Management & Technology, Krishnagar, West Bengal, India*

[2] *Department of Electronics and Communication Engineering, Jalpaiguri Government Engineering College, Jalpaiguri, India*

[3] *Department of Electronics and Communication Engineering, Kalyani Government. Engineering College, Kalyani, India*

Abstract: In this paper, a rectangular microstrip patch antenna with a triangular polygon at the top of the right side is designed. FR-4 is used as a substrate material with a relative permittivity of 4.3. The inset feeding technique is used to construct the proposed patch antenna. By changing three parameters, namely patch width (W_p), substrate height (h), and width of feedline (W_f), a dataset is created to achieve the resonant frequency of 26 GHz and a bandwidth of 2.5 GHz. ANOVA is employed to find out two equations for the resonant frequency (F_r) and bandwidth (BW) to obtain target outcomes. All the simulations and calculations of the dataset are made using the CST Studio Suite version 2023, and ANOVA is carried out in Minitab version 21.

Keywords: ANOVA, Bandwidth, CST microwave studio, Industry 5.0, Resonant frequency, Rectangular microstrip patch, Triangular polygon.

INTRODUCTION

An antenna is an essential device to communicate a message from the sender to the receiver. In today's fast-paced life, mobile phones have become an indispensable tool to connect with the world. The extensive use of mobile phones requires a miniaturized antenna. The most often searched topic in the communication system industry is wireless technology, which is a relatively new field that creates portable devices. Although there are many other types of antennas utilized in wireless applications today, microstrip antennas are highly regarded. Microstrip patch antennas' compact length, low cost, light weight, and ease of fabrication allow them to serve a vital role in a wide range of applications,

* **Corresponding author Sudip Mandal:** Department of Electronics and Communication Engineering, Jalpaiguri Government Engineering College, Jalpaiguri, India; E-mail: sudip.mandal007@gmail.com

Pijush Dutta, Sudip Mondal, Korhan Cengiz and S. Balamurugan (Eds.)

including cellular communication, satellite communication, radar, and aircraft. The most commonly used microstrip patch antennas are rectangular, square, and circular. Despite this, microstrip patch antennas come in a variety of shapes, including hexagonal, triangular, elliptical, etc. The overcrowded spectrum of 4G technologies and the demand for higher data rates, good bandwidth, low latency, and high-resolution video streaming made the way for 5G technology. In order to improve coverage at a cheaper cost and with greater dependability, 5G delivers fast connections, strong throughput capabilities, large bandwidth, and low power consumption.

A typical microstrip patch antenna is made up of three parts: substrate, patch, and ground. The metallic patch is placed on the insulating material and supported by the ground plane. The substrate's relative permittivity (ε_r) can be anywhere between 2.2 and 12 when constructing a microstrip antenna. The quality of the substrate additionally determines the radiation, improves effectiveness, and ensures more extensive data transfer capacity and a greater size of the receiving wire. The feeding of a microstrip patch antenna can be taken care of through various procedures, including coaxial feed, inset feed, microstrip line, and others. A fringe field forms and radiates from the discontinuity side of the patch antenna. The microstrip patch antenna offers a narrow bandwidth and low gain. In order to address the inadequacies, the patch is designed with various slots, slits, and notches. Astuti *et al.* [1] demonstrated a bow-tie microstrip patch antenna that improved bandwidth at 3.67 GHz from 2.6% to 10.45%. Verma *et al.* proposed a T-shaped patch antenna that increased the bandwidth from 40.05 to 81.34% in the frequency range of 1.682–3.988 GHz [2] utilizing FR-4 substrate. Saha *et al.* [3] presented a rectangular slotted microstrip patch antenna at 27 GHz with a bandwidth of 1.51 GHz and a gain of 6.85 dBi. A rectangular patch antenna was reported by Darboe *et al.* [4] at 28 GHz using an inset feedline with 70.18% efficiency and 8.37 dBi directivity. A wearable microstrip antenna was reported by Ateeyah [5] at 28 GHz, which was found to enhance performance by modifying antenna dimensions. Djouimaa and Bencherif [6] introduced a circular patch antenna with a bandwidth of 1.76 GHz and a gain of 0.1573 dBi, operating at 28 GHz. Sadoon *et al.* [7] highlighted three slots in the patch side of the antenna and achieved -39 dB return loss and 753 MHz of bandwidth. There are various optimization methods that can be applied to boost bandwidth. A microstrip patch antenna with an inverted E-shape, PSO, and a 15% bandwidth increase was simplified, according to Islam *et al.* [8]. Dual-band and multiband applications can also be utilized in the design of microstrip patch antennas. Punith *et al.* proposed a microstrip patch antenna operating at 23.9 GHz, 35.5 GHz, and 70.9 GHz, suitable for 5G and space applications [9]. A rectangular patch antenna designed for dual-band 5G cellular communication (38 GHz and 54 GHz) was developed by Imran *et al.* [10]. Syahbana *et al.* [11] presented a rectangular microstrip patch antenna at a frequency of 26-28 GHz with a centre frequency of 26 GHz and a gain of 6.846 dBi. Colaco *et al.* [12] proposed a multiband (26GHz,40 GHz,53.5GHz) rectangular microstrip patch antenna with a metamaterial structure to enhance the bandwidth from 5.368 GHz to 5.630 GHz. Kenari *et al.* [13] proposed a miniaturized composite right/left-handed UWB antenna using a metamaterial structure with a fractional bandwidth of 111% and a peak gain of 9.41 dBi. Nahas [14] demonstrated an antenna that incorporated two symmetric L-shaped slots and a centrally placed square slot into a single rectangular patch operating at 26 GHz and 28 GHz.

In this present research, a rectangular microstrip patch antenna with a triangular polygon at the right upper side of the patch is constructed using the CST Studio Suite version 2023, and three variables are used, namely substrate height(h), width of the patch (W_p) and width of the feedline (W_f), to increase the bandwidth close to the target resonant frequency. A regression model with ANOVA for both bandwidth and resonant frequency is created using Minitab (version 21) to design several antennas with variations in these four variables. From two equations for bandwidth and resonant frequency, the model is well-suited and validates the enhancement of bandwidth and achieves the desired resonant frequency of 26 GHz, which is appropriate for 5G applications and is very useful for Industry 5.0.

METHODOLOGY

Rectangular patch having dimensions of width (W_p), length (L_p), substrate thickness (h), and relative permittivity (ε_r) of the dielectric substrate are used to create the proposed rectangular microstrip patch antennas. A triangular polygon (1.2 mm x 1.2 mm x 1.7 mm) is created for better impedance matching. Utilizing FR-4 substrate with a relative permittivity of 4.3 and a loss tangent ($tan\delta$) of 0.02 has allowed for the modeling of the proposed rectangular patch antenna. The inset feed technique is used to feed the suggested patch antenna. A ground layer of copper is designed with dimensions of 7.74 mm x 6.65 mm. The patch antenna's length and width can be calculated using the following formulas [15].

$$W = \frac{C}{2f_r}\sqrt{\frac{2}{\varepsilon_r+1}} \tag{1}$$

Where C is the speed of light, f_r is the resonant frequency, ε_r is the relative permittivity of the substrate

$$L = L_{eff} - 2\Delta L \tag{2}$$

Where L_{effis} the effective length of the patch, which can be expressed as

$$L_{eff} = \frac{c}{2f_r\sqrt{\epsilon_{eff}}} \tag{3}$$

Where ϵ_{effis} the effective relative permittivity given as follows:

$$\epsilon_{eff} = \frac{\epsilon_r+1}{2} + \frac{\epsilon_r-1}{2}(1+\frac{12h}{W})^{-\frac{1}{2}} \tag{4}$$

And ΔL is the length extension given as follows:

$$\Delta L = 0.412h\frac{(\epsilon_{eff}+0.3)(\frac{W}{h}+0.264)}{(\epsilon_{eff}-0.258)(\frac{W}{h}+0.8)} \tag{5}$$

The patch antenna's dimensions (length ×width ×height) are roughly indicated by the matching length L_g, width W_g, and height of the substrate h. These values are determined using the following equations.

$$L_g = L + 6h \tag{6}$$

$$W_g = W + 6h \tag{7}$$

The proposed rectangular microstrip patch antenna with a triangular polygon is designed as shown in Fig. (**1**). The recommended antenna's inset feeding approach has a length (L_f) and width (W_f) of 3.10 mm and 1.30 mm, respectively. The fundamental parameters of the proposed rectangular patch antenna are shown in Table **I**.

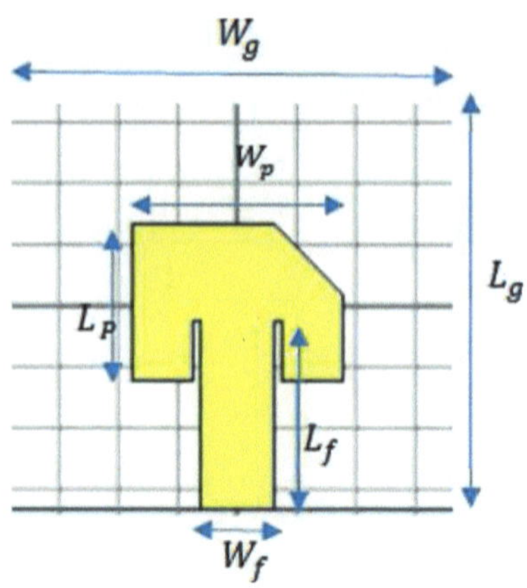

Fig. (1). Geometry of the suggested microstrip patch antenna.

Table 1. The parameters for the proposed microstrip patch antenna

Parameters	Values (mm)
Width (*Wp*)	3.54
LLength (*Lp*)	2.58
Width of ground (*Wg*)	7.74
Length of ground (*Lg*)	6.65
Width of feed (*Wf*)	1.30
Length of feed (*Lf*)	3.10
Height of Substrate (*h*)	0.80

The substrate height (*h*) in this suggested design is 0.80 mm, and the patch thickness (*t*) is assumed to be 0.035 mm. The CST Studio Suite [16] is used to simulate the rectangular microstrip patch antenna, which resonates at 26.126 GHz with a return loss of -31.39 dB and a bandwidth of 1.910 GHz. The traditional rectangular patch antenna with a triangular polygon has a higher cut-off frequency of 27.125 GHz and a lower cut-off frequency of 25.215 GHz. The proposed patch antenna is designed to operate between 23 and 30 GHz. A typical rectangular patch antenna return loss graph is displayed in Fig. (**2**). Regression analysis with ANOVA is carried out to significantly improve the resonant frequency, bringing it closer to the desired frequency of 26 GHz, and enhance the bandwidth. As illustrated in Fig. (**3**), the VSWR of the rectangular microstrip patch antenna at 26.126 GHz is 1.05. As illustrated in Fig. (**4**), the yield gain of the suggested patch antenna at the resonance frequency of 26.126 GHz is 3.13dBi. The Z parameter of the proposed patch antenna is 54.123 - *j*0.929Ω at the resonant frequency of 26.126. It indicates a mismatch of only 4.123Ω as shown in Fig. (**5**).

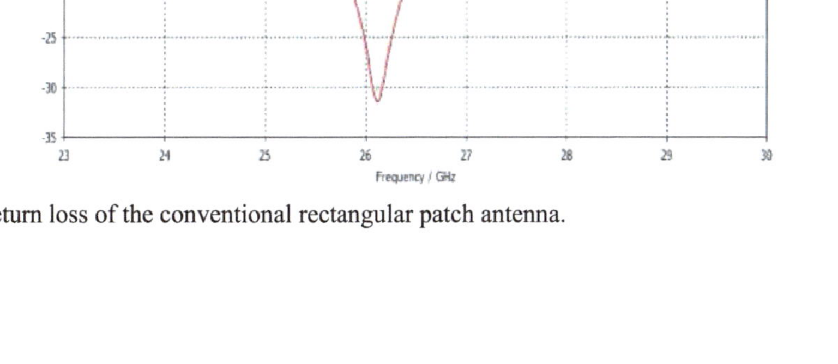

Fig. (2). Return loss of the conventional rectangular patch antenna.

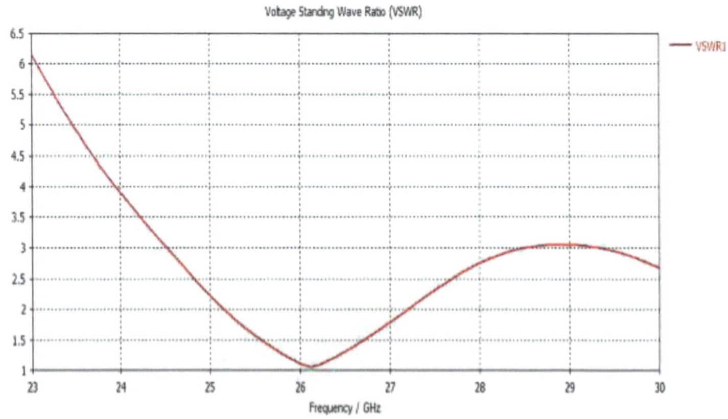

Fig. (3). VSWR of the conventional proposed patch antenna.

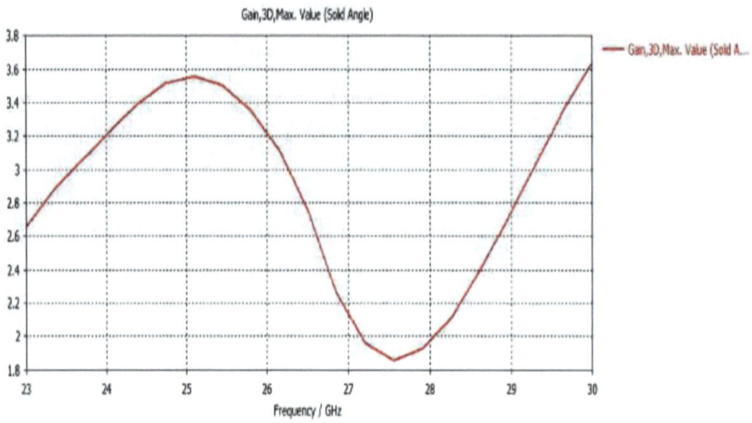

Fig. (4). Gain of the conventional proposed patch antenna.

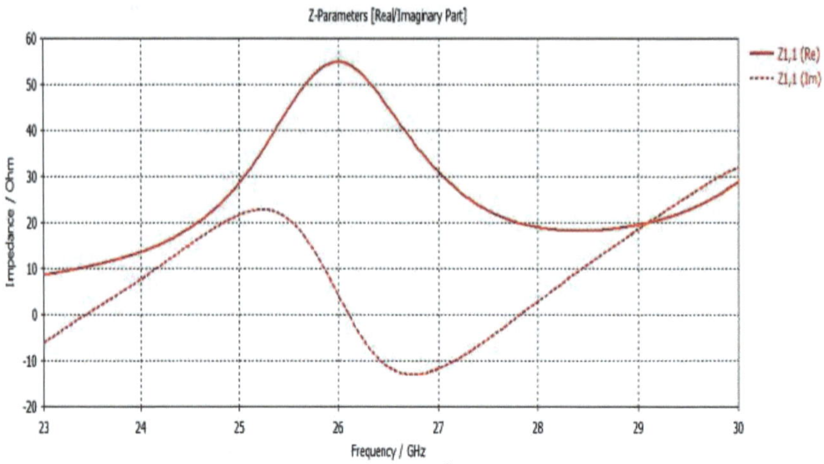

Fig. (5). Z parameter plots (real and imaginary) of the conventional proposed patch antenna.

VARIATION OF THREE PARAMETERS

Three variables or parameters out of the seven parameters change, as they affect the bandwidth of the proposed patch antenna. Three parameters are the width of the patch (W_p), substrate thickness (h), and width of the feedline (W_f). To generate a dataset for ANOVA, these three parameters are changed. Width of the patch (W_p) varies from 3.48 mm to 3.57 mm, substrate thickness (h) changes from 0.73 mm to 0.82 mm, and the width of the feedline (W_f) varies from 1.24 mm to 1.32 mm. Table **2** displays the fluctuation of these three parameters as well as the resonant frequency (F_r), bandwidth (BW), and return loss. Variations in these four factors result in variations in bandwidth, resonant frequency, and return loss.

Table 2. Results of the simulation with changes to the antenna parameters

W_p(mm)	h(mm)	W_f(mm)	Return Loss (dB)	F_r(GHz)	BW(GHz)
3.48	0.73	1.275	-36.95	26.275	1.621
3.49	0.74	1.285	-49.87	26.278	1.693
3.5	0.75	1.28	-47.61	26.222	1.706
3.505	0.755	1.28	-44.57	26.193	1.699
3.5	0.76	1.26	-29.23	26.07	1.607
3.51	0.76	1.27	-33.27	26.109	1.654
3.52	0.77	1.27	-33.3	26.054	1.673
3.52	0.78	1.29	-47.29	26.269	1.794
3.53	0.78	1.3	-40.14	26.314	1.848
3.53	0.79	1.31	-27.28	26.243	1.947
3.54	0.8	1.3	-31.39	26.126	1.91
3.54	0.81	1.31	-27.24	26.06	2.154
3.55	0.81	1.315	-25.99	26.08	2.191
3.55	0.82	1.315	-25.13	26.047	2.27
3.55	0.79	1.32	-16.95	26.677	2.425
3.56	0.82	1.305	-28.86	25.948	2.169
3.515	0.775	1.28	-45.3	26.125	1.749
3.525	0.795	1.285	-46.46	26.075	1.82
3.535	0.805	1.285	-47.69	25.914	1.959
3.555	0.81	1.29	-43.84	25.887	1.995
3.545	0.805	1.29	-41.81	25.925	1.989
3.54	0.8	1.25	-25.67	25.831	1.632
3.55	0.79	1.24	-22.82	25.788	1.546

(Table 2) cont.....

W_p(mm)	h(mm)	W_f(mm)	Return Loss (dB)	F_r(GHz)	BW(GHz)
3.55	0.8	1.24	-23.23	25.756	1.572
3.57	0.8	1.24	-22.46	25.721	1.552

The dataset shown in Table **2** is statistically evaluated using Minitab Software version 21. The three factors, taken separately and in combination, help increase the forecast accuracy of the answer values. A first-order polynomial equation is used to build a model that correlates the responses with the independent variables. Mathematically, the first-order polynomial may be expressed as:

$$\bar{y} = a_0 + a_1x_1 + a_2x_2^2 + .. + a_kx_k^k \quad \textbf{(8)}$$

Where ȳ is the predicted outcome value for the polynomial model with regression coefficients a_1 to k for each degree and ȳ intercept a_0. First-order polynomial equations for resonant frequency (F_r) and bandwidth (BW) related to the independent variables are written as:

$$F_r = 295 - 124W_p + 442h - 364W_f - 67.5W_ph + 142.4W_pW_f - 167.2hW_f \quad \textbf{(9)}$$

$$BW = 751 - 231.6W_p - 41.5h - 527W_f + 33.4W_ph + 164.3W_pW_f - 59.4hW_f \quad \textbf{(10)}$$

ANOVA ANALYSIS

Analysis of variance (ANOVA) and residual analysis are used to assess the model's appropriateness and fitness. The results of the analysis of variance (ANOVA) for $F_r$and BW are shown in Table **3**. Coefficients of determination (R^2) for the resonant frequency (F_r) and bandwidth (BW) are 91.51% and 95.41%, respectively. The sufficiency of the suggested model is also shown by the coefficients of determination (R^2). For this model, the adjustedR^2 is nearly equal to R^2. P-values less than 0.05 ($p<0.05$) are regarded as significant terms. For resonant frequency (F_r 0.05)), the significant terms are the width of the patch(W_p), substrate thickness (h 0.05)>), interaction between the width of the patch and substrate thickness (W_p h), interaction between the width of the patch and the width of the feedline (W_p W_f), and interaction between substrate thickness and the width of the feedline (hW_f). For bandwidth (BW), the significant terms are patch width (W_p), width of the feedline (W_f), and interaction between the width of the patch and the width of the feedline (W_p W_f). Table **3** displays a polynomial model of the coefficients of determination (R^2) for resonant frequency (F_r) and bandwidth (BW) with an experimental dataset.

Table 3. ANOVA for the polynomial models of resonating frequency and impedance bandwidth.

Source	DF	Resonant Frequency (F_r)				Bandwidth (BW)			
		Adj SS	Adj MS	F-value	p-value	Adj SS	Adj MS	F-value	p-value
W_p (mm)	1	0.00992	0.009919	1.95	0.18	0.03456	0.034563	9.32	0.007
h(mm)	1	0.08247	0.082474	16.21	0.001	0.00073	0.000729	0.2	0.663
W_f(mm)	1	0.0187	0.018701	3.68	0.071	0.0392	0.039197	10.57	0.004
W_p* h(mm)	1	0.02248	0.022481	4.42	0.05	0.0055	0.005501	1.48	0.239
W_p* W_f(mm)	1	0.02582	0.025824	5.08	0.037	0.03438	0.034379	9.27	0.007
h* W_f(mm)	1	0.02519	0.025186	4.95	0.039	0.00318	0.003179	0.86	0.367
-	R^2	91.51%	Adj R^2	88.69%	-	R^2	95.41%	AdjR^2	93.88%

Where SS is the sum of squares and DF is the degree of freedom. For a given answer, the parameters in Table **3** are effective within a 95% confidence interval.

The residual against observation order and residual against normal probability plots for the resonant frequency (F_r) are shown in Fig. (**6**). Nearly every point on the graph is in line with the straight line. Every point on the second graph crosses the residual value of zero. It suggests that the model is a good fit. Fig. (**7**) displays the residual versus observation order plot and residual against normal probability plot for bandwidth (BW).

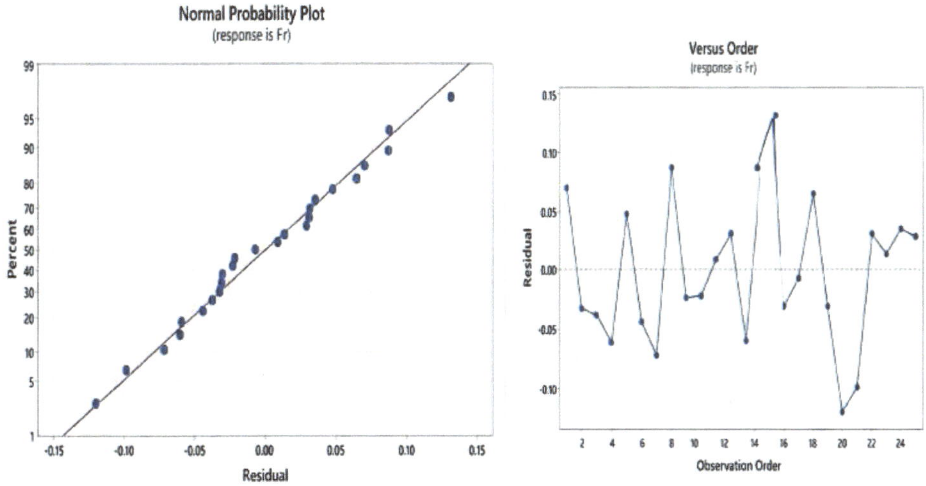

(a) (b)

Fig. (6). For resonant frequency (**a**) residual *vs*. normal probability graph and (**b**) residual *vs*. observation order graph.

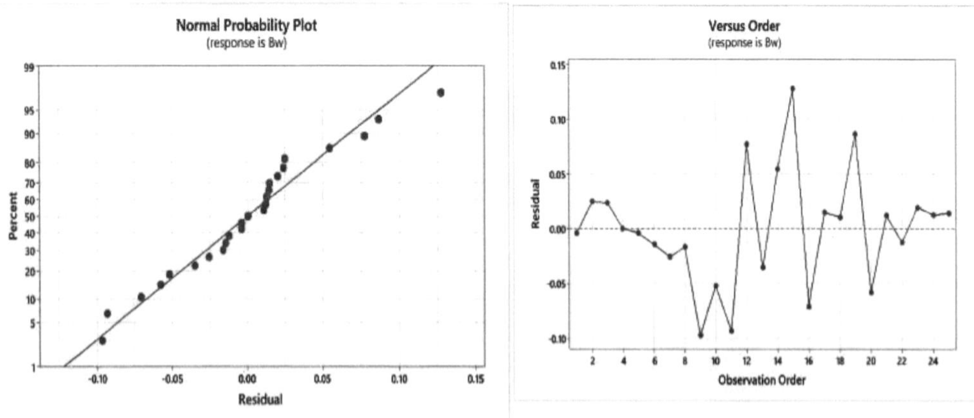

(a) (b)

Fig. (7). For bandwidth (**a**) residual vs. normal probability graph and (**b**) residual vs. observation order graph.

Figs. (**8** and **9**) display the contour plot and surface plot, respectively, of the resonant frequency (F_r) and bandwidth (BW). 2D contour and 3D surface plots are the graphical representations of the regression equation that show the function of two components at a time while keeping other factors at a fixed level. Fig. (**8**) displays the contour plot of the interaction between substrate thickness and feedline width and the interaction between patch width and feedline width for the resonant frequency (F_r), as well as a contour plot of interaction between patch width and feedline width for bandwidth (BW). Fig. (**9**) shows a surface plot of the patch width and substrate thickness for resonant frequency (F_r) and also a surface plot of the patch width and feedline width interaction for bandwidth (BW).

These two polynomial equations for resonant frequency (F_r) and bandwidth (BW), as well as Analysis of variance (ANOVA) and residual analysis, suggest that the model is well fitted and validates the target outcome of achieving 2.5 GHz of bandwidth (BW) and close to the desired resonant frequency (F_r) of 26 GHz.

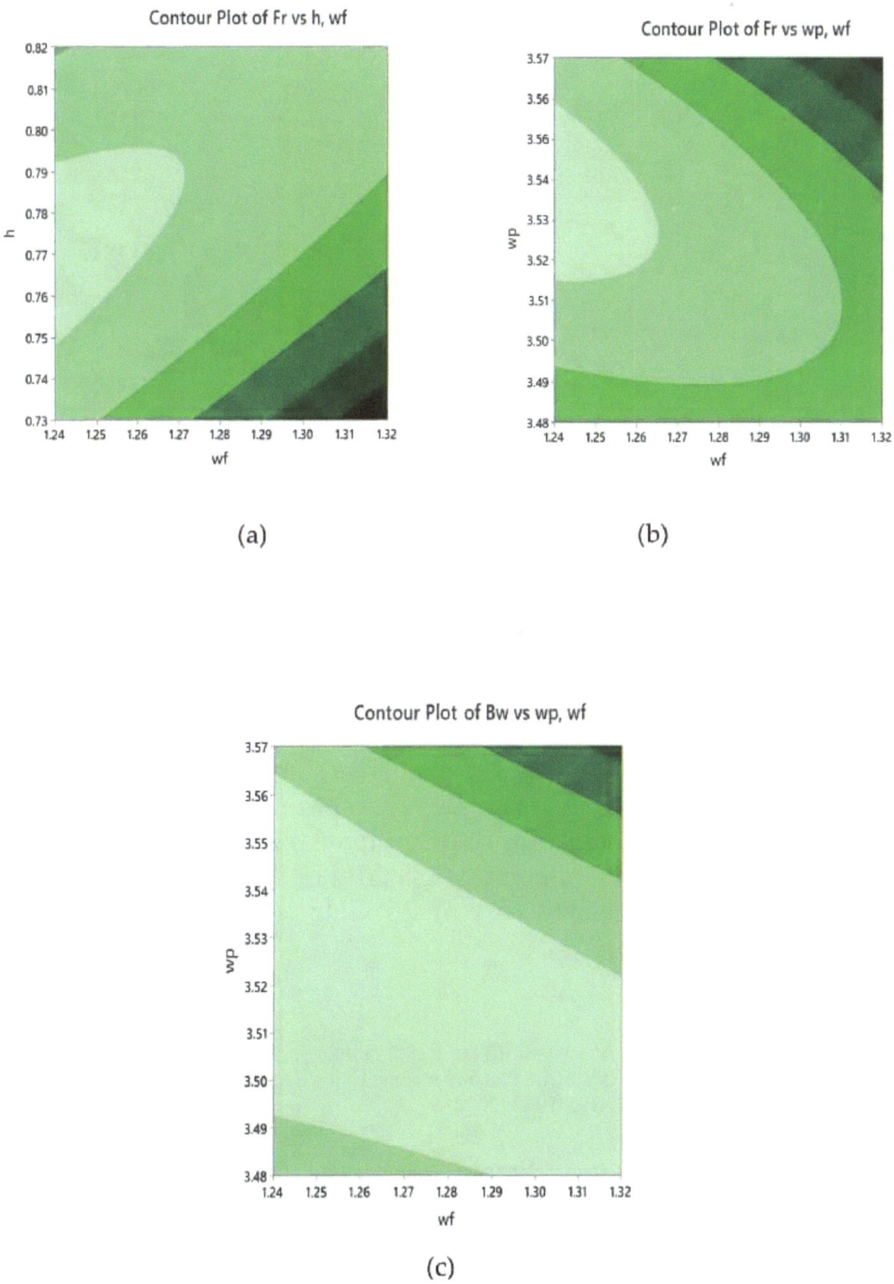

Fig. (8). Contour plot (**a**) F_r*vs.* hW_f, (**b**) F_r *vs.* W_p W_f and (c) BW *vs.* W_p W_f

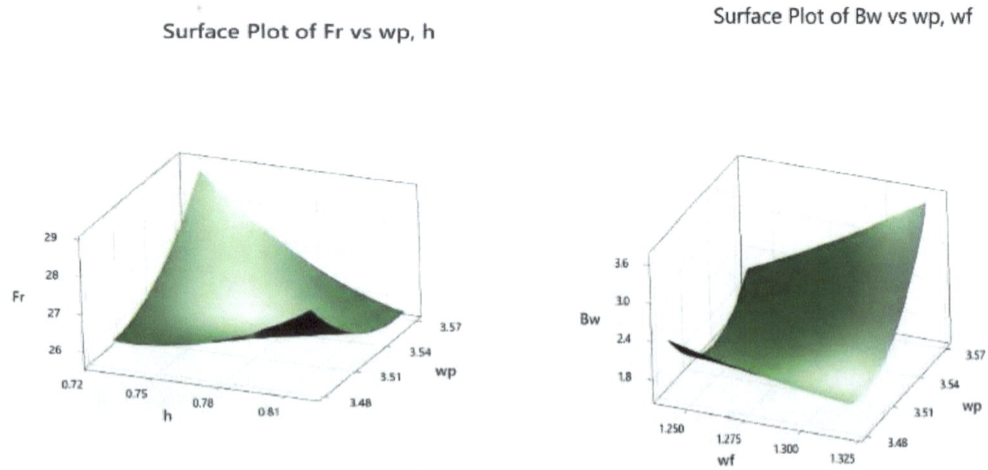

Fig. (9). Surface plot (**a**) F_r *vs.* W_p h and (**b**) BW *vs.* W_p W_f

CONCLUSION

A rectangular microstrip patch antenna using a triangular polygon is designed using a CST Studio Suite, with a return loss of -31.39 dB, a bandwidth of 1.910 GHz, and a gain of 3.13 dBi at a resonant frequency of 26.126 GHz. Twenty-five (25) different antennas have been configured by changing three parameters, namely patch width (W_p), substrate height (h), and width of feedline (W_f). Analysis of variance (ANOVA) is employed to evaluate the fitness of the model. From two polynomial equations for resonant frequency (F_r) and bandwidth (BW), it is validated that the target outcome of 2.5 GHz of bandwidth (BW) and close to the desired resonant frequency (F_r) of 26 GHz is obtained and suitable for Industry 5.0.

REFERENCES

[1] D.W. Astuti, R. Fadilah, M. Muslim, D. Rusdiyanto, S. Alam, and Y. Wahyu, "Bandwidth Enhancement of Bow-tie Microstrip Patch Antenna Using Defected Ground Structure for 5G", *J. Commun.*, vol. 17, no. 12, pp. 995-1002, 2022.
[http://dx.doi.org/10.12720/jcm.17.12.995-1002]

[2] R.K. Verma, and D.K. Srivastava, "Bandwidth enhancement of a slot loaded T-shape patch antenna", *J. Comput. Electron.*, vol. 18, no. 1, pp. 205-210, 2019.
[http://dx.doi.org/10.1007/s10825-018-1277-7]

[3] D. Saha, S. Mandal, and K. Purkait, "Design of Rectangular Slotted Microstrip Patch antenna for 5G applications at 27GHz", *2022 International Conference on Intelligent Innovations in Engineering and Technology (ICIIET)*, pp. 15-19, 2022.
[http://dx.doi.org/10.1109/ICIIET55458.2022.9967679]

[4] O. Darboe, D.B.O. Konditi, and F. Manene, "A 28 GHz rectangular microstrip patch antenna for 5G applications", *Int. J. Eng. Res. Technol. (Ahmedabad)*, vol. 12, no. 6, pp. 854-857, 2019.

[5] E. Ateeyah, "Design and optimization of a wearable microstrip patch antenna for 28 GHz 5G applications". *Int. J. Electr. Eng. and Sustain.*, 95-102.

[6] A. Djouimaa, and K. Bencherif, "Design of a Compact Circular Microstrip Patch Antenna for 5G Applications", *Engineering, Technology & Appl. Sci. Res.,* vol. 14, no. 4, pp. 16020-16024, 2024.

[7] Z. Saadoon, H.A. Abbood, and D.S. Wais, "New Design and Simulation of 28GHz Microstrip Patch Antenna for 5G Applications", *Academic Journal of Electrical and Computer Engineering,* vol. 1, no. 01, pp. 12-17, 2024. [http://dx.doi.org/10.31272/ajece.12]

[8] M.T. Islam, M. Moniruzzaman, N. Misran, and M.N. Shakib, "Curve fitting based particle swarm optimization for UWB patch antenna", *J. Electromagn. Waves Appl.,* vol. 23, no. 17-18, pp. 2421-2432, 2009.

[9] S. Punith, S.K. Praveenkumar, A.A. Jugale, and M.R. Ahmed, "A novel multiband microstrip patch antenna for 5G communications", *Procedia Comput. Sci.,* vol. 171, pp. 2080-2086, 2020. [http://dx.doi.org/10.1016/j.procs.2020.04.224]

[10] Imran, D., Farooqi, M. M., Khattak, M. I., Ullah, Z., Khan, M. I., Khattak, M. A., & Dar, H. (2018, February). Millimeter wave microstrip patch antenna for 5G mobile communication. In 2018 international conference on engineering and emerging technologies (ICEET) (pp. 1-6). IEEE.

[11] D. Syahbana, S. Rahmatia, and P. Wulandari, "An improved design of multiband patch antenna at 26 GHz for 5G mobile", *Proceedings of the 2020 International Conference on Engineering and Information Technology for Sustainable Industry,* pp. 1-5, 2020. [http://dx.doi.org/10.1145/3429789.3429839]

[12] J. Colaco, and R.B. Lohani, "Metamaterial based multiband microstrip patch antenna for 5G wireless technology-enabled IoT devices and its applications", *J. Phys. Conf. Ser.,* vol. 2070, no. 1, p. 012116, 2021. [http://dx.doi.org/10.1088/1742-6596/2070/1/012116]

[13] M. Alibakhshi-Kenari, M. Naser-Moghadasi, R.A. Sadeghzadeh, B.S. Virdee, and E. Limiti, "Miniature CRLH-based ultra wideband antenna with gain enhancement for wireless communication applications", *ICT Express,* vol. 2, no. 2, pp. 75-79, 2016. [http://dx.doi.org/10.1016/j.icte.2016.04.001]

[14] M. Nahas, "A super high gain l-slotted microstrip patch antenna for 5G mobile systems operating at 26 and 28 GHz. Engineering, Technology &", *Appl. Sci. Res.,* vol. 12, no. 1, pp. 8053-8057, 2022.

[15] Balanis, C. A. (2016). Antenna theory: analysis and design. John wiley & sons.

[16] CST Studio Suite, Available from:https://edu.3ds.com/en/software/cst-studio-suite-students

SUBJECT INDEX

G

H

I

J

K

L

M

N

O

P

R

S

T

V

W

X

www.ingramcontent.com/pod-product-compliance
Lightning Source LLC
LaVergne TN
LVHW070950210926
848482LV00002B/167

* 9 7 9 8 8 9 8 8 1 4 1 0 6 *